MW00397238

* 1,000,000 *

Free E-Books

@

www.ForgottenBooks.org

* Alchemy *

The Secret is Revealed

@

www.TheBookofAquarius.com

Forgotten Books

The Aquarian Gospel of Jesus the Christ

By

Levi

Published by Forgotten Books 2012

Originally Published 1911

PIBN 1000412011

Copyright © 2012 Forgotten Books
www.forgottenbooks.org

THE AQUARIAN GOSPEL

of

JESUS THE CHRIST

*The Philosophic and Practical Basis of the Religion
of the Aquarian Age of the World*

AND OF

THE CHURCH UNIVERSAL

TRANSCRIBED FROM THE BOOK OF GOD'S REMEMBRANCES,
KNOWN AS THE AKASHIC RECORDS,

BY
LEVI

2 6 0 (n)

WITH

INTRODUCTION
BY
EVA S. DOWLING, A. Ph. D.

LONDON:
L. N. FOWLER AND COMPANY

E. S. DOWLING, PUBLISHER,
Los Angeles, California
1911

FOR SALE BY
E. S. DOWLING
Los Angeles, California.

Copyright 1911, by

MRS. EVA S. DOWLING

Copyright in England, 1911
Entered at Stationers' Hall, London

ALL RIGHTS RESERVED
including rights of translation

CONTENTS

M735971

INTRODUCTION

BY

EVA S. DOWLING, A. Ph.D.,

SCRIBE TO THE MESSENGER.

THE BOOK.

The full title of this book is "The Aquarian Age Gospel of Jesus, the Christ of the Piscean Age," and the critical reader is apt to ask a number of pertinent questions concerning it. Among the many anticipated questions these are perhaps the most important:

1 What is an Age?
2 What is the Piscean Age?
3 What is the Aquarian Age?
4 What is meant by the Christ as the word is used in this book?
5 What relationship existed between Jesus of Nazareth and the Christ?
6 Who is Levi, the transcriber of this book?
7 What are the Akashic Records?

1 *What is an Age?* Astronomers tell us that our sun and his family of planets revolve around a central sun, which is millions of miles distant, and that it requires something less than 26,000 years to make one revolution. His orbit is called the Zodiac, which is divided into twelve signs, familiarly known as Aries, Taurus, Gemini, Cancer, Leo, Virgo, Libra, Scorpio, Sagittarius, Capricorn, Aquarius and Pisces. It requires our Solar System a little more than 2100 years to pass through one of these signs, and this time is the measurement of an Age or Dispensation. Because of what Astronomers call "the precession of the Equinoxes" the movement of the sun through the signs of the Zodiac is in order reverse from that given above.

Exact Time of the Beginning of an Age. Regarding this matter there is a disagreement among astronomers; but in this Introduction we are not called upon to give the reasons of the various investigators for their opinions; there are enough well authenticated facts for our present purposes. It is conceded by all critical students that the sun entered the zodiacal sign Taurus in the days of our historic Adam when the Taurian Age began; that Abraham lived not far from the beginning of the Arian Age, when the sun entered the sign Aries. About the time of the rise of the Roman empire the sun entered the sign Pisces, the Fishes, and the Piscean Age began, so that early in this Age Jesus of Nazareth lived.

2 *What is the Piscean Age?* This question requires further consideration. The Piscean Age is identical with the Christian Dispensation. The word Pisces means fish. The sign is known as a water sign, and the Piscean Age has been distinctly the age of the fish and its element, water.

In the establishment of their great institutions John the Harbinger and Jesus both introduced the rite of water baptism, which has been used in some form in all the so-called Christian Churches and cults, even to the present time. Water is the true symbol of purification. Jesus himself said to the Harbinger before he was baptized: "All men must be washed, symbolic of the cleansing of the soul." (Aquarian Gospel 64:7.)

Fish was a Christian Symbol. In the earlier centuries of the Christian Dispensation the fish was everywhere used as a symbol. In his remarkable book, "Christian Iconography," Didron says:

"The fish, in the opinion of antiquarians generally, is the symbol of Jesus Christ. The fish is sculptured upon a number of Christian monuments, and more particularly upon the ancient sarcophagi. It is also upon medals, bearing the name of our Savior and also upon engraved stones, cameos and intaglios   The fish is also to be remarked upon the amulets worn suspended from the necks by children, and upon ancient glasses and sculptured lamps.

"Baptismal fonts are more particularly ornamented with the fish. The fish is constantly exhibited placed upon a dish in the middle of the table, at the Last Supper, among the loaves, knives and cups used at the banquet."

In the writings of Tertullian we find this statement: "We are little fishes in Christ our great fish."

The last two thousand years, comprising the Piscean Age, has certainly been one of water and the many uses of that element have been emphasized, and sea and lake and river navigation has been brought to a high degree of efficiency.

3 *What is the Aquarian Age?* The human race is today standing upon the cusp of the Piscean-Aquarian Ages. Aquarius is an air sign and the New Age is already noted for remarkable inventions for the use of air, electricity, magnetism, etc. Men navigate the air as fish do the sea, and send their thoughts spinning around the world with the speed of lightning.

The word Aquarius is derived from the Latin word aqua, meaning water. Aquarius is, however, the *water bearer*, and the symbol of the sign, which is the eleventh sign of the Zodiac, is a man carrying in his right hand a pitcher of water. Jesus referred to the beginning of the Aquarian Age in these words:

"And then the man who bears the pitcher will walk forth across an arc of heaven; the sign and signet of the Son of Man will stand forth in the eastern sky. The wise will then lift up their heads and know that the redemption of the earth is near." (Aquarian Gospel 157:29, 30.)

The Aquarian Age is pre-eminently a spiritual age, and the spiritual side of the great lessons that Jesus gave to the world may now be comprehended by multitudes of people for the many are now coming into an advanced stage of spiritual consciousness; so with much propriety this book is called "The Aquarian (or Spiritual) Gospel of Jesus, the Christ."

An Important Event. The transfer of dominion from one Age to another is an important event in the world of Cherubim and Seraphim. Among the manuscripts of Levi we have found a most remarkable paper describing the transfer of dominion from the Piscean Age to the Aquarian Age, but it is difficult to determine whether it is a recital of facts or a prophetic statement. We reproduce the paper in full.

THE CUSP OF THE AGES.

"In Spirit I was caught away into the realms of Akasha; I stood alone within the circle of the sun.

"And there I found the secret spring that opens up the door to Wisdom and an understanding heart.

"I entered in and then I knew.

"I saw the four and twenty Cherubim and Seraphim that guard the circle of the sun, the mighty ones who were proclaimed by masters long ago 'the four and twenty ancient ones.'

"I heard the names of every Cherubim and Seraphim, and learned that every sign in all the Zodiac is ruled by two—a Cherubim and Seraphim.

"And then I stood upon the cusp where Ages meet. The Piscean Age had passed; the Aquarian Age had just begun.

"I saw the guardian Spirits of the Piscean Age; Ramasa is the Cherubim; Vacabiel is Seraphim.

"I saw the guardian Spirits of the Aquarian Age, and Archer is the Cherubim; Sakmaquil is the Seraphim.

"These four great spirits of the Triune God stood close together on the cusp, and in the presence of the sacred Three—the God of Might, the God of Wisdom, and the God of Love—the scepter of Domain, of Might, of Wisdom and of Love was there transferred.

"I heard the charges of the Triune God; but these I may not now reveal.

"I heard the history of the Piscean Age from Piscean Cherubim and Seraphim, and when I took my pen to write Ramasa said:

"Not now, my son, not now; but you may write it down for men when men have learned the sacred laws of Brotherhood, of Peace on earth, good-will to every living thing.

"And then I heard the Aquarian Cherubim and Seraphim proclaim the Gospel of the coming Age, the age of Wisdom, of the Son of Man.

"And when the crown was lifted from the head of Ramasa and placed upon the head of Archer of the Aquarian Age; and when the royal scepter was transferred from Seraphim Vacabiel to Seraphim Sakmaquil there was deep silence in the courts of heaven.

"And then the goddess Wisdom spoke, and with her hands outstretched she poured the benedictions of the Holy Breath upon the rulers of Aquarius.

"I may not write the words she spoke, but I may tell the Gospel of the coming age that Archer told when he received the crown.

"And I may breathe to men the song of praise that Seraphim Sakmaquil sung when she received the royal scepter of the newborn age.

"This Gospel I will tell, and I will sing this song in every land, to all the people, tribes and tongues of earth."

4   *What is Meant by "the Christ," as the Word is Used in This Book?* The word Christ is derived from the Greek word Kristos and means anointed. It is identical with the Hebrew word Messiah. The word Christ, per se, does not refer to any particular person; every anointed person is christed. When the definite article "the" is placed before the word christ a definite personality is indicated, and this personality is none other than a member of the Trinity, the Son who had a glory with the Father-Mother before the worlds were formed.

According to the teachings of all ancient masters this Son is Love; so the Christ is Love, and Love is God, since God is Love.

Another remarkable manuscript found in Levi's Akashic portfolio gives the clearest possible ideal of the Christ, or Love of God. It is presumed that this manuscript is a direct transcription from the Akashic Records and its importance demands its reproduction here in full.

THE CHRIST

"Before creation was the Christ walked with the Father God and Mother God in Akasha.

"The Christ is son, the only son begotten by Almighty God, the God of Force and God omniscient, God of thought; and Christ is God, the God of Love.

"Without the Christ there was no light. Through Christ all life was manifest; and so through him all things were done, and naught was done in forming worlds or peopling worlds without the Christ.

"Christ is the Logos of Infinities and through the word alone are Thought and Force made manifest.

"The Son is called the Christ, because the Son, the Love, the universal Love, was set apart, ordained to be creator, Lord, preserver and redeemer of all things, of everything that is, or evermore will be.

"Through Christ, the protoplast, the earth, the plant, the beast, the man, the angel and the cherubim took up their stations on their planes of life.

"Through Christ they are preserved; and if they fall it is the Christ who lifts them up; and if they sell themselves to sin the Christ redeems.

"Now Christ, the universal Love, pervades all spaces of infinity, and so there is no end to love.

"From the great heart of Love unnumbered spirits were sent forth to demonstrate the height, the depth, the width, the boundlessness of Love.

"To every world and star and moon and sun a master spirit of this Love divine was sent; and all were full anointed with the oil of helpfulness, and each became a Christ.

"All glorious in his majesty is Christ, who spread the pure white robe of Love o'er all the planes of earth— The Christ of earth, its heaven, its graves.

"In course of time the protoplast, the earth, the plant, the beast, the man sold out their birthrights unto sin; but Christ was present to redeem.

"Hid in the holiest place in all infinities is locked the scroll that bears the record of the purposes of God, the Triune God, and there we read:

"Perfection is the ultimate of life. A seed is perfect in its embryotic life, but it is destined to unfold, to grow.

"Into the soil of every plane these seeds, which were the Thoughts of God, were cast—the seeds of protoplast, of earth, of plant, of beast, of man, of angel and of cherubim, and they who sowed the seeds, through Christ, ordained that they should grow, and should return at last, by effort of unnumbered years, to the great granary of thought, and each be a perfection of its kind.

"And in the boundless blessedness of Love the man was made the Lord of protoplast, of earth, of plant, of beast; and Christ proclaimed: Man shall have full dominion over everything that is upon these planes of life; and it was so.

"And he who gave the lordship unto man declared that he must rule by Love.

"But men grew cruel and they lost their power to rule, and protoplast, and earth, and plant and beast became at enmity with man; he lost his heritage; but Christ was present to redeem.

"But man had lost his consciousness of right; he could no longer comprehend the boundlessness of Love; he could see naught but self, and things of self; but Christ was there to seek the lost and save.

"So that he might be close to man in all the ways of life, that man might comprehend the mighty spirit of the Love, the Christ of earth made manifest to human eyes and ears by taking his abode in some pure person, well prepared by many lives to be a fit abiding place of Love.

"Thus Christ made manifest Love's power to save; but men forgot so soon, and so Christ must manifest again, and then again.

"And ever since man took his place in form of flesh the Christ has been manifest in flesh at first of every age."

5 *What relationship existed between Jesus of Nazareth and the Christ?* Orthodox Christian ecclesiastics tell us that Jesus of Nazareth and the Christ were one; that the true name of this remarkable person was Jesus Christ. They tell us that this man of Galilee was the very eternal God clothed in flesh of man that men might see his glory. Of course this doc-

trine is wholly at variance with the teachings of Jesus himself and of his apostles. The Aquarian Masters in council have formulated an answer to this question that so well covers all the information required that we give it in full:

"Jesus was an ideal Jew, born in Bethlehem of Judea. His mother was a beautiful Jewish girl named Mary. As a child Jesus differed but little from other children only that in past lives he had overcome carnal propensities to such an extent that he could be tempted like others and not yield. Paul was right when to the Hebrews he said: 'He was in all points tempted like as we are, yet without sin.'—Hebrews 4:15.

"Jesus suffered as other men suffer, and was made perfect through suffering; for this is the only way to perfection. His life was an example of attainment by the way of crosses and cruel treatment. Paul was right again when he said: 'It became him, for whom are all things and by whom are all things, in bringing many sons into glory to make the captain of their salvation perfect through suffering.'—Hebrews 2:10.

"In many respects Jesus was a remarkable child, for by ages of strenuous preparation he was qualified to be an avatar, a savior of the world, and from childhood he was endowed with superior wisdom and was conscious of the fact that he was competent to lead the race into the higher ways of spiritual living. But he was conscious also of the fact that he must attain the mastery by trials, buffetings, temptations and sufferings. And all his life was spent in attaining. After his death, burial and resurrection he appeared in materialized form before the Silent Brothers in the temple of Heliopolis, in Egypt, and said:

"'My human life was wholly given to bring my will to tune with the deific will; when this was done my earth-tasks all were done.

"'You know that all my life was one great drama for the sons of men; a pattern for the sons of men. I lived to show the possibilities of man.

"'What I have done all men can do, and what I am all men shall be.'"— Aquarian Gospel 178:43,46.

"Jesus was the name of the man and it was the only appropriate name for this kind of a man. The word means Savior and Jesus was in more senses than one a savior.

The word Christ means "the anointed one," and then it is an official title. It means, The Master of Love. When we say "Jesus the Christ" we refer to the man and to his office; just as we do when we say Edward, the King, or Lincoln, the President. Edward was not always King, and Lincoln was not always President, and Jesus was not always Christ. Jesus won his Christship by a strenuous life, and in the Aquarian Gospel, chapter 55, we have a record of the events of his christing, or receiving the degree Christ. Here is where he was coronated by the highest earth authorities as the Christ-King; properly speaking, 'The Master of Love'; and after this was done he entered at once upon his Judean and Galilean ministry.

"We recognize the facts that Jesus was man and that Christ was God, so that in very truth Jesus the Christ was the God-man of the ages."

The Nazarene's Testimony. Jesus himself made the matter clear. Once when he was speaking to a congregation in Bethany the people called him King and he stood forth and said:

"'I am not sent to sit upon a throne to rule as Caesar rules; and you may tell the ruler of the Jews that I am not a claimant for his throne.

"'Men call me Christ, and God has recognized the name; but Christ is not a man. The Christ is universal Love, and Love is King.

"'This Jesus is but man who has been fitted by temptations overcome, by trials multiform, to be the temple through which the Christ can manifest to men.

"'Then hear, you men of Israel, hear! Look not upon the flesh; it is not king. Look to the Christ within who shall be formed in every one of you, as he is formed in me.

"'When you have purified your hearts by faith, the king will enter in and you will see his face.'"—Aquarian Gospel 68:10-14.

Surely this question has been answered. Jesus was man; Christ was Divine Love—the Love of God, and after thirty years of strenuous life the man had made his body fit to be the temple of the holy breath and Love took full possession, and John well said when he declared:

" 'And the Word was made flesh and dwelt among us and we beheld the glory of the only begotten of the Father, full of grace and truth.' "

6 *Who was Levi, the Transcriber of this Book?* Regarding the personality of Levi we are permitted to write but little. Suffice it to say that he is an American citizen, and has been a close student of the religions of the world from childhood. When but a boy he was impressed with the sensitiveness of the finer ethers and believed that in some manner they were sensitized plates on which sounds, even thoughts, were recorded. With avidity he entered into the deeper studies of etheric vibration, determined to solve the great mysteries of the heavens for himself. Forty years he spent in study and silent meditation, and then he found himself in that stage of spiritual consciousness that permitted him to enter the domain of these superfine ethers and become familiar with their mysteries. He then learned that the imaginings of his boyhood days were founded upon veritable facts, and that every thought of every living thing is there recorded.

In his manuscript entitled "The Cusp of the Ages," a part of which we have already reproduced in this Introduction, we find the following copy of the Commission, which Levi received from Visel, the Goddess of Wisdom, or the Holy Breath.

LEVI'S COMMISSION.

"And then Visel the holy one stood forth and said:

"O Levi, son of man, behold, for you are called to be the message bearer of the coming age—the age of spirit blessedness.

"Give heed, O son of man, for men must know the Christ, the Love of God; for Love is sovereign balm for all the wounds of men, the remedy for every ill.

"And man must be endowed with Wisdom and with Power and with an Understanding heart.

"Behold the Akasha! Behold the Record Galleries of Visel where every thought and word and deed of every living thing is written down.

"The needs of men are manifold, and men must know their needs.

"Now, Levi, hearken to my words: go forth into these mystic Galleries and read. There you will find a message for the world; for every man; for every living thing.

"I breathe upon you now the Holy Breath; you will discriminate, and you will know the lessons that these Record Books of God are keeping now for men of this new age.

"This age will be an age of splendor and of light, because it is the home age of the Holy Breath; and Holy Breath will testify anew for Christ, the Logos of eternal Love.

"At first of every age this Logos is made manifest in flesh so man can see and know and comprehend a Love that is not narrow, circumscribed.

"Twelve times in every revolution of the sun this christed Love of God is made full manifest in flesh upon the planes of earth, and you may read in Akasha the wondrous lessons that these Christs have taught to men; but you shall publish not to men the lessons of the Christs of ancient times.

"Now, Levi, message bearer of the Spirit Age, take up your pen and write.

"Write full the story of The Christ who built upon the Solid Rock of yonder circle of the sun—the Christ who men have known as Enoch the Initiate.

"Write of his works as prophet, priest and seer; write of his life of purity and love, and how he changed his carnal flesh to flesh divine without descending through the gates of death.

"And you may write the story of Melchizedec, the Christ who lived when Abram lived, and pointed out to men the way to life through sacrifice; who gave his life a willing sacrifice for men.

"And you may write the story of the Prince of Peace, The Christ who came as babe in Bethlehem, and traveled every way of life that man must tread.

"He was despised, rejected and abused; was spit upon, was crucified, was buried in a tomb; but he revived and rose a conqueror over death that he might show the possibilities of man —

"A thousand times he said to men; 'I came to show the possibilities of man; what I have done all men may do, and what I am all men shall be.'

"These stories of The Christ will be enough, for they contain the true philosophy of life, of death and of the resurrection of the dead.

"They show the spiral journey of the soul until the man of earth and God are one forevermore."

Levi in Prophecy. About two thousand years ago Elihu, who conducted a school of the prophets in Zoan, Egypt, referred to Levi thus:

"This age will comprehend but little of the works of Purity and Love; but not a word is lost, for in the Book of God's Remembrance a registry is made of every thought and word and deed;

"And when the world is ready to receive, lo, God will send a messenger to open up the book and copy from its sacred pages all the messages of Purity and Love.

"Then every man of earth will read the words of life in the language of his native land, and men will see the light.

"And man again will be at one with God."—Aquarian Gospel 7:25-28.

Further references to the personality of Levi are, seemingly, unnecessary. It matters but little who he is; his work in the transcription of the Aquarian Gospel of Jesus, the Christ, stands unimpeachable. The lessons of this book all bear the stamp of the Nazarene, for no man except the world's greatest master could have touched the high chords of divine Love and Wisdom which characterize the pages of this marvelous book.

7 *What are the Akashic Records?* Akasha is a Sanskrit word, and means "Primary substance," that out of which all things are formed. According to Aquarian philosophy, it is the first stage of the crystallization of spirit. This philosophy recognizes the fact that all primordial substance is spirit; that matter is spirit moving at a lower rate of vibration, becoming, as one master expressed it, a coagulum.

This Akashic, or primary substance, is of exquisite fineness and is so sensitive that the slightest vibrations of an ether any place in the universe registers an indelible impression upon it.

This primal substance is not relegated to any particular part of the universe, but is everywhere present. It is in very fact the "Universal Mind" of which our metaphysicians speak.

When the mind of man is in exact accord with the Universal Mind man enters into a conscious recognition of these Akashic impressions, and may collect them and translate them into any language of earth with which he is familiar.

In the infinite One manifest we note the attributes of Force, Intelligence and Love, and a person may be in full accord with one of these attributes and not with the others. One may enter fully into the spirit of the God of Force and not be imbued with the spirit of Intelligence; or one may be wholly absorbed with the spirit of Divine Love and be far removed from both Intelligence and Force.   Furthermore, a person may enter fully into the consciousness of Holy Breath, or Supreme Intelligence, and be not at all in rapport with either Love or Force.   Knowledge is not gained through the spirit of either Force or Love.   It is only from Universal Mind, which is Supreme Intelligence, called by Oriental scholars the Akashic Records, and by Hebrew masters, the Book of God's Remembrance, that knowledge of any kind can be obtained.

Consciousness; we note three phases of it:

1   Consciousness of the omnipotence of God and man.
2   Christ consciousness, or consciousness of Divine Love.
3   Consciousness of the Holy Breath, or of Supreme Intelligence.

We must bear in mind that one of these phases of consciousness does not necessarily imply either of the others.   People are frequently found who are completely filled with the Love of God, are far advanced in the science of Christ consciousness, who are absolutely ignorant; have not the slightest conception of the laws of natural things or of spiritual things; are not in rapport with the great Teacher which is the Holy Spirit.

The Akashic Records.   The imperishable records of life, known as the Akashic Records, are wholly in the domain of Supreme Intelligence, or Universal Mind, and the Akashic Record reader must be in such close touch with the Holy Spirit, or the Holy Breath, as the ancient masters call this spirit of Supreme Intelligence, that every thought vibration is instantly felt in every fibre of his being.

Differentiation.   Since all space is charged with the vibrations of thoughts of all kinds how may the Akashic Record reader differentiate and gather only the thoughts and life events of a particular person or group of persons?

Every person has his own distinct vibration and when the reader fully understands the law of discrimination his whole being is tuned for the reception of the one particular tone and rhythm, and it is impossible for any other tone or rhythm to make the slightest impression upon him.   This principle is demonstrated in wireless telegraphy.

It required many years for Levi to learn the Law of Differentiation, and to come in rapport with the tones and rhythms of Jesus of Nazareth, Enoch and Melchizedec and their co-laborers.   But under the direction of the Spirit of Supreme Intelligence, he has attained unto this accomplishment, and now he instantly feels in all his being the slightest vibrations that come from any of these great centers and, of course, all of his transcriptions are true to the letter.

MAN.

"What is man that thou art mindful of him, or the son of man that thou visiteth him?"   This was the earnest question of David, the Hebrew Psalmist, and the 8th Psalm is given wholly to the contemplation of man, the crowning work of manifest creation.   Among the many great lessons that Levi has been permitted to gather from the Akashic Records, or the

Universal Mind, we find one on *Man* in which his descent into physical matter and his final ascent into an eternal oneness with God is so graphically described that it certainly merits a place in this Introduction, and we give it in full:

"Time never was when man was not.

"If life of man at any time began a time would come when it would end.

"The thoughts of God cannot be circumscribed. No finite mind can comprehend things infinite.

"All finite things are subject unto change. All finite things will cease to be, because there was a time when they were not.

"The bodies and the soul of men are finite things, and they will change, yea, from the finite point of view the time will come when they will be no more.

"But man himself is not the body, nor the soul; he is a spirit and is part of God.

"Creative Fiat gave to man, to spirit man, a soul that he might function on the plane of soul; gave him a body of the flesh, that he might function on the plane of things made manifest.

"Why did creative Fiat give to spirit man a soul that he might function on the plane of soul?

"Why did creative Fiat give to soul a body of the flesh that it might function on the plane of things that are made manifest?

"Hear, now, ye worlds, dominions, powers and thrones!

"Hear, now, ye cherubim, ye seraphim, ye angels and ye men!

"Hear, now, O protoplast, and earth, and plant and beast!

"Hear, now, ye creeping things of earth, ye fish that swim, ye birds that fly!

"Hear, now, ye winds that blow, ye thunders and ye lightnings of the sky!

"Hear, now, ye spirits of the fire, of water, earth and air!

"Hear, now, O everything that is, or was, or evermore will be, for Wisdom speaks from out the highest plane of spirit life:

"Man is a thought of God; all thoughts of God are infinite; they are not measured up by time, for things that are concerned with time begin and end.

"The thoughts of God are from the everlasting of the past unto the never ending days to come—And so is man, the Spirit-man.

"But man, like every other thought of God, was but a seed, a seed that held within itself the potencies of God, just as the seed of any plant of earth holds deep within itself the attributes of every part of that especial plant.

"So spirit-man, as seed of God, held deep within himself the attributes of every part of God.

"Now, seeds are perfect, yea, as perfect as the source from which they come; but they are not unfolded into life made manifest.

"The child in utero is perfect as the mother is.

"So man, the seed, must be deep planted in a soil that he might grow, unfold, as does the bud unfold to show the flower.

"The human seed that came forth from the heart of God was full ordained to be the lord of plane of soul, and of the plane of things made manifest.

"So God, the husbandman of every thing that is, threw forth this human seed into the soil of soul; it grew apace, and man became a living soul; and he became the lord of all the kingdom of the soul.

"Hark, now, let every creature hear, The plane of soul is but the ether of the spirit plane vibrating not so fast, and in the slower rhythm of this plane the essences of life are manifest; the perfumes and the odors, the true sensations and the all of love are manifest.

"And these soul attributes become a body beautiful.

"A multitude of lessons man must learn upon the plane of soul; and here he tarries many ages until his lessons are all learned.

"Upon the boundary of the plane of soul the ether began to vibrate slower still, and then the essences took on a garb; the perfumes and the odors and the true sensations and the all of love were clothed in flesh; and man was clothed in flesh.

"Perfected man must pass through all the ways of life, and so a carnal nature was full manifest, a nature that sprang forth from fleshly things.

"Without a foe a soldier never knows his strength, and thought must be developed by the exercise of strength.

"And so this carnal nature soon became a foe that man must fight, that he might be the strength of God made manifest.

"Let every living thing stand still and hear!

"Man is the lord of all the plane of manifests; of protoplast, of mineral, of plant, of beast; but he has given up his birthright, just to gratify his lower self, his carnal self.

"But man will full regain his lost estate, his heritage; but he must do it in a conflict that cannot be told in words.

"Yea, he must suffer trials and temptations manifold; but let him know that cherubim and seraphim that rule the stations of the sun, and spirits of the mighty God who rule the solar stars are his protectors and his guides, and they will lead to victory.

"Man will be fully saved, redeemed, perfected by the things he suffers on the plane of flesh, and on the plane of soul.

"When man has conquered carnal things his garb of flesh will then have served its purpose wel' and it will fall, will be no more.

"Then he will stand untrammeled on the plane of soul where he must full complete his victories."

"Unnumbered foes will stand before the man upon the plane of soul; there he must overcome, yea, overcome them every one.

"Thus hope will ever be his beacon light; there is no failure for the human soul, for God is leading on and victory is sure.

"Man cannot die; the spirit man is one with God, and while God lives man cannot die.

"When man has conquered every foe upon the plane of soul the seed will have full opened out, will have unfolded in the Holy Breath.

"The garb of soul will then have served its purpose well, and man will need it never more, and it will pass and be no more.

"And man will then attain unto the blessedness of perfectness and be at one with God."

SUBJECT INDEX

A general outline of the incidents and topics of the book will be found in the Contents which appears in the first part of the volume.

THE AQUARIAN GOSPEL
OF JESUS THE CHRIST.

SECTION I.

ALEPH.

Birth and Early Life of Mary, Mother of Jesus.

CHAPTER 1.

Palestine. Birth of Mary. Joachim's feast. Mary is blest by the priests. His prophecy. Mary abides in the temple. Is betrothed to Joseph.

AUGUSTUS Cæsar reigned and Herod Antipas was ruler of Jerusalem.

2 Three provinces comprised the land of Palestine: Judea, and Samaria, and Galilee.

3 Joachim was a master of the Jewish law, a man of wealth; he lived in Nazareth of Galilee; and Anna, of the tribe of Judah, was his wife.

4 To them was born a child, a goodly female child, and they were glad; and Mary was the name they gave the child.

5 Joachim made a feast in honor of the child; but he invited not the rich, the honored and the great; he called the poor, the halt, the lame, the blind, and to each one he gave a gift of raiment, food, or other needful thing.

6 He said, The Lord has given me this wealth; I am his steward by his grace, and if I give not to his children when in need, then he will make this wealth a curse.

7 Now, when the child was three years old her parents took her to Jerusalem, and in the temple she received the blessings of the priests.

8 The high priest was a prophet and a seer, and when he saw the child he said,

9 Behold, this child will be the mother of an honored prophet and a master of the law; she shall abide within this holy temple of the Lord.

10 And Mary did abide within the temple of the Lord; and Hillel, chief of the Sanhedrim, taught her all the precepts of the Jews, and she delighted in the law of God.

11 When Mary reached the age of womanhood she was betrothed to Joseph, son of Jacob, and a carpenter of Nazareth.

12 And Joseph was an upright man, and a devoted Essenes.

SECTION II.

BETH.

Birth and Infancy of John, the Harbinger, and of Jesus.

CHAPTER 2.

Zacharias and Elizabeth. Prophetic messages of Gabriel to Zacharias, Elizabeth and Mary. Birth of John. Prophecy of Zacharias.

NEAR Hebron in the hills of Judah, Zacharias and Elizabeth abode.

2 They were devout and just, and every day they read the Law, the Prophets and the Psalms which told of one to come, strong to redeem; and they were waiting for the king.

3 Now, Zacharias was a priest, and in his turn he led the temple service in Jerusalem.

4 It came to pass as Zacharias stood before the Lord and burned the incense in the Holy Place, that Gabriel came and stood before his face.

5 And Zacharias was afraid; he thought that some great evil was about to come upon the Jews.

6 But Gabriel said, O man of God, fear not; I bring to you, and all the world, a message of good will, and peace on earth.

7 Behold, the Prince of Peace, the king you seek, will quickly come.

8 Your wife will bear to you a son, a holy son, of whom the prophet wrote,

9 Behold, I send Elijah unto you again before the coming of the Lord; and he will level down the hills and fill the valleys up, and pave the way for him who shall redeem.

10 From the beginning of the age your son has borne the name of John, the mercy of the Lord; his name is John.

11 He will be honored in the sight of God, and he will drink no wine, and from his birth he will be filled with Holy Breath.

12 And Gabriel stood before Elizabeth as she was in the silence in her home, and told her all the words that he had said to Zacharias in Jerusalem.

13 When he had done the service of his course, the priest went home, and with Elizabeth rejoiced.

14 Five months passed by and Gabriel came to Mary in her home in Nazareth and said,

15 Hail Mary, hail! Once blessed in the name of God; twice blessed in the name of Holy Breath; thrice blessed in the name of Christ; for you are worthy, and will bear a son who shall be called Immanuel.

16 His name is Jesus, for he saves his people from their sins.

17 When Joseph's daily task was done he came, and Mary told him all the words that Gabriel spoke to her, and they rejoiced; for they believed that he, the man of God, had spoken words of truth.

18 And Mary went with haste to tell Elizabeth about the promises of Gabriel; together they rejoiced.

19 And in the home of Zacharias and Elizabeth did Mary tarry ninety days; then she returned to Nazareth.

20 To Zacharias and Elizabeth a son was born, and Zacharias said,

21 Most blessed be the name of God, for he has opened up the fount of blessings for his people, Israel.

22 His promises are verified;

for he has brought to pass the words which holy prophets spoke in olden times.

23 And Zacharias looked upon the infant John, and said,

24 You will be called the prophet of the Holy One; and you will go before his face, and will prepare his way.

25 And you will give a knowledge of salvation unto Israel; and you will preach the gospel of repentance and the blotting out of sins.

26 Behold, for soon the Day Star from on high will visit us, to light the way for those who sit within the darkness of the shadowland, and guide our feet unto the ways of peace.

CHAPTER 3.

Birth of Jesus. Masters honor the child. The shepherds rejoice. Zacharias and Elizabeth visit Mary. Jesus is circumcised.

THE time was nearly due for Jesus to be born, and Mary longed to see Elizabeth, and she and Joseph turned their faces toward the Judean hills.

2 And when upon their way they came to Bethlehem the day was done, and they must tarry for the night.

3 But Bethlehem was thronged with people going to Jerusalem; the inns and homes were filled with guests, and Joseph and his wife could find no place to rest but in a cave where animals were kept; and there they slept.

4 At midnight came a cry, A child is born in yonder cave among the beasts. And lo, the promised son of man was born.

5 And strangers took the little one and wrapped him in the dainty robes that Mary had prepared and laid him in a trough from which the beasts of burden fed.

6 Three persons clad in snow-white robes came in and stood before the child and said,

7 All strength, all wisdom and all love be yours, Immanuel.

8 Now, on the hills of Bethlehem were many flocks of sheep with shepherds guarding them.

9 The shepherds were devout, were men of prayer, and they were waiting for a strong deliverer to come.

10 And when the child of promise came a man in snow-white robe appeared to them, and they fell back in fear. The man stood forth and said,

11 Fear not! behold I bring you joyful news. At midnight in a cave in Bethlehem was born the prophet and the king that you have long been waiting for.

12 And then the shepherds all were glad; they felt that all the hills were filled with messengers of light, who said,

13 All glory be to God on high; peace, peace on earth, good will to men.

14 And then the shepherds came with haste to Bethlehem and to the cave, that they might see and honor him whom men had called Immanuel.

15 Now, when the morning came, a shepherdess whose home was near, prepared a room for Mary, Joseph and the child; and here they tarried many days.

16 And Joseph sent a messenger in haste to Zacharias and Elizabeth to say, The child is born in Bethlehem.

17 And Zacharias and Elizabeth took John and came to Bethlehem with words of cheer.

18　And Mary and Elizabeth recounted all the wondrous things that had transpired. The people joined with them in praising God.

19　According to the custom of the Jews, the child was circumcised; and when they asked, What will you call the child? the mother said, His name is Jesus, as the man of God declared.

CHAPTER 4.

Consecration of Jesus. Mary offers sacrifices. Simeon and Anna prophesy. Anna is rebuked for worshipping the child. The family returns to Bethlehem.

NOW, Mary took her son, when he was forty days of age, up to the temple in Jerusalem, and he was consecrated by the priest.

2　And then she offered purifying sacrifices for herself, according to the custom of the Jews; a lamb and two young turtle doves.

3　A pious Jew named Simeon was in the temple serving God.

4　From early youth he had been looking for Immanuel to come, and he had prayed to God that he might not depart until his eyes had seen Messiah in the flesh.

5　And when he saw the infant Jesus he rejoiced and said, I now am ready to depart in peace, for I have seen the king.

6　And then he took the infant in his arms and said, Behold, this child will bring a sword upon my people, Israel, and all the world; but he will break the sword and then the nations will learn war no more.

7　The master's cross I see upon the forehead of this child, and he will conquer by this sign.

8　And in the temple was a widow, four and eighty years of age, and she departed not, but night and day she worshipped God.

9　And when she saw the infant Jesus she exclaimed, Behold Immanuel! Behold the signet cross of the Messiah on his brow!

10　And then the woman knelt to worship him, as God with us, Immanuel; but one, a master clothed in white, appeared and said,

11　Good woman, stay; take heed to what you do; you may not worship man; this is idolatry.

12　This child is man, the son of man, and worthy of all praise. You shall adore and worship God; him only shall you serve.

13　The woman rose and bowed her head in thankfulness and worshipped God.

14　And Mary took the infant Jesus and returned to Bethlehem.

CHAPTER 5.

Three magian priests honor Jesus. Herod is alarmed. Calls a council of the Jews. Is told that prophets had foretold the coming of a king. Herod resolves to kill the child. Mary and Joseph take Jesus and flee into Egypt.

BEYOND the river Euphrates the magians lived; and they were wise, could read the language of the stars and they divined that one, a master soul, was born; they saw his star above Jerusalem.

2　And there were three among the magian priests who longed to see the master of the coming age; and they took costly gifts and hastened to the West in search of him, the new-born king, that they might honor him.

3　And one took gold, the symbol of nobility; another myrrh, the symbol of dominion and of power; gum-thus the other took, the symbol of the wisdom of the sage.

4 Now when the magians reached Jerusalem the people were amazed, and wondered who they were and why they came.

5 And when they asked, Where is the child that has been born a king? the very throne of Herod seemed to shake.

6 And Herod sent a courtier forth to bring the magians to his court.

7 And when they came they asked again, Where is the new born king? And then they said, While yet beyond the Euphrates we saw his star arise, and we have come to honor him.

8 And Herod blanched with fear. He thought, perhaps, the priests were plotting to restore the kingdom of the Jews, and so he said within himself, I will know more about this child that has been born a king.

9 And so he told the magian priests to tarry in the city for a while and he would tell them all about the king.

10 He called in council all the Jewish masters of the law and asked, What have the Jewish prophets said concerning such a one?

11 The Jewish masters answered him and said, The prophets long ago foretold that one would come to rule the tribes of Israel; that this Messiah would be born in Bethle-

12 They said, The prophet Micah wrote, O Bethlehem Judea, a little place among the Judean hills, yet out of you will one come forth to rule my people, Israel; yea, one who lived in olden times, in very ancient days.

13 Then Herod called the magian priests again and told them

what the masters of the Jewish law had said; and then he sent them on the way to Bethlehem.

14 He said, Go search, and if you find the child that has been born a king, return and tell me all, that I may go and honor him.

15 The magians went their way and found the child with Mary in the shepherd's home.

16 They honored him; bestowed upon him precious gifts and gave him gold, gum-thus and myrrh.

17 These magian priests could read the hearts of men; they read the wickedness of Herod's heart, and knew that he had sworn to kill the new born king.

18 And so they told the secret to the parents of the child, and bid them flee beyond the reach of harm.

19 And then the priests went on their homeward way; they went not through Jerusalem.

20 And Joseph took the infant Jesus and his mother in the night and fled to Egypt land, and with Elihu and Salome in ancient Zoan they abode.

CHAPTER 6.

Herod learns of the supposed mission of John. The infants of Bethlehem are massacred by Herod's order. Elizabeth escapes with John. Because Zacharias cannot tell where his son is hidden, he is murdered. Herod dies.

NOW, when the magian priests did not return to tell him of the child that had been born a king, King Herod was enraged.

2 And then his courtiers told him of another child in Bethlehem, one born to go before and to prepare the people to receive the king.

3 This angered more and more

the king; he called his guards and bid them go to Bethlehem and slay the infant John, as well as Jesus who was born to be a king.

4 He said, Let no mistake be made, and that you may be sure to slay these claimants to my throne, slay all male children in the town not yet two years of age.

5 The guards went forth and did as Herod bade them do.

6 Elizabeth knew not that Herod sought to slay her son, and she and John were yet in Bethlehem; but when she knew, she took the infant John and hastened to the hills.

7 The murderous guards were near; they pressed upon her hard; but then she knew the secret caves in all the hills, and into one she ran and hid herself and John until the guards were gone.

8 Their cruel task was done; the guards returned and told the story to the king.

9 They said, We know that we have slain the infant king; but John, his harbinger, we could not find.

10 The king was angry with his guards because they failed to slay the infant John; he sent them to the tower in chains.

11 And other guards were sent to Zacharias, father of the harbinger, while he was serving in the Holy Place, to say, The king demands that you shall tell where is your son.

12 But Zacharias did not know, and he replied, I am a minister of God, a servant in the Holy Place;

how could I know where they have taken him?

13 And when the guards returned and told the king what Zacharias said, he was enraged and said,

14 My guards, go back and tell that wily priest that he is in my hands; that if he does not tell the truth, does not reveal the hiding place of John, his son, then he shall die.

15 The guards went back and told the priest just what the king had said.

16 And Zacharias said, I can but give my life for truth; and if the king does shed my blood the Lord will save my soul.

17 The guards again returned and told the king what Zacharias said.

18 Now, Zacharias stood before the altar in the Holy Place engaged in prayer.

19 A guard approached and with a dagger thrust him through; he fell and died before the curtain of the sanctuary of the Lord.

20 And when the hour of salutation came, for Zacharias daily blessed the priests, he did not come.

21 And after waiting long the priests went to the Holy Place and found the body of the dead.

22 And there was grief, deep grief, in all the land.

23 Now Herod sat upon his throne; he did not seem to move; his courtiers came; the king was dead. His sons reigned in his stead.

SECTION III.

GIMEL.

Education of Mary and Elizabeth in Zoan.

CHAPTER 7.

Archelaus reigns. Mary and Elizabeth with their sons are in Zoan and are taught by Elihu and Salome. Elihu's introductory lesson. Tells of an interpreter.

THE son of Herod, Archelaus, reigned in Jerusalem. He was a selfish, cruel king; he put to death all those who did not honor him.

2 He called in council all the wisest men and asked about the infant claimant to his throne.

3 The council said that John and Jesus both were dead; then he was satisfied.

4 Now Joseph, Mary and their son were down in Egypt in Zoan, and John was with his mother in the Judean hills.

5 Elihu and Salome sent messengers in haste to find Elizabeth and John. They found them and they brought them to Zoan.

6 Now, Mary and Elizabeth were marveling much because of their deliverance.

7 Elihu said, It is not strange; there are no happenings; law governs all events.

8 From olden times it was ordained that you should be with us, and in this sacred school be taught.

9 Elihu and Salome took Mary and Elizabeth out to the sacred grove near by where they were wont to teach.

10 Elihu said to Mary and Elizabeth, You may esteem yourselves thrice blest, for you are chosen mothers of long promised sons,

11 Who are ordained to lay in solid rock a sure foundation stone

on which the temple of the perfect man shall rest—a temple that shall never be destroyed.

12 We measure time by cycle ages, and the gate to every age we deem a mile stone in the journey of the race.

13 An age has passed; the gate unto another age flies open at the touch of time. This is the preparation age of soul, the kingdom of Immanuel, of God in man;

14 And these, your sons, will be the first to tell the news, and preach the gospel of good will to men, and peace on earth.

15 A mighty work is theirs; for carnal men want not the light; they love the dark, and when the light shines in the dark they comprehend it not.

16 We call these sons, Revealers of the Light; but they must have the light before they can reveal the light.

17 And you must teach your sons, and set their souls on fire with love and holy zeal, and make them conscious of their missions to the sons of men.

18 Teach them that God and man were one; but that through carnal thoughts and words and deeds, man tore himself away from God; debased himself.

19 Teach that the Holy Breath would make them one again, restoring harmony and peace;

20 That naught can make them one but love; that God so loved the world that he has clothed his son in flesh that man may comprehend.

21 The only Savior of the world is love, and Jesus, son of Mary,

comes to manifest that love to men.

22   Now, love cannot be manifest until its way has been prepared, and naught can rend the rocks and bring down lofty hills and fill the valleys up, and thus prepare the way, but purity.

23   But purity in life men do not comprehend; and so, it, too, must come in flesh.

24   And you, Elizabeth, are blest because your son is purity made flesh, and he shall pave the way for love.

25   This age will comprehend but little of the works of Purity and Love; but not a word is lost, for in the Book of God's Remembrance a registry is made of every thought, and word, and deed;

26   And when the world is ready to receive, lo, God will send a messenger to open up the book and copy from its sacred pages all the messages of Purity and Love.

27   Then every man of earth will read the words of life in language of his native land, and men will see the light, walk in the light and be the light.

28   And man again will be at one with God.

CHAPTER 8.

Elihu's lessons.   The unity of life.
The two selfs.   The devil.   Love
the savior of men.   The David of
the light.   Goliath of the dark.

AGAIN Elihu met his pupils in the sacred grove and said,

2   No man lives unto himself; for every living thing is bound by cords to every other living thing.

3   Blest are the pure in heart; for they will love and not demand love in return.

4   They will not do to other men what they would not have other men do unto them.

5   There are two selfs; the higher and the lower self.

6   The higher self is human spirit clothed with soul, made in the form of God.

7   The lower self, the carnal self, the body of desires, is a reflexion of the higher self, distorted by the murky ethers of the flesh.

8   The lower self is an illusion, and will pass away; the higher self is God in man, and will not pass away.

9   The higher self is the embodiment of truth; the lower self is truth reversed, and so is falsehood manifest.

10   The higher self is justice, mercy, love and right; the lower self is what the higher self is not.

11   The lower self breeds hatred, slander, lewdness, murders, theft, and everything that harms; the higher self is mother of the virtues and the harmonies of life.

12   The lower self is rich in promises, but poor in blessedness and peace; it offers pleasure, joy and satisfying gains; but gives unrest and misery and death.

13   It gives men apples that are lovely to the eye and pleasant to the smell; their cores are full of bitterness and gall.

14   If you would ask me what to study I would say, yourselfs; and when you well had studied them, and then would ask me what to study next, I would reply, your-

15   He who knows well his lower self, knows the illusions of the world, knows of the things that pass away; and he who knows his higher self, knows God; knows well the things that cannot pass away.

16   Thrice blessed is the man who has made purity and love his

very own; he has been ransomed from the perils of the lower self and is himself his higher self.

17 Men seek salvation from an evil that they deem a living monster of the nether world; and they have gods that are but demons in disguise; all powerful, yet full of jealousy and hate and lust;

18 Whose favors must be bought with costly sacrifice of fruits, and of the lives of birds, and animals, and human kind.

19 And yet these gods possess no ears to hear, no eyes to see, no heart to sympathize, no power to save.

20 This evil is a myth; these gods are made of air, and clothed with shadows of a thought.

21 The only devil from which men must be redeemed is self, the lower self. If man would find his devil he must look within; his name is self.

22 If man would find his savior he must look within; and when the demon self has been dethroned the savior, Love, will be exalted to the throne of power.

23 The David of the light is Purity, who slays the strong Goliath of the dark, and seats the savior, Love, upon the throne.

CHAPTER 9.

Salome's lessons. The man and the woman. Philosophy of human moods. The triune God. The Septonate. The God Tao.

SALOME taught the lesson of the day. She said, All times are not alike. Today the words of man may have the greatest power; tomorrow women teaches best.

2 In all the ways of life the man and woman should walk hand in hand; the one without the other is but half; each has a work to do.

3 But all things teach; each has a time and season for its own. The sun, the moon have lessons of their own for men; but each one teaches at the appointed time.

4 The lessons of the sun fall down on human hearts like withered leaves upon a stream, if given in the season of the moon; and so with lessons of the moon and all the stars.

5 Today one walks in gloom, downhearted and oppressed; tomorrow that same one is filled with joy.

6 Today the heavens seem full of blessedness and hope; tomorrow hope has fled, and every plan and purpose comes to naught.

7 Today one wants to curse the very ground on which he treads; tomorrow he is full of love and praise.

8 Today one hates and scorns and envies and is jealous of the child he loves; tomorrow he has risen above his carnal self, and breathes forth gladness and good will.

9 A thousand times men wonder why these heights and depths, these light hearts and these sad, are found in every life.

10 They do not know that there are teachers everywhere, each busy with a God-appointed task, and driving home to human hearts the truth.

11 But this is true, and every one receives the lessons that he needs.

12 And Mary said, Today I am in exaltation great; my thoughts and all my life seem lifted up; why am I thus inspired?

13 Salome replied, This is a day of exaltation; day of worship and of praise; a day when, in a measure, we may comprehend our Father-God.

14   Then let us study God, the One, the Three, the Seven.

15   Before the worlds were formed all things were One; just Spirit, Universal Breath.

16   And Spirit breathed, and that which was not manifest became the Fire and Thought of heaven, the Father-God, the Mother-God.

17   And when the Fire and Thought of heaven in union breathed, their son, their only son, was born. This son is Love whom men have called the Christ.

18   Men call the Thought of heaven the Holy Breath.

19   And when the Triune God breathed forth, lo, seven Spirits stood before the throne. These are the Elohim, creative spirits of the universe.

20   And these are they who said, Let us make man; and in their image man was made.

21   In early ages of the world the dwellers in the farther East said, Tao is the name of Universal Breath; and in the ancient books we read,

22   No manifesting form has Tao Great, and yet he made and keeps the heavens and earth.

23   No passion has our Tao Great, and yet he causes sun and moon and all the stars to rise and set.

24   No name has Tao Great, and yet he makes all things to grow; he brings in season both the seed time and the harvest time.

25   And Tao Great was One; the One became the Two; the Two became the Three, the Three evolved the Seven, which filled the universe with manifests.

26   And Tao Great gives unto all, the evil and the good, the rain, the dew, the sunshine and the flow-

ers; from his rich stores he feeds them all.

27   And in the same old book we read of man: He has a spirit knit to Tao Great; a soul which lives within the seven Breaths of Tao Great; a body of desires that springs up from the soil of flesh.

28   Now spirit loves the pure, the good, the true; the body of desires extols the selfish self; the soul becomes the battle ground between the two.

29   And blessed is the man whose spirit is triumphant and whose lower self is purified; whose soul is cleansed, becoming fit to be the council chamber of the manifests of Tao Great.

30   Thus closed the lesson of Salome.

CHAPTER 10.

Elihu's lessons. The Brahmic religion. Life of Abram. Jewish sacred books. The Persian religion.

ELIHU taught; he said, In ancient times a people in the East were worshippers of God, the One, whom they called Brahm.

2   Their laws were just; they lived in peace; they saw the light within; they walked in wisdom's ways.

3   But priests with carnal aims arose, who changed the laws to suit the carnal mind; bound heavy burdens on the poor, and scorned the rules of right; and so the Brahms became corrupt.

4   But in the darkness of the age a few great masters stood unmoved; they loved the name of Brahm; they were great beacon lights before the world.

5   And they preserved inviolate the wisdom of their holy Brahm,

and you may read this wisdom in their sacred books.

6 And in Chaldea, Brahm was known. A pious Brahm named Terah lived in Ur; his son was so devoted to the Brahmic faith that he was called A-Brahm; and he was set apart to be the father of the Hebrew race.

7 Now, Terah took his wife and sons and all his flocks and herds to Haran in the West; here Terah died.

8 And Abram took the flocks and herds, and with his kindred journeyed further west;

9 And when he reached the Oaks of Morah in the land of Canaan, he pitched his tents and there abode.

10 A famine swept the land and Abram took his kindred and his flocks and herds and came to Egypt, and in these fertile plains of Zoan pitched his tent, and here abode.

11 And men still mark the place where Abram lived—across the plain.

12 You ask why Abram came to Egypt land? This is the cradle-land of the initiate; all secret things belong to Egypt land; and this is why the masters come.

13 In Zoan Abram taught his science of the stars, and in that sacred temple over there he learned the wisdom of the wise.

14 And when his lessons all were learned, he took his kindred and his flocks and herds and journeyed back to Canaan, and in the plains of Mamre pitched his tent, and there he lived, and there he died.

15 And records of his life and works and of his sons, and of the tribes of Israel, are well preserved in Jewish sacred books.

16 In Persia Brahm was known,

and feared. Men saw him as the One, the causeless Cause of all that is, and he was sacred unto them, as Tao to the dwellers of the farther East.

17 The people lived in peace, and justice ruled.

18 But, as in other lands, in Persia priests arose imbued with self and self desires, who outraged Force, Intelligence and Love;

19 Religion grew corrupt, and birds and beasts and creeping things were set apart as gods.

20 In course of time a lofty soul, whom men called Zarathustra, came in flesh.

21 He saw the causeless Spirit, high and lifted up; he saw the weakness of all man appointed gods.

22 He spoke and all of Persia heard; and when he said, One God, one people and one shrine, the altars of the idols fell, and Persia was redeemed.

23 But men must see their God with human eyes, and Zarathustra said,

24 The greatest of the Spirits standing near the throne is the Ahura Mazda, who manifests in brightness of the sun.

25 And all the people saw Ahura Mazda in the sun, and they fell down and worshipped him in temples of the sun.

26 And Persia is the magian land where live the priests who saw the star arise to mark the place where Mary's son was born, and were the first to greet him as the Prince of Peace.

27 The precepts and the laws of Zarathustra are preserved in the Avesta which you can read and make your own.

28 But you must know that words are naught till they are made alive; until the lessons they contain

become a part of head and heart.

29   Now truth is one; but no one knows the truth until he is the truth. It is recorded in an ancient book,

30   Truth is the leavening power of God; it can transmute the all of life into itself; and when the all of life is truth, then man is truth.

CHAPTER 11.

Elihu's lessons.   Buddhism and the precepts of Buddha.   The mysteries of Egypt.

AGAIN Elihu taught; he said, The Indian priests became corrupt; Brahm was forgotten in the streets; the rights of men were trampled in the dust.

2   And then a mighty master came, a Buddha of enlightenment, who turned away from wealth and all the honors of the world, and found the Silence in the quiet groves and caves; and he was blest.

3   He preached a gospel of a higher life, and taught man how to honor man.

4   He had no doctrine of the gods to teach; he just knew man, and so his creed was justice, love and right-eousness.

5   I quote for you a few of many of the helpful words which Buddha spoke:

6   Hate is a cruel word. If men hate you, regard it not; and you can turn the hate of men to love and mercy and good will, and mercy is as large as all the heavens.

7   And there is good enough for all. With good destroy the bad; with generous deeds make avarice ashamed; with truth make straight the crooked lines that error draws, for error is but truth distorted, gone astray.

8   And pain will follow him who speaks or acts with evil thoughts,

as does the wheel the foot of him who draws the cart.

9   He is a greater man who conquers self than he who kills a thousand men in war.

10   He is the noble man who is himself what he believes that other men should be.

11   Return to him who does you wrong your purest love, and he will cease from doing wrong; for love will purify the heart of him who is beloved as truly as it purifies the heart of him who loves.

12   The words of Buddha are recorded in the Indian sacred books; attend to them, for they are part of the instructions of the Holy Breath.

13   The land of Egypt is the land of secret things.

14   The mysteries of the ages lie lock-bound in our temples and our shrines.

15   The masters of all times and climes come here to learn; and when your sons have grown to manhood they will finish all their studies in Egyptian schools.

16   But I have said enough. Tomorrow at the rising of the sun we meet again.

CHAPTER 12.

Salome's lessons.   Prayer.   Elihu's concluding lessons.   Sums up the three years' course of study.   The pupils return to their homes.

NOW, when the morning sun arose the masters and their pupils all were in the sacred grove.

2   Salome was the first to speak; she said, Behold the sun! It manifests the power of God who speaks to us through sun and moon and stars;

3   Through mountain, hill and

vale; through flower, and plant and tree.

4 God sings for us through bird, and harpsichord, and human voice; he speaks to us through wind and rain and thunder roll; why should we not bow down and worship at his feet?

5 God speaks to hearts apart; and hearts apart must speak to him; and this is prayer.

6 It is not prayer to shout at God, to stand, or sit, or kneel and tell him all about the sins of men.

7 It is not prayer to tell the Holy One how great he is, how good he is, how strong and how compassionate.

8 God is not man to be bought up by praise of man.

9 Prayer is the ardent wish that every way of life be light; that every act be crowned with good; that every living thing be prospered by our ministry.

10 A noble deed, a helpful word is prayer; a fervent, an effectual prayer.

11 The fount of prayer is in the heart; by thought, not words, the heart is carried up to God, where it is blest. Then let us pray.

12 They prayed, but not a word was said; but in that holy Silence every heart was blest.

13 And then Elihu spoke. He said to Mary and Elizabeth, Our words are said; you need not tarry longer here; the call has come; the way is clear, you may return unto your native land.

14 A mighty work is given you to do; you shall direct the minds that will direct the world.

15 Your sons are set apart to lead men up to righteous thoughts, and words, and deeds;

16 To make men know the sinfulness of sin; to lead them from the adoration of the lower self, and all illusive things, and make them conscious of the self that lives with Christ in God.

17 In preparation for their work your sons must walk in many thorny paths.

18 Fierce trials and temptations they will meet, like other men; their loads will not be light, and they will weary be, and faint.

19 And they will know the pangs of hunger and of thirst; and without cause they will be mocked, imprisoned, scourged.

20 To many countries they will go, and at the feet of many masters they will sit, for they must learn like other men.

21 But we have said enough. The blessings of the Three and of the Seven, who stand before the throne, will surely rest upon you evermore.

22 Thus closed the lessons of Elihu and Salome. Three years they taught their pupils in the sacred grove, and if their lessons all were written in a book, lo, it would be a mighty book; of what they said we have the sum.

23 Now, Mary, Joseph and Elizabeth with Jesus and his harbinger, set forth upon their homeward way. They went not by Jerusalem, for Archelaus reigned.

24 They journeyed by the Bitter Sea, and when they reached Engedi hills they rested in the home of Joshua, a near of kin; and here Elizabeth and John abode.

25 But Joseph, Mary and their son went by the Jordan way, and after certain days they reached their home in Nazareth.

SECTION IV.

DALETH.

Childhood and Early Education of John the Harbinger.

CHAPTER 13.

Elizabeth in Engedi. Teaches her son. John becomes the pupil of Matheno, who reveals to him the meaning of sin and the law of forgiveness.

ELIZABETH was blest; she spent her time with John, and gave to him the lessons that Elihu and Salome had given her.

2 And John delighted in the wildness of his home and in the lessons that he learned.

3 Now in the hills were many caves. The cave of David was a-near in which the Hermit of Engedi lived.

4 This hermit was Matheno, priest of Egypt, master from the temple of Sakara.

5 When John was seven years of age Matheno took him to the wilderness and in the cave of David they abode.

6 Matheno taught, and John was thrilled with what the master said, and day by day Matheno opened up to him the mysteries of life.

7 John loved the wilderness; he loved his master and his simple fare. Their food was fruits, and nuts, wild honey and the carob bread.

8 Matheno was an Israelite, and he attended all the Jewish feasts.

9 When John was nine years old Matheno took him to a great feast in Jerusalem.

10 The wicked Archelaus had been deposed and exiled to a distant land because of selfishness and cruelty, and John was not afraid.

11 John was delighted with his visit to Jerusalem. Matheno told him all about the service of the Jews; the meaning of their sacrifices and their rites.

12 John could not understand how sin could be forgiven by killing animals and birds and burning them before the Lord.

13 Matheno said, The God of heaven and earth does not require sacrifice. This custom with its cruel rites was borrowed from the idol worshippers of other lands.

14 No sin was ever blotted out by sacrifice of animal, of bird, or man.

15 Sin is the rushing forth of man into the fens of wickedness. If one would get away from sin he must retrace his steps, and find his way out of the fens of wickedness.

16 Return and purify your hearts by love and righteousness and you shall be forgiven.

17 This is the burden of the message that the harbinger shall bring to men.

18 What is forgiveness? John inquired.

19 Matheno said, It is the paying up of debts. A man who wrongs another man can never be forgiven until he rights the wrong.

20 The Vedas says that none can right the wrong but him who does the wrong.

21 John said, If this be true where is the power to forgive except the power that rests in man himself? Can man forgive himself?

22 Matheno said, The door is wide ajar; you see the way of man's

return to right, and the forgiveness of his sins.

CHAPTER 14.

Matheno's lessons. The doctrine of universal law. The power of man to choose and to attain. The benefits of antagonisms. Ancient sacred books. The place of John and Jesus in the world's history.

MATHENO and his pupil, John, were talking of the sacred books of olden times, and of the golden precepts they contained, and John exclaimed,

2 These golden precepts are sublime; what need have we of other sacred books?

3 Matheno said, The Spirits of the Holy One cause every thing to come and go in proper time.

4 The sun has his own time to set, the moon to rise, to wax and wane, the stars to come and go, the rain to fall, the winds to blow;

5 The seed times and the harvest times to come; man to be born and man to die.

6 These mighty Spirits cause the nations to be born; they rock them in their cradles, nurture them to greatest power, and when their tasks are done they wrap them in their winding sheets and lay them in their tombs.

7 Events are many in a nation's life, and in the life of man, that are not pleasant for the time; but in the end the truth appears: whatever comes is for the best.

8 Man was created for a noble part; but he could not be made a free man filled with wisdom, truth and might.

9 If he were hedged about, confined in straits from which he could not pass, then he would be a toy, a mere machine.

10 Creative spirits gave to man a will; and so he has the power to choose.

11 He may attain the greatest heights, or sink to deepest depths; for what he wills to gain he has the power to gain.

12 If he desires strength he has the power to gain that strength; but he must overcome resistances to reach the goal; no strength is ever gained in idleness.

13 So, in the whirl of many-sided conflicts man is placed where he must strive to extricate himself.

14 In every conflict man gains strength; with every conquest he attains to greater heights. With every day he finds new duties and new cares.

15 Man is not carried over dangerous pits, nor helped to overcome his foes. He is himself his army, and his sword and shield; and he is captain of his hosts.

16 The Holy Ones just light his way. Man never has been left without a beacon light to guide.

17 And he has ever had a lighted lamp in hand that he may see the dangerous rocks, the turbid streams and treacherous pits.

18 And so the Holy Ones have judged; when men have needed added light a master soul has come to earth to give that light.

19 Before the Vedic days the world had many sacred books to light the way; and when man needed greater light the Vedas, the Avesta and the books of Tao Great appeared to show the way to greater heights.

20 And in the proper place the Hebrew Bible, with its Law, its Prophets and its Psalms, appeared for man's enlightenment.

21 But years have passed and men have need of greater light.

22 And now the Day Star from on high begins to shine; and Jesus is the flesh-made messenger to show that light to men.

23 And you, my pupil, you have been ordained to harbinger the coming day.

24 But you must keep that purity of heart you now possess; and you must light your lamp directly from the coals that burn upon the altar of the Holy Ones.

25 And then your lamp will be transmuted to a boundless flame, and you will be a living torch whose light will shine wherever man abides.

26 But in the ages yet to come, man will attain to greater heights, and lights still more intense will come.

27 And then, at last, a mighty master soul will come to earth to light the way up to the throne of perfect man.

CHAPTER 15.

Death and burial of Elizabeth. Matheno's lessons. The ministry of death. The mission of John. Institution of the rite of baptism. Matheno takes John to Egypt, and places him in the temple at Sakara, where he remains eighteen years.

WHEN John was twelve years old his mother died, and neighbors laid her body in a tomb among her kindred in the Hebron burying ground, and near to Zacharias' tomb.

2 And John was deeply grieved; he wept. Matheno said, It is not well to weep because of death.

3 Death is no enemy of man; it is a friend who, when the work of life is done, just cuts the cord that binds the human boat to earth, that it may sail on smoother seas.

4 No language can describe a mother's worth, and yours was tried and true. But she was not called hence until her tasks were done.

5 The calls of death are always for the best, for we are solving problems there as well as here; and one is sure to find himself where he can solve his problems best.

6 It is but selfishness that makes one wish to call again to earth departed souls.

7 Then let your mother rest in peace. Just let her noble life be strength and inspiration unto you.

8 A crisis in your life has come, and you must have a clear conception of the work that you are called to do.

9 The sages of the ages call you harbinger. The prophets look to you and say, He is Elijah come again.

10 Your mission here is that of harbinger; for you will go before Messiah's face to pave his way, and make the people ready to receive their king.

11 This readiness is purity of heart; none but the pure in heart can recognize the king.

12 To teach men to be pure in heart you must yourself be pure in heart, and word, and deed.

13 In infancy the vow for you was made and you became a Nazarite. The razor shall not touch your face nor head, and you shall taste not wine nor fiery drinks.

14 Men need a pattern for their lives; they love to follow, not to lead.

15 The man who stands upon the corners of the paths and points the way, but does not go, is just a pointer; and a block of wood can do the same.

16 The teacher treads the way;

on every span of ground he leaves his footprints clearly cut, which all can see and be assured that he, their master, went that way.

17 Men comprehend the inner life by what they see and do. They come to God through ceremonies and forms.

18 And so when you would make men know that sins are washed away by purity in life, a rite symbolic may be introduced.

19 In water wash the bodies of the people who would turn away from sin and strive for purity in life.

20 This rite of cleansing is a preparation rite and they who thus are cleansed comprise the Church of Purity.

21 And you shall say, You men of Israel, hear; Reform and wash; become the sons of purity, and you shall be forgiven.

22 This rite of cleansing and this church are but symbolic of the cleansing of the soul by purity in life, and of the kingdom of the soul, which does not come with outward show, but is the church within.

23 Now, you may never point the way and tell the multitudes to do what you have never done; but you must go before and show the way.

24 You are to teach that men must wash; so you must lead the way, your body must be washed, symbolic of the cleansing of the soul.

25 John said, Why need I wait? May I not go at once and wash?

26 Matheno said, 'Tis well, and then they went down to the Jordan ford, and east of Jericho, just where the hosts of Israel crossed when first they entered Canaan, they tarried for a time.

27 Matheno taught the harbinger, and he explained to him the inner meaning of the cleansing rite and how to wash himself and how to wash the multitude.

28 And in the river Jordan John was washed; then they returned unto the wilderness.

29 Now in Engedi's hills Matheno's work was done and he and John went down to Egypt. They rested not until they reached the temple of Sakara in the valley of the Nile.

30 For many years Matheno was a master in this temple of the Brotherhood, and when he told about the life of John and of his mission to the sons of men, the hierophant with joy received the harbinger and he was called the Brother Nazarite.

31 For eighteen years John lived and wrought within these temple gates; and here he conquered self, became a master mind and learned the duties of the harbinger.

SECTION V.

. HE.

Childhood and Early Education of Jesus.

CHAPTER 16.

The home of Joseph. Mary teaches her son. Jesus' grandparents give a feast in his honor. Jesus has a dream. His grandmother's interpretation. His birthday gift.

THE home of Joseph was on Marmion Way in Nazareth; here Mary taught her son the lessons of Elihu and Salome.

2 And Jesus greatly loved the Vedic hymns and the Avesta; but more than all he loved to read the Psalms of David and the pungent words of Solomon.

3 The Jewish books of prophecy were his delight; and when he reached his seventh year he needed not the books to read, for he had fixed in memory every word.

4 Joachim and his wife, grandparents of child Jesus, made a feast in honor of the child, and all their near of kin were guests.

5 And Jesus stood before the guests and said, I had a dream, and in my dream I stood before a sea, upon a sandy beach.

6 The waves upon the sea were high; a storm was raging on the deep.

7 Some one above gave me a wand. I took the wand and touched the sand, and every grain of sand became a living thing; the beach was all a mass of beauty and of song.

8 I touched the waters at my feet, and they were changed to trees, and flowers, and singing birds, and every thing was praising God.

9 And some one spoke, I did not see the one who spoke, I heard the voice, which said, There is no death.

10 Grandmother Anna loved the child; she laid her hand on Jesus' head and said, I saw you stand beside the sea; I saw you touch the sand and waves; I saw them turn to living things and then I knew the meaning of the dream.

11 The sea of life rolls high; the storms are great. The multitude of men are idle, listless, waiting, like dead sand upon the beach.

12 Your wand is truth. With this you touch the multitudes, and every man becomes a messenger of holy light and life.

13 You touch the waves upon the sea of life; their turmoils cease; the very winds become a song of praise.

14 There is no death, because the wand of truth can change the dryest bones to living things, and bring the lovliest flowers from stagnant ponds, and turn the most discordant notes to harmony and praise.

15 Joachim said, My son, today you pass the seventh milestone of your way of life, for you are seven years of age, and we will give to you, as a remembrance of this day, whatever you desire; choose that which will afford you most delight.

16 And Jesus said, I do not want a gift, for I am satisfied. If I could make a multitude of children glad upon this day I would be greatly pleased.

17 Now, there are many hungry boys and girls in Nazareth who would be pleased to eat with us this feast and share with us the pleasures of this day.

18 The richest gift that you can

give to me is your permission to go out and find these needy ones and bring them here that they may feast with us.

19 Joachim said, 'Tis well; go out and find the needy boys and girls and bring them here; we will prepare enough for all.

20 And Jesus did not wait; he ran; he entered every dingy hut and cabin of the town; he did not waste his words; he told his mission everywhere.

21 And in a little time one hundred and three-score of happy, ragged boys and girls were following him up Marmion Way.

22 The guests made way; the banquet hall was filled with Jesus' guests, and Jesus and his mother helped to serve.

23 And there was food enough for all, and all were glad; and so the birthday gift of Jesus was a crown of righteousness.

CHAPTER 17.

Jesus talks with the rabbi of the synagogue of Nazareth. He criticises the narrowness of Jewish thought.

NOW, Rabbi Barachia of the synagogue of Nazareth, was aid to Mary in the teaching of her son.

2 One morning after service in the synagogue the rabbi said to Jesus as he sat in silent thought, Which is the greatest of the Ten Commands?

3 And Jesus said, I do not see a greatest of the Ten Commands. I see a golden cord that runs through all the Ten Commands that binds them fast and makes them one.

4 This cord is love, and it belongs to every word of all the Ten Commands.

5 If one is full of love he can do nothing else than worship God; for God is love.

6 If one is full of love, he cannot kill; he cannot falsely testify; he cannot covet; can do naught but honor God and man.

7 If one is full of love he does not need commands of any kind.

8 And Rabbi Barachia said, Your words are seasoned with the salt of wisdom that is from above. Who is the teacher who has opened up this truth to you?

9 And Jesus said, I do not know that any teacher opens up this truth for me. It seems to me that truth was never shut; that it was always opened up, for truth is one and it is everywhere.

10 And if we open up the windows of our minds the truth will enter in and make herself at home; for truth can find her way through any crevice, any window, any open door.

11 The rabbi said, What hand is strong enough to open up the windows and the doors of mind so truth can enter in?

12 And Jesus said, It seems to me that love, the golden cord that binds the Ten Commands in one, is strong enough to open any human door so that the truth can enter in and cause the heart to understand.

13 Now, in the evening Jesus and his mother sat alone, and Jesus said,

14 The rabbi seems to think that God is partial in his treatment of the sons of men; that Jews are favored and are blest above all other men.

15 I do not see how God can have his favorites and be just.

16 Are not Samaritans and Greeks and Romans just as much the children of the Holy One as are the Jews?

17 I think the Jews have built a wall about themselves, and they see nothing on the other side of it.

18 They do not know that flowers are blooming over there; that sowing times and reaping times belong to anybody but the Jews.

19 It surely would be well if we could break these barriers down so that the Jews might see that God has other children that are just as greatly blest.

20 I want to go from Jewry land and meet my kin in other countries of my Fatherland.

CHAPTER 18.

Jesus at a feast in Jerusalem. Is grieved by the cruelties of the sacrificers. Appeals to Hillel, who sympathizes with him. He remains in the temple a year.

THE great feast of the Jews was on, and Joseph, Mary and their son, and many of their kin, went to Jerusalem. The child was ten years old.

2 And Jesus watched the butchers kill the lambs and birds and burn them on the altar in the name of God.

3 His tender heart was shocked at this display of cruelty; he asked the serving priest, What is the purpose of this slaughter of the beasts and birds? Why do you burn their flesh before the Lord?

4 The priest replied, This is our sacrifice for sin. God has commanded us to do these things, and said that in these sacrifices all our sins are blotted out.

5 And Jesus said, Will you be kind enough to tell when God proclaimed that sins are blotted out by sacrifice of any kind?

6 Did not David say that God requires not a sacrifice for sin? that it is sin itself to bring before his face burnt offerings, as offerings for sin? Did not Isaiah say the same?

7 The priest replied, My child, you are beside yourself. Do you know more about the laws of God than all the priests of Israel? This is no place for boys to show their wit.

8 But Jesus heeded not his taunts; he went to Hillel, chief of the Sanhedrim, and he said to him,

9 Rabboni, I would like to talk with you; I am disturbed about this service of the pascal feast. I thought the temple was the house of God where love and kindness dwell.

10 Do you not hear the bleating of those lambs, the pleading of those doves that men are killing over there? Do you not smell that awful stench that comes from burning flesh?

11 Can man be kind and just, and still be filled with cruelty?

12 A God that takes delight in sacrifice, in blood and burning flesh, is not my Father-God.

13 I want to find a God of love, and you, my master, you are wise, and surely you can tell me where to find the God of love.

14 But Hillel could not give an answer to the child. His heart was stirred with sympathy. He called the child to him; he laid his hand upon his head and wept.

15 He said, There is a God of love, and you shall come with me; and hand in hand we will go forth and find the God of love.

16 And Jesus said, Why need we go? I thought that God is everywhere. Can we not purify our hearts and drive out cruelty, and every wicked thought, and make within, a temple where the God of love can dwell?

17 The master of the great Sanhedrim felt as though he was himself the child, and that before him stood Rabboni, master of the higher law.

18 He said within himself, This child is surely prophet sent from God.

19 Then Hillel sought the parents of the child, and asked that Jesus might abide with him, and learn the precepts of the law, and all the lessons of the temple priests.

20 His parents gave consent, and Jesus did abide within the holy temple in Jerusalem, and Hillel taught him every day.

21 And every day the master learned from Jesus many lessons of the higher life.

22 The child remained with Hillel in the temple for a year, and then returned unto his home in Nazareth; and there he wrought with Joseph as a carpenter.

CHAPTER 19.

Jesus at the age of twelve in the temple. Disputes with the doctors of the law. Reads from a book of prophecy. By request of Hillel he interprets the prophecies.

AGAIN the great feast in Jerusalem was on, and Joseph, Mary and their son were there. The child was twelve years old.

2 And there were Jews and proselytes from many countries in Jerusalem.

3 And Jesus sat among the priests and doctors in the temple hall.

4 And Jesus opened up a book of prophecy and read:

5 Woe, woe, to Ariel, the town where David dwelt! I will dismantle Ariel, and she shall groan and weep;

6 And I will camp against her round about with hostile posts;

7 And I will bring her low and she shall speak out of the earth; with muffled voice like a familiar spirit shall she speak; yea, she shall only whisper forth her speech;

8 And foes unnumbered, like the grains of dust, shall come upon her suddenly.

9 The Lord of hosts will visit her with thunder and with tempest, and with storm; with earthquake, and with devouring flames.

10 Lo, all these people have deserted me. They draw to me with speech, and with their lips they honor me; their hearts are far removed from me; their fear for me is that inspired by man.

11 And I will breathe an adverse breath upon my people, Israel; the wisdom of their wise men shall be lost; the understanding of their prudent men shall not be found.

12 My people seek to hide their counsel from the Lord, so that their works may not be seen. They fain would cover up their works with darkness of the night, and say, Who sees us now? Who knows us now?

13 Poor, foolish men! shall that which has been made say of its maker, He is naught, I made myself?

14 Or shall the pot speak out and say to him, who made the pot, You have no skill; you do not know?

15 But this will not forever be; the time will come when Lebanon will be a fruitful field, and fruitful fields will be transformed to groves.

16 And on that day the deaf will hear the words of God; the blind will read the Book of God's Remembrance.

17 And suffering ones will be relieved, and they will have abundant

joy; and every one that needs will be supplied; and it will come to pass that all the foolish will be wise.

18 The people will return and sanctify the Holy One, and in their heart of hearts, lo, they will reverence him.

19 When Jesus had thus read he put aside the book and said, You masters of the law, will you make plain for us the prophet's words?

20 Now, Hillel sat among the masters of the law, and he stood forth and said, Perhaps our young rabboni who has read the word will be interpreter.

21 And Jesus said, The Ariel of the prophet is our own. Jerusalem.

22 By selfishness and cruelty this people has become a stench unto the Elohim.

23 The prophet saw these days from far, and of these times he wrote.

24 Our doctors, lawyers, priests and scribes oppress the poor, while they themselves in luxury live.

25 The sacrifices and the offerings of Israel are but abomination unto God. The only sacrifice that God requires is self.

26 Because of this injustice and this cruelty of man to man, the Holy One has spoken of this common-w

27 Lo, I will overturn, yes, I will overturn, it shall be overturned, and it shall be no more until he comes whose right it is and I will give it unto him.

28 In all the world there is one law of right, and he who breaks that law will suffer grief; for God is just.

29 And Israel has gone far astray; has not regarded justice, nor the rights of man, and God demands that Israel shall reform, and turn again to ways of holiness.

30 And if our people will not hear the voice of God, lo, nations from afar will come and sack Jerusalem, and tear our temple down, and take our people captive into foreign lands.

31 But this will not forever be; though they be scattered far and wide, and wander here and there among the nations of the earth, like sheep that have no shepherd guide,

32 The time will come when God will bring again the captive hosts; for Israel shall return and dwell in peace.

33 And after many years our temple shall be built again, and one whom God will honor, one in whom the pure in heart delights will come and glorify the house of God, and reign in righteousness.

34 When Jesus had thus said, he stepped aside, and all the people were amazed and said, This surely is the Christ.

CHAPTER 20.

After the feast. The homeward journey. The missing Jesus. The search for him. His parents find him in the temple. He goes with them to Nazareth. Symbolic meaning of carpenter's tools.

THE great feast of the pasch was ended and the Nazarenes were journeying toward their homes.

2 And they were in Samaria, and Mary said, Where is my son? No one had seen the boy.

3 And Joseph sought among their kindred who were on their way to Galilee; but they had seen him not.

4 Then Joseph, Mary, and a son of Zebedee, returned and sought through all Jerusalem, but they could find him not.

5   And then they went up to the temple courts and asked the guards, Have you seen Jesus, a fair-haired boy, with deep blue eyes, twelve years of age, about these courts?

6   The guards replied, Yes, he is in the temple now disputing with the doctors of the law.

7   And they went in, and found him as the guards had said.

8   And Mary said, Why Jesus, why do you treat your parents thus? Lo, we have sought two days for you. We feared that some great harm had overtaken you.

9   And Jesus said, Do you not know that I must be about my Father's work?

10   But he went round and pressed the hand of every doctor of the law and said, I trust that we may meet again.

11   And then he went forth with his parents on their way to Nazareth; and when they reached their home he wrought with Joseph as a carpenter.

12   One day as he was bringing forth the tools for work he said,

13   These tools remind me of the ones we handle in the workshop of the mind where things are made of thought and where we build up character.

14   We use the square to measure all our lines, to straighten out the crooked places of the way, and make the corners of our conduct square.

15   We use the compass to draw circles round our passions and desires to keep them in the bounds of righteousness.

16   We use the ax to cut away the knotty, useless and ungainly parts and make the character symmetrical.

17   We use the hammer to drive home the truth, and pound it in until it is a part of every part.

18   We use the plane to smooth the rough, uneven surfaces of joint, and block, and board that go to build the temple for the truth.

19   The chisel, line, the plummet and the saw all have their uses in the workshop of the mind.

20   And then this ladder with its trinity of steps, faith, hope and love; on it we climb up to the dome of purity in life.

21   And on the twelve-step ladder we ascend until we reach the pinnacle of that which life is spent to build—the Temple of Perfected Man.

SECTION VI.

VAU.

Life and Works of Jesus in India.

CHAPTER 21.

Ravanna sees Jesus in the temple and is captivated. Hillel tells him about the boy. Ravanna finds Jesus in Nazareth and gives a feast in his honor. Ravanna becomes patron of Jesus, and takes him to India to study the Brahmic religion.

A ROYAL prince of India, Ravanna of Orissa in the south, was at the Jewish feast.

2   Ravanna was a man of wealth; and he was just, and with a band of Brahmic priests sought wisdom in the West.

3   When Jesus stood among the

Jewish priests and read and spoke, Ravanna heard and was amazed.

4 And when he asked who Jesus was, from whence he came and what he was, chief Hillel said,

5 We call this child the Day Star from on high, for he has come to bring to men a light, the light of life; to lighten up the way of men and to redeem his people, Israel.

6 And Hillel told Ravanna all about the child; about the prophecies concerning him; about the wonders of the night when he was born; about the visit of the magian priests;

7 About the way in which he was protected from the wrath of evil men; about his flight to Egyptland, and how he then was serving with his father as a carpenter in Nazarᵃᵗʰ

8 Ravanna was entranced, and asked to know the way to Nazareth, that he might go and honor such a one as son of God.

9 And with his gorgeous train he journeyed on the way and came to Nazareth of Galilee.

10 He found the object of his search engaged in building dwellings for the sons of men.

11 And when he first saw Jesus he was climbing up a twelve-step ladder, and he carried in his hands a compass, square and ax.

12 Ravanna said, All hail, most favored son of heaven!

13 And at the inn Ravanna made a feast for all the people of the town; and Jesus and his parents were the honored guests.

14 For certain days Ravanna was a guest in Joseph's home on Marmion Way; he sought to learn the secret of the wisdom of the son; but it was all too great for him.

15 And then he asked that he might be the patron of the child;

might take him to the East where he could learn the wisdom of the Brahms.

16 And Jesus longed to go that he might learn: and after many days his parents gave consent.

17 Then, with proud heart, Ravanna with his train, began the journey toward the rising sun; and after many days they crossed the Sind, and reached the province of Orissa, and the palace of the prince.

18 The Brahmic priests were glad to welcome home the prince; with favor they received the Jewish boy.

19 And Jesus was accepted as a pupil in the temple Jagannath; and here he learned the Vedas and the Manic laws.

20 The Brahmic masters wondered at the clear conceptions of the child, and often were amazed when he explained to them the meaning of the laws.

CHAPTER 22.

The friendship of Jesus and Lamaas. Jesus explains to Lamaas the meaning of truth, man, power, understanding, wisdom, salvation and faith.

AMONG the priests of Jagannath was one who loved the Jewish boy. Lamaas Bramas was the name by which the priest was known.

2 One day as Jesus and Lamaas walked alone in plaza Jagannath, Lamaas said, My Jewish master, what is truth?

3 And Jesus said, Truth is the only thing that changes not.

4 In all the world there are two things; the one is truth; the other falsehood is; and truth is that which is, and falsehood that which seems to be.

5 Now truth is aught, and has no cause, and yet it is the cause of everything.

6 Falsehood is naught, and yet it is the manifest of aught.

7 Whatever has been made will be unmade; that which begins must end.

8 All things that can be seen by human eyes are manifests of aught, are naught, and so must pass away.

9 The things we see are but reflexes just appearing, while the ethers vibrate so and so, and when conditions change they disappear.

10 The Holy Breath is truth; is that which was, and is, and evermore shall be; it cannot change nor pass away.

11 Lamaas said, You answer well; now, what is man?

12 And Jesus said, Man is the truth and falsehood strangely mixed.

13 Man is the Breath made flesh; so truth and falsehood are conjoined in him; and then they strive, and naught goes down and man as truth abides.

14 Again Lamaas asked, What do you say of power?

15 And Jesus said, It is a manifest; is the result of force; it is but naught; it is illusion, nothing more. Force changes not, but power changes as the ethers change.

16 Force is the will of God and is omnipotent, and power is that will in manifest, directed by the Breath.

17 There is a power in the winds, a power in the waves, a power in the lightning's stroke, a power in the human arm, a power in the eye.

18 The ethers cause these powers to be, and thought of Elohim, of angel, man, or other thinking thing, directs the force; when it has done its work the power is no more.

19 Again Lamaas asked, Of understanding what have you to say?

20 And Jesus said, It is the rock on which man builds himself; it is the gnosis of the aught and of the naught, of falsehood and of truth.

21 It is the knowledge of the lower self; the sensing of the powers of man himself.

22 Again Lamaas asked, Of wisdom what have you to say?

23 And Jesus said, It is the consciousness that man is aught; that God and man are one;

24 That naught is naught; that power is but illusion; that heaven and earth and hell are not above, around, below, but in; which in the light of aught becomes the naught, and God is all.

25 Lamaas asked, Pray, what is faith?

26 And Jesus said, Faith is the surety of the omnipotence of God and man; the certainty that man will reach deific life.

27 Salvation is a ladder reaching from the heart of man to heart of God.

28 It has three steps; Belief is first, and this is what man thinks, perhaps, is truth.

29 And faith is next, and this is what man knows is truth.

30 Fruition is the last, and this is man himself, the truth.

31 Belief is lost in faith; and in fruition faith is lost; and man is saved when he has reached deific life; when he and God are one.

CHAPTER 23.

Jesus and Lamaas among the sudras and visyas. In Benares. Jesus becomes a pupil of Udraka. The lessons of Udraka.

NOW, Jesus with his friend Lamaas went through all the regions of Orissa, and the valley of the Ganges, seeking wisdom from the sudras and the visyas and the masters.

2   Benares of the Ganges was a city rich in culture and in learning; here the two rabbonis tarried many days.

3   And Jesus sought to learn the Hindu art of healing, and became the pupil of Udraka, greatest of the Hindu healers.

4   Udraka taught the uses of the waters, plants and earths; of heat and cold; sunshine and shade; of light and dark.

5   He said, The laws of nature are the laws of health, and he who lives according to these laws is never sick.

6   Transgression of these laws is sin, and he who sins is sick.

7   He who obeys the laws, maintains an equilibrium in all his parts, and thus insures true harmony; and harmony is health, while discord is disease.

8   That which produces harmony in all the parts of man is medicine, insuring health.

9   The body is a harpsichord, and when its strings are too relaxed, or are too tense, the instrument is out of tune, the man is sick.

10   Now, everything in nature has been made to meet the wants of man; so everything is found in medical arcanes.

11   And when the harpsichord of man is out of tune the vast expanse of nature may be searched for remedy; there is a cure for every ailment of the flesh.

12   Of course the will of man is remedy supreme; and by the vigorous exercise of will, man may make tense a chord that is relaxed, or may relax one that is too tense, and thus may heal himself.

13   When man has reached the place where he has faith in God, in nature and himself, he knows the Word of power; his word is balm for every wound, is cure for all the ills of life.

14   The healer is the man who can inspire faith. The tongue may speak to human ears, but souls are reached by souls that speak to souls.

15   He is the forceful man whose soul is large, and who can enter into souls, inspiring hope in those who have no hope, and faith in those who have no faith in God, in nature, nor in man.

16   There is no universal balm for those who tread the common walks of life.

17   A thousand things produce inharmony and make men sick; a thousand things may tune the harpsichord, and make men well.

18   That which is medicine for one is poison for another one; so one is healed by what would kill another one.

19   An herb may heal the one; a drink of water may restore another one; a mountain breeze may bring to life one seeming past all help;

20   A coal of fire, or bit of earth, may cure another one; and one may wash in certain streams, or pools, and be made whole.

21   The virtue from the hand or breath may heal a thousand more; but love is queen. Thought, reinforced by love, is God's great sovereign balm.

22   But many of the broken chords in life, and discords that so vex the soul, are caused by evil spirits of the air that men see not; that lead men on through ignorance to break the laws of nature and of God.

23   These powers act like de-

mons, and they speak; they rend the man; they drive him to despair.

24 But he who is a healer, true, is master of the soul, and can, by force of will, control these evil ones.

25 Some spirits of the air are master spirits and are strong, too strong for human power alone; but man has helpers in the higher realms that may be importuned, and they will help to drive the demons out.

26 Of what this great physician said, this is the sum. And Jesus bowed his head in recognition of the wisdom of this master soul, and went his way.

CHAPTER 24.

The Brahmic doctrine of castes. Jesus repudiates it and teaches human equality. The priests are offended and drive him from the temple. He abides with the sudras and teaches them.

FOUR years the Jewish boy abode in temple Jagannath.

2 One day he sat among the priests and said to them, Pray, tell me all about your views of castes; why do you say that all men are not equal in the sight of God?

3 A master of their laws stood forth and said, The Holy One whom we call Brahm, made men to suit himself, and men should not complain.

4 In the beginning days of human life Brahm spoke, and four men stood before his face.

5 Now, from the mouth of Parabrahm the first man came; and he was white, was like the Brahm himself; a brahman he was called.

6 And he was high and lifted up; above all want he stood; he had no need of toil.

7 And he was called the priest of Brahm, the holy one to act for Brahm in all affairs of earth.

8 The second man was red, and from the hand of Parabrahm he came; and he was called shatriya.

9 And he was made to be the king, the ruler and the warrior, whose highest ordained duty was, protection of the priest.

10 And from the inner parts of Parabrahm the third man came; and he was called a visya.

11 He was a yellow man, and his it was to till the soil, and keep the flocks and herds.

12 And from the feet of Parabrahm the fourth man came; and he was black; and he was called the sudras, one of low estate.

13 The sudras is the servant of the race of men; he has no rights that others need respect; he may not hear the Vedas read, and it means death to him to look into the face of priest, or king, and naught but death can free him from his state of servitude.

14 And Jesus said, Then Parabrahm is not a God of justice and of right; for with his own strong hand he has exalted one and brought another low.

15 And Jesus said no more to them, but looking up to heaven he said,

16 My Father-God, who was, and is, and ever more shall be; who holds within thy hands the scales of justice and of right;

17 Who in the boundlessness of love has made all men to equal be. The white, the black, the yellow and the red can look up in thy face and say, Our Father-God.

18 Thou Father of the human race, I praise thy name.

19 And all the priests were angered by the words which Jesus spoke; they rushed upon him,

seized him, and would have done him harm.

20 But then Lamaas raised his hand and said, You priests of Brahm, beware! you know not what you do; wait till you know the God this youth adores.

21 I have beheld this boy at prayer when light above the light of sun surrounded him, Beware! his God may be more powerful than Brahm.

22 If Jesus speaks the truth, if he is right, you cannot force him to desist; if he is wrong and you are right, his words will come to naught, for right is might, and in the end it will prevail.

23 And then the priests refrained from doing Jesus harm; but one spoke out and said,

24 Within this holy place has not this reckless youth done violence to Parabrahm? The law is plain; it says, He who reviles the name of Brahm shall die.

25 Lamaas plead for Jesus' life; and then the priests just seized a scourge of cords and drove him from the place.

26 And Jesus went his way and found a shelter with the black and yellow men, the servants and the tillers of the soil.

27 To them he first made known the gospel of equality; he told them of the Brotherhood of Man, the Fatherhood of God.

28 The common people heard him with delight, and learned to pray, Our Father-God who art in heaven.

CHAPTER 25.

Jesus teaches the sudras and farmers. Relates a parable of a nobleman and his unjust sons. Makes known the possibilities of all men.

WHEN Jesus saw the sudras and the farmers in such multitudes draw near to hear his words, he spoke a parable to them; he said:

2 A nobleman possessed a great estate; he had four sons, and he would have them all grow strong by standing forth and making use of all the talents they possessed.

3 And so he gave to each a share of his great wealth, and bade them go their way.

4 The eldest son was full of self; he was ambitious, shrewd and quick of thought.

5 He said within himself, I am the oldest son, and these, my brothers, must be servants at my feet,

6 And then he called his brothers forth; and one he made a puppet king; gave him a sword and charged him to defend the whole estate.

7 To one he gave the use of lands and flowing wells, and flocks and herds, and bade him till the soil, and tend the flocks and herds and bring to him the choicest of his gains.

8 And to the other one he said, You are the youngest son; the broad estate has been assigned; you have no part nor lot in anything that is.

9 And then he took a chain and bound his brother to a naked rock upon a desert plain, and said to him,

10 You have been born a slave; you have no rights, and you must be contented with your lot, for there is no release for you until you die and go from hence.

11 Now, after certain years the day of reckoning came; the nobleman called up his sons to render their accounts.

12 And when he knew that one, his eldest son, had seized the whole estate and made his brothers slaves,

13 He seized him, tore his priestly robes away and put him in a prison cell, where he was forced to stay until he had atoned for all the wrongs that he had done.

14 And then, as though they were but toys, he threw in air the throne and armor of the puppet king; he broke his sword, and put him in a prison cell.

15 And then he called his farmer son and asked him why he had not rescued from his galling chains his brother on the desert sands.

16 And when the son made answer not, the father took unto himself the flocks and herds, the fields and flowing wells,

17 And sent his farmer son to live out on the desert sands, until he had atoned for all the wrongs that he had done.

18 And then the father went and found his youngest son in cruel chains; with his own hands he broke the chains and bade his son to go in peace.

19 Now, when the sons had all paid up their debts they came again and stood before the bar of right.

20 They all had learned their lessons, learned them well; and then the father once again divided the estate.

21 He gave to each an equal share, and bade them recognize the law of equity and right, and live in peace.

22 And one, a sudras, spoke and said, May we who are but slaves, who are cut down like beasts to satisfy the whims of priests—may we have hope that one will come to break our chains and set us free?

23 And Jesus said, The Holy One has said, that all his children shall be free; and every soul is child of God

24 The sudras shall be free as priest; the farmer shall walk hand in hand with king; for all the world will own the brotherhood of man. -

25 O men, arise! be conscious of your powers, for he who wills need not remain a slave.

26 Just live as you would have your brother live; unfold each day as does the flower; for earth is yours, and heaven is yours, and God will bring you to your own.

27 And all the people cried, Show us the way that like the flower we may unfold and come unto our own.

CHAPTER 26.

Jesus at Katak. The car of Jagannath. Jesus reveals to the people the emptiness of Brahmic rites, and how to see God in man. Teaches them the divine law of sacrifice.

IN all the cities of Orissa Jesus taught. At Katak, by the river side, he taught, and thousands of the people followed him.

2 One day a car of Jagannath was hauled along by scores of frenzied men, and Jesus said,

3 Behold, a form without a spirit passes by; a body with no soul; a temple with no altar fires.

4 This car of Krishna is an empty thing, for Krishna is not there.

5 This car is but an idol of a people drunk on wine of carnal things.

6 God lives not in the noise of tongues; there is no way to him from any idol shrine.

7 God's meeting place with man is in the heart, and in a still small voice he speaks; and he who hears is still.

8 And all the people said, Teach us to know the Holy One who

speaks within the heart, God of the still small voice.

9   And Jesus said, The Holy Breath cannot be seen with mortal eyes; nor can men see the Spirits of the Holy One;

10   But in their image man was made, and he who looks into the face of man, looks at the image of the God who speaks within.

11   And when man honors man he honors God, and what man does for man, he does for God.

12   And you must bear in mind that when man harms in thought, or word or deed another man, he does a wrong to God.

13   If you would serve the God who speaks within the heart, just serve your near of kin, and those that are no kin, the stranger at your gates, the foe who seeks to do you harm;

14   Assist the poor, and help the weak; do harm to none, and covet not what is not yours;

15   Then, with your tongue the Holy One will speak; and he will smile behind your tears, will light your countenance with joy, and fill your hearts with peace.

16   And then the people asked, To whom shall we bring gifts? Where shall we offer sacrifice?

17   And Jesus said, Our Father-God asks not for needless waste of plant, of grain, of dove, of lamb.

18   That which you burn on any shrine you throw away. No blessings can attend the one who takes the food from hungry mouths to be destroyed by fire.

19   When you would offer sacrifice unto our God, just take your gift of grain, or meat and lay it on the table of the poor.

20   From it an incense will arise to heaven, which will return to you with blessedness.

21   Tear down your idols; they can hear you not; turn all your sacrificial altars into fuel for the flames.

22   Make human hearts your altars, and burn your sacrifices with the fire of love.

23   And all the people were entranced, and would have worshipped Jesus as a God; but Jesus said,

24   I am your brother man just come to show the way to God; you shall not worship man; praise God, the Holy One.

CHAPTER 27.

Jesus attends a feast in Behar. Preaches a revolutionary sermon on human equality. Relates the parable of the broken blades.

THE fame of Jesus as a teacher spread through all the land, and people came from near and far to hear his words of truth.

2   At Behar, on the sacred river of the Brahms, he taught for many days.

3   And Ach, a wealthy man of Behar, made a feast in honor of his guest, and he invited every one to come.

4   And many came; among them thieves, extortioners, and courtesans. And Jesus sat with them and taught; but they who followed him were much aggrieved because he sat with thieves and courtesans.

5   And they upbraided him; they said, Rabboni, master of the wise, this day will be an evil day for you.

6   The news will spread that you consort with courtesans and thieves, and men will shun you as they shun an asp.

7   And Jesus answered them and said, A master never screens him-

self for sake of reputation or of fame.

8 These are but worthless baubles of the day; they rise and sink, like empty bottles on a stream; they are illusions and will pass away;

9 They are the indices to what the thoughtless think; they are the noise that people make; and shallow men judge merit by the noise.

10 God and all master men judge men by what they are and not by what they seem to be; not by their reputation and their fame.

11 These courtesans and thieves are children of my Father-God; their souls are just as precious in his sight as yours, or of the Brahmic priests.

12 And they are working out the same life sums that you, who pride yourselves on your respectability and moral worth, are working out.

13 And some of them have solved much harder sums than you have solved, you men who look at them with scorn.

14 Yes, they are sinners, and confess their guilt, while you are guilty, but are shrewd enough to have a polished coat to cover up your guilt.

15 Suppose you men who scorn these courtesans, these drunkards and these thieves, who know that you are pure in heart and life, that you are better far than they, stand forth that men may know just who you are.

16 The sin lies in the wish, in the desire, not in the act.

17 You covet other people's wealth; you look at charming forms, and deep within your hearts you lust for them.

18 Deceit you practice every day, and wish for gold, for honor and for fame, just for your selfish selves.

19 The man who covets is a thief, and she who lusts is courtesan. You who are none of these speak out.

20 Nobody spoke; the accusers held their peace.

21 And Jesus said, The proof this day is all against those who have accused.

22 The pure in heart do not accuse. The vile in heart who want to cover up their guilt with holy smoke of piety are ever loathing drunkard, thief and courtesan.

23 This loathing and this scorn is mockery, for if the tinseled coat of reputation could be torn away, the loud professor would be found to revel in his lust, deceit, and many forms of secret sin.

24 The man who spends his time in pulling other people's weeds can have no time to pull his own, and all the choicest flowers of life will soon be choked and die, and nothing will remain but darnel, thistles, burs.

25 And Jesus spoke a parable: he said, Behold, a farmer had great fields of ripened grain, and when he looked he saw that blades of many stalks of wheat were bent and broken down.

26 And when he sent his reapers forth he said, We will not save the stalks of wheat that have the broken blades.

27 Go forth and cut and burn the stalks with broken blades.

28 And after many days he went to measure up his grain, but not a kernel could he find.

29 And then he called the harvesters and said to them, Where is my grain?

30 They answered him and said, We did according to your word; we

gathered up and burned the stalks with broken blades, and not a stalk was left to carry to the barn.

31 And Jesus said, If God saves only those who have no broken blades, who have been perfect in his sight, who will be saved?

32 And the accusers hung their heads in shame; and Jesus went his way.

CHAPTER 28.

Udraka gives a feast in Jesus' honor. Jesus speaks on the unity of God and the brotherhood of life. Criticises the priesthood. Becomes the guest of a farmer.

BENARES is the sacred city of the Brahms, and in Benares Jesus taught; Udraka was his host.

2 Udraka made a feast in honor of his guest, and many high born Hindu priests and scribes were there.

3 And Jesus said to them, With much delight I speak to you concerning life—the brotherhood of life.

4 The universal God is one, yet he is more than one; all things are God; all things are one.

5 By the sweet breaths of God all life is bound in one; so if you touch a fiber of a living thing you send a thrill from center to the outer bounds of life.

6 And when you crush beneath your foot the meanest worm, you shake the throne of God, and cause the sword of right to tremble in its sheath.

7 The bird sings out its song for men, and men vibrate in unison to help it sing.

8 The ant constructs her home, the bee its sheltering comb, the spider weaves her web, and flowers breathe to them a spirit in their sweet perfumes that gives them strength to toil.

9 Now, men and birds and beasts and creeping things are deities, made flesh; and how dare men kill anything?

10 'Tis cruelty that makes the world awry. When men have learned that when they harm a living thing they harm themselves, they surely will not kill, nor cause a thing that God has made to suffer pain.

11 A lawyer said, I pray you, Jesus, tell who is this God you speak about; where are his priests, his temples and his shrines?

12 And Jesus said, The God I speak about is every where; he cannot be compassed with walls, nor hedged about with bounds of any kind.

13 All people worship God, the One; but all the people see him not alike.

14 This universal God is wisdom, will and love.

15 All men see not the Triune God. One sees him as the God of might; another as the God of thought; another as the God of love.

16 A man's ideal is his God, and so, as man unfolds, his God unfolds. Man's God today, tomorrow is not God.

17 The nations of the earth see God from different points of view, and so he does not seem the same to every one.

18 Man names the part of God he sees, and this to him is all of God; and every nation sees a part of God, and every nation has a name for God.

19 You Brahmans call him Parabrahm; in Egypt he is Thoth; and Zeus is his name in Greece; Jehovah is his Hebrew name; but everywhere he is the causeless Cause, the

rootless Root from which all things have grown.

20 When men become afraid of God, and take him for a foe, they dress up other men in fancy garbs and call them priests,

21 And charge them to restrain the wrath of God by prayers; and when they fail to win his favor by their prayers, to buy him off with sacrifice of animal, or bird,

22 When man sees God as one with him, as Father-God, he needs no middle man, no priest to intercede;

23 He goes straight up to him and says, My Father-God! and then he lays his hand in God's own hand, and all is well.

24 And this is God. You are, each one, a priest, just for yourself; and sacrifice of blood God does not want.

25 Just give your life in sacrificial service to the all of life, and God is pleased.

26 When Jesus had thus said he stood aside; the people were amazed, but strove among themselves.

27 Some said, He is inspired by Holy Brahm; and others said, He is insane; and others said, He is obsessed; he speaks as devils speak.

28 But Jesus tarried not. Among the guests was one, a tiller of the soil, a generous soul, a seeker after truth, who loved the words that Jesus spoke; and Jesus went with him, and in his home abode.

CHAPTER 29.

Ajainin, a priest from Lahore, comes to Benares to see Jesus, and abides in the temple. Jesus refuses an invitation to visit the temple. Ajainin visits him at night in the farmer's home, and accepts his philosophy.

AMONG Benares' temple priests was one, a guest, Ajainin, from Lahore.

2 By merchantmen Ajainin heard about the Jewish boy, about his words of wisdom, and he girt himself and journeyed from Lahore that he might see the boy, and hear him speak.

3 The Brahmic priests did not accept the truth that Jesus brought, and they were angered much by what he said at the Udraka feast.

4 But they had never seen the boy, and they desired much to hear him speak, and they invited him to be a temple guest.

5 But Jesus said to them, The light is most abundant, and it shines for all; if you would see the light come to the light.

6 If you would hear the message that the Holy One has given me to give to men, come unto me.

7 Now, when the priests were told what Jesus said they were enraged.

8 Ajainin did not share their wrath, and he sent forth another messenger with costly gifts to Jesus at the farmer's home; he sent this message with the gifts:

9 I pray you, master, listen to my words; The Brahmic law forbids that any priest shall go into the home of any one of low estate; but you can come to us;

10 And I am sure these priests will gladly hear you speak. I pray that you will come and dine with us this day.

11 And Jesus said, The Holy One regards all men alike; the dwelling of my host is good enough for any council of the sons of men.

12 If pride of caste keeps you away, you are not worthy of the light. My Father-God does not regard the laws of man.

13 Your presents I return; you cannot buy the knowledge of the Lord with gold, or precious gifts.

14 These words of Jesus angered more and more the priests, and they began to plot and plan how they might drive him from the land.

15 Ajainin did not join with them in plot and plan; he left the temple in the night, and sought the home where Jesus dwelt.

16 And Jesus said, There is no night where shines the sun; I have no secret messages to give; in light all secrets are revealed.

17 Ajainin said, I came from far-away Lahore, that I might learn about this ancient wisdom, and this kingdom of the Holy One of which you speak.

18 Where is the kingdom? where the king? Who are the subjects? what its laws?

19 And Jesus said, This kingdom is not far away, but man with mortal eyes can see it not; it is within the heart.

20 You need not seek the king in earth, or sea, or sky; he is not there, and yet is everywhere. He is the Christ of God; is universal love.

21 The gate of this dominion is not high, and he who enters it must fall down on his knees. It is not wide, and none can carry carnal bundles through.

22 The lower self must be transmuted into spirit-self; the body must be washed in living streams of purity.

23 Ajainin asked, Can I become a subject of this king?

24 And Jesus said, You are yourself a king, and you may enter through the gate and be a subject of the King of kings.

25 But you must lay aside your priestly robes; must cease to serve the Holy One for gold; must give your life, and all you have, in willing service to the sons of men.

26 And Jesus said no more; Ajainin went his way; and while he could not comprehend the truth that Jesus spoke, he saw what he had never seen before.

27 The realm of faith he never had explored; but in his heart the seeds of faith and universal brotherhood had found good soil.

28 And as he journeyed to his home he seemed to sleep, to pass through darkest night, and when he woke the Sun of Righteousness had arisen; he had found the king.

29 Now, in Benares Jesus tarried many days and taught.

CHAPTER 30.

Jesus receives news of the death of his father. He writes a letter to his mother. The letter. He sends it on its way by a merchant.

ONE day as Jesus stood beside the Ganges busy with his work, a caravan, returning from the West, drew near.

2 And one, approaching Jesus, said, We come to you just from your native land and bring unwelcome news.

3 Your father is no more on earth; your mother grieves; and none can comfort her. She wonders whether you are still alive or not; she longs to see you once again.

4 And Jesus bowed his head in silent thought; and then he wrote. Of what he wrote this is the sum:

5 My mother, noblest of woman kind; A man just from my native land has brought me word that father is no more in flesh, and that you grieve, and are disconsolate.

6 My mother, all is well; is well

for father and is well for you.

7 His work in this earth-round is done, and it is nobly done.

8 In all the walks of life men cannot charge him with deceit, dishonesty, nor wrong intent.

9 Here in this round he finished many heavy tasks, and he has gone from hence prepared to solve the problems of the round of soul.

10 Our Father-God is with him there, as he was with him here; and there his angel guards his footsteps lest he goes astray.

11 Why should you weep? Tears cannot conquer grief. There is no power in grief to mend a broken heart.

12 The plane of grief is idleness; the busy soul can never grieve; it has no time for grief.

13 When grief comes trooping through the heart, just lose yourself; plunge deep into the ministry of love, and grief is not.

14 Yours is a ministry of love, and all the world is calling out for love.

15 Then let the past go with the past; rise from the cares of carnal things and give your life for those who live.

16 And if you lose your life in serving life you will be sure to find in it the morning sun, the evening dews, in song of bird, in flowers, and in the stars of night.

17 In just a little while your problems of this earth-round will be solved; and when your sums are all worked out it will be pleasure unalloyed for you to enter wider fields of usefulness, to solve the greater problems of the soul.

18 Strive, then, to be content, and I will come to you some day and bring you richer gifts than gold or precious stones.

19 I'm sure that John will care

for you, supplying all your needs: and I am with you all the way, Jehoshua.

20 And by the hand of one, a merchant, going to Jerusalem, he sent this letter on its way.

CHAPTER 31.

Brahmic priests are enraged because of Jesus' teaching and resolve to drive him from India. Lamaas pleads for him. Priests employ a murderer to kill him. Lamaas warns him and he flees to Nepel.

THE words and works of Jesus caused unrest through all the land.

2 The common people were his friends, believed in him, and followed him in throngs.

3 The priests and rulers were afraid of him; his very name sent terror to their hearts.

4 He preached the brotherhood of life, the righteousness of equal rights, and taught the uselessness of priests, and sacrificial rites.

5 He shook the very sand on which the Brahmic system stood; he made the Brahmic idols seem so small, and sacrifice so fraught with sin, that shrines and wheels of prayer were all forgot.

6 The priests declared that if this Hebrew boy should tarry longer in the land a revolution would occur; the common people would arise and kill the priests, and tear the temples down.

7 And so they sent a call abroad, and priests from every province came. Benares was on fire with Brahmic zeal.

8 Lamaas from the temple Jagannath, who knew the inner life of Jesus well, was in their midst, and heard the rantings of the priests,

9 And he stood forth and said,

My brother priests, take heed, be careful what you do; this is a record-making day.

10 The world is looking on; the very life of Brahmic thought is now on trial.

11 If we are reason-blind; if prejudice be king today; if we resort to beastly force, and dye our hands in blood that may, in sight of Brahm, be innocent and pure,

12 His vengeance may fall down on us; the very rock on which we stand may burst beneath our feet; and our beloved priesthood, and our laws and shrines will go into decay.

13 But they would let him speak no more. The wrathful priests rushed up and beat him, spit upon him, called him traitor, threw him, bleeding, to the street.

14 And then confusion reigned; the priests became a mob; the sight of human blood led on to fiendish acts, and called for more.

15 The rulers, fearing war, sought Jesus, and they found him calmly teaching in the market-place.

16 They urged him to depart, that he might save his life; but he refused to go.

17 And then the priests sought cause for his arrest; but he had done no crime.

18 And then false charges were preferred; but when the soldiers went to bring him to the judgment hall they were afraid, because the people stood in his defense.

19 The priests were baffled, and they resolved to take his life by stealth.

20 They found a man who was a murderer by trade, and sent him out by night to slay the object of their wrath.

21 Lamaas heard about their plotting and their plans, and sent a messenger to warn his friend; and

Jesus hastened to depart.

22 By night he left Benares, and with haste he journeyed to the north; and everywhere, the farmers, merchants and the sudras helped him on his way.

23 And after many days he reached the mighty Himalayas, and in the city Kapivastu he abode.

24 The priests of Buddha opened wide their temple doors for him.

CHAPTER 32.

Jesus and Barata. Together they read the sacred books. Jesus takes exception to the Buddhist doctrine of evolution and reveals the true origin of man. Meets Vidyapati, who becomes his co-laborer.

AMONG the Buddhist priests was one who saw a lofty wisdom in the words that Jesus spoke. It was Barata Arabo.

2 Together Jesus and Barata read the Jewish Psalms and Prophets; read the Vedas, the Avesta and the wisdom of Guatama.

3 And as they read and talked about the possibilities of man, Barata said,

4 Man is the marvel of the universe. He is a part of everything, for he has been a living thing on every plane of life.

5 Time was when man was not; and then he was a bit of formless substance in the molds of time; and then a protoplast.

6 By universal law all things tend upward to a state of perfectness. The protoplast evolved, becoming worm, then reptile, bird and beast, and then at last it reached the form of man.

7 Now, man himself is mind, and mind is here to gain perfection by experience; and mind is often manifest in fleshy form, and in the

form best suited to its growth. So mind may manifest as worm, or bird, or beast, or man.

8 The time will come when everything of life will be evolved unto the state of perfect man.

9 And after man is man in perfectness, he will evolve to higher forms of life.

10 And Jesus said, Barata Arabo, who taught you this, that mind, which is the man, may manifest in flesh of beast, or bird, or creeping thing?

11 Barata said, From times which man remembers not our priests have told us so, and so we know.

12 And Jesus said, Enlightened Arabo, are you a master mind and do not know that man knows naught by being told?

13 Man may believe what others say; but thus he never knows. If man would know, he must himself be what he knows.

14 Do you remember, Arabo, when you was ape, or bird, or worm?

15 Now, if you have no better proving of your plea than that the priests have told you so, you do not know; you simply guess.

16 Regard not, then, what any man has said; let us forget the flesh, and go with mind into the land of fleshless things; mind never does forget.

17 And backward through the ages master minds can trace themselves; and thus they know.

18 Time never was when man was not.

19 That which begins will have an end. If man was not, the time will come when he will not exist.

20 From God's own Record Book we read: The Triune God breathed forth, and seven Spirits stood before his face. (The Hebrews call these seven Spirits, Elohim.)

21 And these are they who, in their boundless power, created everything that is, or was.

22 These Spirits of the Triune God moved on the face of boundless space and seven ethers were, and every ether had its form of life.

23 These forms of life were but the thoughts of God, clothed in the substance of their ether planes.

24 (Men call these ether planes the planes of protoplast, of earth, of plant, of beast, of man, of angel and of cherubim.)

25 These planes with all their teeming thoughts of God, are never seen by eyes of man in flesh; they are composed of substance far too fine for fleshly eyes to see, and still they constitute the soul of things;

26 And with the eyes of soul all creatures see these ether planes, and all the forms of life.

27 Because all forms of life on every plane are thoughts of God, all creatures think, and every creature is possessed of will, and, in its measure, has the power to choose,

28 And in their native planes all creatures are supplied with nourishment from the ethers of their planes.

29 And so it was with every living thing until the will became a sluggish will, and then the ethers of the protoplast, the earth, the plant, the beast, the man, began to vibrate very slow.

30 The ethers all became more dense, and all the creatures of these planes were clothed with coarser garbs, the garbs of flesh, which men can see; and thus this coarser manifest, which men call physical, appeared.

31 And this is what is called the

fall of man; but man fell not alone for protoplast, and earth, and plant and beast were all included in the fall.

32 The angels and the cherubim fell not; their wills were ever strong, and so they held the ethers of their planes in harmony with God.

33 Now, when the ethers reached the rate of atmosphere, and all the creatures of these planes must get their food from atmosphere, the conflict came; and then that which the finite man has called, survival of the best, became a law,

34 The stronger ate the bodies of the weaker manifests; and here is where the carnal law of evolution had its rise.

35 And now man, in his utter shamelessness, strikes down and eats the beasts, the beast consumes the plant, the plant thrives on the earth, the earth absorbs the protoplast.

36 In yonder kingdom of the soul this carnal evolution is not known, and the great work of master minds is to restore the heritage of man, to bring him back to his estate that he has lost, when he again will live upon the ethers of his native plane.

37 The thoughts of God change not; the manifests of life on every plane unfold into perfection of their kind; and as the thoughts of God can never die, there is no death to any being of the seven ethers of the seven Spirits of the Triune God.

38 And so an earth is never plant; a beast, or bird, or creeping thing is never man, and man is not, and cannot be, a beast, or bird, or creeping thing.

39 The time will come when all these seven manifests will be absorbed, and man, and beast, and plant, and earth and protoplast will be redeemed.

40 Barata was amazed; the wisdom of the Jewish sage was revelation unto him.

41 Now, Vidyapati, wisest of the Indian sages, chief of temple Kapavistu, heard Barata speak to Jesus of the origin of man, and heard the answer of the Hebrew prophet, and he said,

42 You priests of Kapavistu, hear me speak: We stand today upon a crest of time. Six times ago a master soul was born who gave a glory light to man, and now a master sage stands here in temple Kapavistu.

43 This Hebrew prophet is the rising star of wisdom, deified. He brings to us a knowledge of the secret things of God; and all the world will hear his words, will heed his words, and glorify his name.

44 You priests of temple Kapavistu, stay! be still and listen when he speaks; he is the Living Oracle of God.

45 And all the priests gave thanks, and praised the Buddha of enlightenment.

CHAPTER 33.

Jesus teaches the common people at a spring. Tells them how to attain unto happiness. Relates the parable of the rocky field and the hidden treasure.

IN silent meditation Jesus sat beside a flowing spring. It was a holy day, and many people of the servant caste were near the place.

2 And Jesus saw the hard drawn lines of toil on every brow, in every hand. There was no look of joy in any face. Not one of all the group could think of anything but toil.

3 And Jesus spoke to one and

said, Why are you all so sad? Have you no happiness in life?

4 The man replied, We scarcely know the meaning of that word. We toil to live, and hope for nothing else but toil, and bless the day when we can cease our toil and lay us down to rest in Buddha's city of the dead.

5 And Jesus' heart was stirred with pity and with love for these poor toilers, and he said,

6 Toil should not make a person sad; men should be happiest when they toil. When hope and love are back of toil, then all of life is filled with joy and peace, and this is heaven. Do you not know that such a heaven is for you?

7 The man replied, Of heaven we have heard; but then it is so far away, and we must live so many lives before we reach that place!

8 And Jesus said, My brother, man, your thoughts are wrong; your heaven is not far away; and it is not a place of metes and bounds, is not a country to be reached; it is a state of mind.

9 God never made a heaven for man; he never made a hell; we are creators and we make our own.

10 Now, cease to seek for heaven in the sky; just open up the windows of your hearts, and, like a flood of light, a heaven will come and bring a boundless joy; then toil will be no cruel task.

11 The people were amazed, and gathered close to hear this strange young master speak,

12 Imploring him to tell them more about the Father-God; about the heaven that men can make on earth; about the boundless joy.

13 And Jesus spoke a parable; he said, A certain man possessed a field; the soil was hard and poor.

14 By constant toil he scarcely could provide enough of food to keep his family from want.

15 One day a miner who could see beneath the soil, in passing on his way, saw this poor man and his unfruitful field.

16 He called the weary toiler and he said, My brother, know you not that just below the surface of your barren field rich treasures lie concealed?

17 You plow and sow and reap in scanty way, and day by day you tread upon a mine of gold and precious stones.

18 This wealth lies not upon the surface of the ground; but if you will but dig away the rocky soil, and delve down deep into the earth, you need no longer till the soil for naught.

19 The man believed. The miner surely knows; he said, and I will find the treasures hidden in my field.

20 And then he dug away the rocky soil, and deep down in the earth he found a mine of gold.

21 And Jesus said, The sons of men are toiling hard on desert plains, and burning sands and rocky soils; are doing what their fathers did, not dreaming they can do aught else.

22 Behold, a master comes, and tells them of a hidden wealth; that underneath the rocky soil of carnal things are treasures that no man can count;

23 That in the heart the richest gems abound; that he who wills may open up the door and find them all.

24 And then the people said, Make known to us the way that we may find the wealth that lies within the heart.

25 And Jesus opened up the way; the toilers saw another side of life, and toil became a joy.

CHAPTER 34.

*The Jubilee in Kapavistu. Jesus
teaches in the plaza and the people
are astonished. He relates the parable of the unkept vineyard and the
vine dresser. The priests are angered by his words.*

IT was a gala day in sacred Kapavistu; a throng of Buddhist
worshippers had met to celebrate
a Jubilee.

2 And priests and masters from
all parts of India were there; they
taught; but they embellished little
truth with many words.

3 And Jesus went into an ancient plaza and he taught; he spoke
of Father-Mother-God; he told
about the brotherhood of life.

4 The priests and all the people
were astounded at his words and
said, Is this not Buddha come again
in flesh? No other one could speak
with such simplicity and power.

5 And Jesus spoke a parable;
he said, There was a vineyard all
unkept; the vines were high, the
growth of leaves and branches
great.

6 The leaves were broad and
shut the sunlight from the vines;
the grapes were sour, and few, and
small.

7 The pruner came; with his
sharp knife he cut off every branch,
and not a leaf remained; just root
and stalk, and nothing more.

8 The busy neighbors came with
one accord and were amazed, and
said to him who pruned, You foolish man! the vineyard is despoiled.

9 Such desolation! There is
no beauty left, and when the harvest time shall come the gatherers
will find no fruit.

10 The pruner said, Content
yourselves with what you think, and
come again at harvest time and see.

11 And when the harvest time
came on the busy neighbors came
again; they were surprised.

12 The naked stalks had put
forth branch and leaf, and heavy
clusters of delicious grapes weighed
every branch to earth.

13 The gatherers rejoiced as,
day by day, they carried the rich
fruitage to the press.

14 Behold, the vineyard of the
Lord! the earth is spread with human vines.

15 The gorgeous forms and rites
of men are branches, and their
words are leaves; and these have
grown so great that sunlight can
no longer reach the heart; there is
no fruit.

16 Behold, the pruner comes,
and with a two-edged knife he cuts
away the branches and the leaves
of words,

17 And naught is left but un-
clothed stalks of human life.

18 The priests and they of
pompous show, rebuke the pruner,
and would stay him in his work.

19 They see no beauty in the
stalks of human life; no promises of
fruit.

20 The harvest time will come
and they who scorned the pruner
will look on again and be amazed,
for they will see the human stalks
that seemed so lifeless, bending low
with precious fruit.

21 And they will hear the harvesters rejoice, because the harvest
is so great.

22 The priests were not well
pleased with Jesus' words; but they
rebuked him not; they feared the
multitude.

CHAPTER 35.

*Jesus and Vidyapati consider the
needs of the incoming age of the
world.*

THE Indian sage and Jesus often met and talked about the needs of nations and of men; about the sacred doctrines, forms and rites best suited to the coming age.

2 One day they sat together in a mountain pass, and Jesus said, The coming age will surely not require priests, and shrines, and sacrifice of life.

3 There is no power in sacrifice of beast, or bird, to help a man to holy life.

4 And Vidyapati said, All forms and rites are symbols of the things that men must do within the temple of the soul.

5 The Holy One requires man to give his life in willing sacrifice for men, and all the so-called offerings on altars and on shrines that have been made since time began, were made to teach man how to give himself to save his brother man; for man can never save himself except he lose his life in saving other men.

6 The perfect age will not require forms and rites and carnal sacrifice. The coming age is not the perfect age, and men will call for object lessons and symbolic rites.

7 And in the great religion you shall introduce to men, some simple rites of washings and remembrances will be required; but cruel sacrifice of animals, and birds the gods require not.

8 And Jesus said, Our God must loathe the tinseled show of priests and priestly things.

9 When men array themselves in showy garbs to indicate that they are servants of the gods, and strut about like gaudy birds to be admired by men, because of piety or any other thing, the Holy One must surely turn away in sheer disgust.

10 All people are alike the servants of our Father-God, are kings and priests.

11 Will not the coming age demand complete destruction of the priestly caste, as well as every other caste and inequality among the sons of men?

12 And Vidyapati said, The coming age is not the age of spirit life and men will pride themselves in wearing priestly robes, and chanting pious chants to advertise themselves as saints.

13 The simple rites that you will introduce will be extolled by those who follow you, until the sacred service of the age will far outshine in gorgeousness the priestly service of the Brahmic age.

14 This is a problem men must solve.

15 The perfect age will come when every man will be a priest and men will not array themselves in special garb to advertise their piety.

SECTION VII.

ZAIN.

Life and Works of Jesus in Tibet and Western India.

CHAPTER 36.

Jesus in Lassa. He meets Meng-ste who aids him in reading the ancient manuscripts. He goes to Ladak. Heals a child. Relates the parable of the king's son.

IN Lassa of Tibet there was a master's temple, rich in manuscripts of ancient lore.

2 The Indian sage had read these manuscripts, and he revealed to Jesus many of the secret lessons

they contained; but Jesus wished to read them for himself.

3 Now, Meng-ste, greatest sage of all the farther East, was in this temple of Tibet.

4 The path across Emodus heights was difficult; but Jesus started on his way, and Vidyapati sent with him a trusted guide.

5 And Vidyapati sent a message to Meng-ste, in which he told about the Hebrew sage, and spoke for him a welcome by the temple priests.

6 Now, after many days, and perils great, the guide and Jesus reached the Lassa temple in Tibet.

7 And Meng-ste opened wide the temple doors, and all the priests and masters gave a welcome to the Hebrew sage.

8 And Jesus had access to all the sacred manuscripts, and, with the help of Meng-ste, read them all.

9 And Meng-ste often talked with Jesus of the coming age, and of the sacred service best adapted to the people of the age.

10 In Lassa Jesus did not teach. When he had finished all his studies in the temple schools he journeyed toward the West. In many villages he tarried for a time and taught.

11 At last he reached the pass, and in the Ladak city, Leh, he was received with favor by the monks, the merchants, and the men of low estate.

12 And in the monastery he abode, and taught; and then he sought the common people in the marts of trade; and there he taught.

13 Not far away a woman lived, whose infant son was sick nigh unto death. The doctors had declared, There is no hope; the child must die.

14 The woman heard that Jesus was a teacher sent from God, and she believed that he had power to heal her son.

15 And so she clasped the dying infant in her arms and ran with haste and asked to see the man of God.

16 When Jesus saw her faith he lifted up his eyes to heaven and said,

17 My Father-God, let power divine o'ershadow me, and let the Holy Breath fill full this child that it may live.

18 And in the presence of the multitude he laid his hand upon the child and said,

19 Good woman you are blest; your faith has saved your son. And then the child was well.

20 The people were astonished and they said, This surely is the Holy One made flesh, for man alone cannot rebuke a fever thus and save a child from death.

21 Then many of the people brought their sick, and Jesus spoke the Word, and they were healed.

22 Among the Ladaks Jesus tarried many days; he taught them how to heal; how sins are blotted out, and how to make on earth a heaven of joy.

23 The people loved him for his words and works, and when he must depart they grieved as children grieve when mother goes away.

24 And on the morning when he started on his way the multitudes were there to press his hand.

25 To them he spoke a parable; he said, A certain king so loved the people of his land that he sent forth his only son with precious gifts for all.

26 The son went everywhere and scattered forth the gifts with lavish hand.

27 But there were priests who ministered at shrines of foreign gods,

who were not pleased because the king did not through them bestow the gifts.

28 And so they sought to cause the people all to hate the son. They said, These gifts are not of any worth; they are but counterfeits.

29 And so the people threw the precious gems, and gold and silver in the streets. They caught the son and beat him, spit upon him, drove him from their midst.

30 The son resented not their insults and their cruelties; but thus he prayed, My Father-God, forgive these creatures of thy hand; they are but slaves; they know not what they do.

31 And while they yet were beating him he gave them food, and blest them with a boundless love.

32 In certain cities was the son received with joy, and he would gladly have remained to bless the homes; but he could tarry not, for he must carry gifts to every one in all the king's domain.

33 And Jesus said, My Father-God is king of all mankind, and he has sent me forth with all the bounties of his matchless love and boundless wealth.

34 To all the people of all lands, lo, I must bear these gifts—this water and this bread of life.

35 I go my way, but we will meet again; for in my Fatherland is room for all; I will prepare a place for you.

36 And Jesus raised his hand in silent benediction; then he went his way.

CHAPTER 37.

Jesus is presented with a camel. He goes to Lahore where he abides with Ajainin, whom he teaches. Lesson of the wandering musicians. Jesus resumes his journey.

A CARAVAN of merchantmen were journeying through the Kashmar vale as Jesus passed that way, and they were going to Lahore, a city of the Hand, the five-stream land.

2 The merchantmen had heard the prophet speak, had seen his mighty works in Leh, and they were glad to see him once again.

3 And when they knew that he was going to Lahore and then across the Sind, through Persia and the farther West, and that he had no beast on which to ride,

4 They freely gave to him a noble bactrian beast, well saddled and equipped, and Jesus journeyed with the caravan.

5 And when he reached Lahore, Ajainin and some other Brahmic priests, received him with delight.

6 Ajainin was the priest who came to Jesus in the night time in Benares many months before, and heard his words of truth.

7 And Jesus was Ajainin's guest; he taught Ajainin many things; revealed to him the secrets of the healing art.

8 He taught him how he could control the spirits of the air, the fire, the water and the earth; and he explained to him the secret doctrine of forgiveness, and the blotting out of sins.

9 One day Ajainin sat with Jesus in the temple porch; a band of wandering singers and musicians paused before the court to sing and play.

10 Their music was most rich and delicate, and Jesus said, Among the high-bred people of the land we hear no sweeter music than that these uncouth children of the wilderness bring here to us.

11 From whence this talent and this power? In one short life they

surely could not gain such grace of voice, such knowledge of the laws of harmony and tone.

12 Men call them prodigies. There are no prodigies. All things result from natural law.

13 These people are not young. A thousand years would not suffice to give them such divine expressiveness, and such purity of voice and touch.

14 Ten thousand years ago these people mastered harmony. In days of old they trod the busy thoroughfares of life, and caught the melody of birds, and played on harps of perfect form.

15 And they have come again to learn still other lessons from the varied notes of manifests.

16 These wandering people form a part of heaven's orchestra, and in the land of perfect things the very angels will delight to hear them play and sing.

17 And Jesus taught the common people of Lahore; he healed their sick, and showed to them the way to rise to better things by helpfulness.

18 He said, We are not rich by what we get and hold; the only things we keep are those we give away.

19 If you would live the perfect life, give forth your life in service for your kind, and for the forms of life that men esteem the lower forms of life.

20 But Jesus could not tarry longer in Lahore; he bade the priests and other friends farewell; and then he took his camel and he went his way toward the Sind.

SECTION VIII.

CHETH.

Life and Works of Jesus in Persia.

CHAPTER 38.

Jesus crosses Persia. Teaches and heals in many places. Three magian priests meet him as he nears Persepolis. Kaspar, and two other Persian masters, meet him in Persepolis. The seven masters sit in silence seven days.

FOUR-AND-TWENTY years of age was Jesus when he entered Persia on his homeward way.

2 In many a hamlet, town and neighborhood he paused a while and taught and healed.

3 The priests and ruling classes did not welcome him, because he censured them for cruelty to those of low estate.

4 The common people followed him in throngs.

5 At times the chiefs made bold to try to hinder him, forbidding him to teach or heal the sick. But he regarded not their angry threats; he taught, and healed the sick.

6 In time he reached Persepolis, the city where the kings of Persia were entombed; the city of the learned magi, Hor, and Lun, and Mer, the three wise men,

7 Who, two-and-twenty years before, had seen the star of promise rise above Jerusalem, and who had journeyed to the West to find the new-born king;

8 And were the first to honor Jesus as the master of the age, and gave him gifts of gold, gum-thus and myrrh.

9 These magi knew, by ways that masters always know, when

Jesus neared Persepolis; and then they girt themselves, and went to meet him on the way.

10 And when they met, a light much brighter than the light of day, surrounded them, and men who saw the four stand in the way declared they were transfigured; seeming more like gods than men.

11 Now, Hor and Lun were aged men, and Jesus placed them on his beast to ride into Persepolis; while he and Mer led on the way.

12 And when they reached the magi's home they all rejoiced. And Jesus told the thrilling story of his life, and Hor and Lun and Mer spoke not; they only looked to heaven, and in their hearts praised God.

13 Three wise men from the North were in Persepolis; and they were Kaspar, Zara and Melzone; and Kaspar was the wisest master of the magian land. These three were at the home of Hor and Lun and Mer when Jesus came.

14 For seven days these seven men spoke not; they sat in silence in the council hall in close communion with the Silent Brotherhood.

15 They sought for light, for revelation and for power. The laws and precepts of the coming age required all the wisdom of the masters of the world.

CHAPTER 39.

Jesus attends a feast in Persepolis. Speaks to the people, reviewing the magian philosophy. Explains the origin of evil. Spends the night in prayer.

A FEAST in honor of the magian God was being held, and many men were gathered in Persepolis.

2 And on the great day of the feast the ruling magian master said,

Within these sacred walls is liberty; whoever wills to speak may speak.

3 And Jesus standing in the midst of all the people, said, My brothers, sisters, children of our Father-God:

4 Most blest are you among the sons of men today, because you have such just conceptions of the Holy One and man.

5 Your purity in worship and in life is pleasing unto God; and to your master, Zarathustra, praise is due.

6 Well say you all, There is one God from whose great being there came forth the seven Spirits that created heaven and earth; and manifest unto the sons of men are these great Spirits in the sun, and moon, and stars.

7 But in your sacred books we read that two among these seven are of superior strength; that one of these created all the good; the other one created all that evil is.

8 I pray you, honored masters, tell me how that evil can be born of that which is all good?

9 A magus rose and said, If you will answer me, your problem will be solved.

10 We all do recognize the fact that evil is. Whatever is, must have a cause. If God, the One, made not this evil, then, where is the God who did?

11 And Jesus said, Whatever God, the One, has made is good, and like the great first Cause, the seven Spirits all are good, and everything that comes from their creative hands is good,

12 Now, all created things have colors, tones and forms their own; but certain tones, though good and pure themselves, when mixed, produce inharmonies, discordant tones.

13 And certain things, though

good and pure, when mixed, produce discordant things, yea, poisonous things, that men call evil things.

14   So evil is the inharmonious blending of the colors, tones, or forms of good.

15   Now, man is not all-wise, and yet has will his own.   He has the power, and he uses it, to mix God's good things in a multitude of ways, and every day he makes discordant sounds, and evil things.

16   And every tone and form, be it of good, or ill, becomes a living thing, a demon, sprite, or spirit of a good or vicious kind.

17   Man makes his devil thus; and then becomes afraid of him and flees; his devil is emboldened, follows him away and casts him into torturing fires.

18   The devil and the burning fires are both the works of man, and none can put the fires out and dissipate the evil one, but man who made them both.

19   Then Jesus stood aside, and not a magus answered him.

20   And he departed from the throng and went into a secret place to pray.

CHAPTER 40.

Jesus teaches the magians.   Explains the Silence and how to enter it. Kaspar extols the wisdom of Jesus. Jesus teaches in the groves of Cyrus.

NOW, in the early morning Jesus came again to teach and heal. A light not comprehended shown about, as though some mighty spirit overshadowed him.

2   A magus noted this and asked him privately to tell from whence his wisdom came, and what the meaning of the light.

3   And Jesus said, There is a Si-

lence where the soul may meet its God, and there the fount of wisdom is, and all who enter are immersed in light, and filled with wisdom, love and power.

4   The magus said, Tell me about this Silence and this light, that I may go and there abide.

5   And Jesus said, The Silence is not circumscribed; is not a place closed in with wall, or rocky steeps, nor guarded by the sword of man.

6   Men carry with them all the time the secret place where they may meet their God.

7   It matters not where men abide, on mountain top, in deepest vale, in marts of trade, or in the quiet home; they may at once, at any time, fling wide the door, and find the Silence, find the house of God; it is within the soul.

8   One may not be so much disturbed by noise of business, and the words and thoughts of men if he goes all alone into the valley or the mountain pass.

9   And when life's heavy load is pressing hard, it is far better to go out and seek a quiet place to pray and meditate.

10   The Silence is the kingdom of the soul which is not seen by human eyes.

11   When in the Silence, phantom forms may flit before the mind; but they are all subservient to the will; the master soul may speak and they are gone.

12   If you would find this Silence of the soul you must yourself prepare the way.   None but the pure in heart may enter here.

13   And you must lay aside all tenseness of the mind, all business cares, all fears, all doubts and troubled thoughts.

14   Your human will must be absorbed by the divine; then you will

come into a consciousness of holiness.

15 You are within the Holy Place, and you will see upon a living shrine the candle of the Lord aflame.

16 And when you see it burning there, look deep within the temple of your brain, and you will see it all aglow.

17 In every part, from head to foot, are candles all in place, just waiting to be lighted by the flaming torch of love.

18 And when you see the candles all aflame, just look, and you will see, with eyes of soul, the waters of the fount of wisdom rushing on; and you may drink, and there abide.

19 And then the curtains part, and you are in the Holiest of All, where rests the Ark of God, whose covering is the Mercy Seat.

20 Fear not to lift the sacred board; the Tables of the Law are in the Ark concealed.

21 Take them and read them well; for they contain all precepts and commands that men will ever need.

22 And in the Ark, the magic wand of prophecy lies waiting for your hand; it is the key to all the hidden meanings of the present, future, past.

23 And then, behold, the manna there, the hidden bread of life; and he who eats shall never die.

24 The cherubim have guarded well for every soul this treasure box, and whosoever will may enter in and find his own.

25 Now Kaspar heard the Hebrew master speak and he exclaimed, Behold, the wisdom of the gods has come to men!

26 And Jesus went his way, and in the sacred groves of Cyrus,

where the multitudes were met, he taught and healed the sick.

CHAPTER 41.

Jesus stands by a healing fountain. Reveals the fact that faith is the potent factor in healing and many are healed by faith. A little child teaches a great lesson of faith.

A FLOWING spring that people called the Healing Fount, was near Persepolis.

2 And all the people thought that at a certain time of year their deity came down and gave a virtue to the waters of the fount, and that the sick who then would plunge into the fount and wash would be made whole.

3 About the fount a multitude of people were in waiting for the Holy One to come and potentize the waters of the fount.

4 The blind, the lame, the deaf, the dumb, and those obsessed were there.

5 And Jesus, standing in the midst of them, exclaimed, Behold the spring of life! These waters that will fail are honored as the special blessing of your God.

6 From whence do healing virtues come? Why is your God so partial with his gifts? Why does he bless this spring today, and then tomorrow take his blessings all away?

7 A deity of power could fill these waters full of healing virtue every day.

8 Hear me, you sick, disconsolate: The virtue of this fount is not a special gift of God.

9 Faith is the healing power of every drop of all the waters of this spring.

10 He who believes with all his heart that he will be made whole by

rWashing in this fount will be made whole when he has washed; and he may wash at any time.

11 Let every one who has this faith in God and in himself plunge in these waters now and wash.

12 And many of the people plunged into the crystal fount; and they were healed.

13 And then there was a rush, for all the people were inspired with faith, and each one strove to be among the first to wash, lest all the virtue be absorbed.

14 And Jesus saw a little child, weak, faint and helpless, sitting all alone beyond the surging crowd; and there was none to help her to the fount.

15 And Jesus said, My little one, why do you sit and wait? Why not arise and hasten to the fount and wash, and be made well?

16 The child replied, I need not haste; the blessings of my Father in the sky are measured not in tiny cups; they never fail; their virtues are the same forevermore.

17 When these whose faith is weak must haste to wash for fear their faith will fail, have all been cured, these waters will be just as powerful for me.

18 Then I can go and stay a long, long time within the blessed waters of the spring.

19 And Jesus said, Behold a master soul! She came to earth to teach to men the power of faith.

20 And then he lifted up the child and said, Why wait for anything? The very air we breathe is filled with balm of life. Breathe in this balm of life in faith and be made whole.

21 The child breathed in the balm of life in faith, and she was well.

22 The people marveled much at what they heard and saw; they said, This man must surely be the god of health made flesh.

23 And Jesus said, The fount of life is not a little pool; it is as wide as are the spaces of the heavens.

24 The waters of the fount are love; the potency is faith, and he who plunges deep into the living springs, in living faith, may wash away his guilt and be made whole, and freed from sin.

SECTION IX.

TETH.

Life and Works of Jesus in Assyria.

CHAPTER 42.

Jesus bids the magians farewell. Goes to Assyria. Teaches the people in Ur of Chaldea. Meets Ashbina, with whom he visits many towns and cities, teaching and healing the sick.

IN Persia Jesus' work was done and he resumed his journey towards his native land.

2 The Persian sage went with him to the Euphrates; then with a pledge that they would meet again in Egypt land the masters said, Farewell.

3 And Kaspar went his way unto his home beside the Caspian Sea; and Jesus soon was in Chaldea, cradle land of Israel.

4 In Ur, where Abraham was born, he tarried for a time; and when he told the people who he was,

and why he came, they came from near and far to speak to him.

5 He said to them, We all are kin. Two thousand years and more ago, our Father Abraham lived here in Ur, and then he worshipped God the One, and taught the people in these sacred groves.

6 And he was greatly blessed; becoming father of the mighty hosts of Israel.

7 Although so many years have passed since Abraham and Sarah walked these ways, a remnant of their kindred still abide in Ur.

8 And in their hearts the God of Abraham is still adored, and faith and justice are the rocks on which they build.

9 Behold this land! It is no more the fruitful land that Abraham loved so well; the rains come not as in the former times; the vine is not productive now, and withered are the figs.

10 But this shall not forever be; the time will come when all your deserts will rejoice; when flowers will bloom; when all your vines will bend their heads with luscious fruit; your shepherds will again be glad.

11 And Jesus preached to them the gospel of good will, and peace on earth. He told them of the brotherhood of life, and of the inborn powers of man, and of the kingdom of the soul.

12 And as he spoke, Ashbina, greatest sage of all Assyria, stood before his face.

13 The people knew the sage, for he had often taught them in their sacred halls and groves, and they rejoiced to see his face.

14 Ashbina said, My children of Chaldea, hear! Behold, for you are greatly blest today, because a prophet of the living God has come to you.

15 Take heed to what this master says, for he gives forth the words that God has given him.

16 And Jesus and the sage went through the towns and cities of Chaldea and of the lands between the Tigris and the Euphrates;

17 And Jesus healed a multitude of people who were sick.

CHAPTER 43.

Jesus and Ashbina visit Babylon and remark its desolation. The two masters remain in company seven days; then Jesus resumes his homeward journey. Arrives in Nazareth. His mother gives a feast in his honor. His brothers are displeased. Jesus tells his mother and aunt the story of his journeys.

THE ruined Babylon was near, and Jesus and the sage went through her gates and walked among her fallen palaces.

2 They trod the streets where Israel once was held in base captivity.

3 They saw where Judah's sons and daughters hung their harps upon the willows, and refused to sing.

4 They saw where Daniel and the Hebrew children stood as living witnesses of faith.

5 And Jesus lifted up his hands and said, Behold the grandeur of the works of man!

6 The king of Babylon destroyed the temple of the Lord in old Jerusalem; he burned the holy city, bound in chains my people and my kin, and brought them here as slaves.

7 But retribution comes; for whatsoever men shall do to other men the righteous Judge will do to them.

8 The sun of Babylon has gone

down; the songs of pleasure will be heard no more within her walls.

9 And every kind of creeping thing and unclean bird will, in these ruins, find their homes.

10 And in the temple Belus, Jesus and Ashbina stood in silent thought.

11 Then Jesus spoke and said, Behold this monument of folly and of shame.

12 Man tried to shake the very throne of God, and he assayed to build a tower to reach to heaven, when, lo, his very speech was snatched away, because in lofty words he boasted of his power.

13 And on these heights the heathen Baal stood — the god wrought out by hands of man.

14 Upon yon altar, birds, and beasts, and men, yea children have been burned in awful sacrifice to Baal.

15 But now the gory priests are dead; the very rocks have shuddered and have fallen down; the place is desolate.

16 Now, in the plains of Shinar Jesus tarried yet for seven days, and, with Ashbina, meditated long upon the needs of men, and how the sages could best serve the coming age.

17 Then Jesus went his way, and after many days he crossed the Jordan to his native land. At once he sought his home in Nazareth.

18 His mother's heart was filled with joy; she made a feast for him, inviting all her kindred and her friends.

19 But Jesus' brothers were not pleased that such attention should be paid to one they deemed a sheer adventurer, and they went not in to the feast.

20 They laughed their brother's claims to scorn; they called him indolent, ambitious, vain; a worthless fortune hunter; searcher of the world for fame, who, after many years returns to mother's home with neither gold, nor any other wealth.

21 And Jesus called aside his mother and her sister, Miriam, and told them of his journey to the East.

22 He told them of the lessons he had learned, and of the works that he had done. To others he told not the story of his life.

SECTION X.

JOD.

Life and Works of Jesus in Greece.

CHAPTER 44.

Jesus visits Greece and is welcomed by the Athenians. Meets Apollo. Addresses the Grecian masters in the Amphitheater. The address.

THE Greek philosophy was full of pungent truth, and Jesus longed to study with the masters in the schools of Greece.

2 And so he left his home in Nazareth and crossed the Carmel hills, and at the port took ship, and soon was in the Grecian capital.

3 Now, the Athenians had heard of him as teacher and philosopher, and they were glad to have him come to them that they might hear his words of truth.

4 Among the masters of the Greeks was one, Apollo, who was called, Defender of the Oracle, and

recognized in many lands as Grecian sage.

5 Apollo opened up for Jesus all the doors of Grecian lore, and in the Areopagus he heard the wisest masters speak.

6 But Jesus brought to them a wisdom greater far than theirs; and so he taught.

7 Once in the Amphitheater he stood, and when Apollo bade him speak he said,

8 Athenian masters, hear! In ages long ago, men, wise in nature's laws, sought out and found the place on which your city stands.

9 Full well you know that there are parts of earth where its great beating heart throws heavenward etheric waves that meet the ethers from above;

10 Where spirit-light and understanding, like the stars of night, shine forth.

11 Of all the parts of earth there is no place more sensitized, more truly spirit-blest, than that where Athens stands.

12 Yea, all of Greece is blest. No other land has been the homeland of such mighty men of thought as grace your scrolls of fame.

13 A host of sturdy giants of philosophy, of poetry, of science, and of art, were born upon the soil of Greece, and rocked to manhood in your cradle of pure thought.

14 I come not here to speak of science, of philosophy, or art; of these you are the world's best masters now.

15 But all your high accomplishments are but stepping stones to worlds beyond the realm of sense; are but illusive shadows flitting on the walls of time.

16 But I would tell you of a life beyond, within; a real life that can not pass away.

17 In science and philosophy there is no power strong enough to fit a soul to recognize itself, or to commune with God.

18 I would not stay the flow of your great streams of thought; but I would turn them to the channels of the soul.

19 Unaided by the Spirit-breath, the work of intellection tends to solve the problems of the things we see, and nothing more.

20 The senses were ordained to bring into the mind mere pictures of the things that pass away; they do not deal with real things; they do not comprehend eternal law.

21 But man has something in his soul, a something that will tear the veil apart that he may see the world of real things.

22 We call this something, spirit consciousness; it sleeps in every soul, and cannot be awakened till the Holy Breath becomes a welcome guest.

23 This Holy Breath knocks at the door of every soul, but cannot enter in until the will of man throws wide the door.

24 There is no power in intellect to turn the key; philosophy and science both have toiled to get a glimpse behind the veil; but they have failed.

25 The secret spring that throws ajar the door of soul is touched by nothing else than purity in life, by prayer and holy thought.

26 Return, O mystic stream of Grecian thought, and mingle your clear waters with the flood of Spirit-life; and then the spirit consciousness will sleep no more, and man will know, and God will bless.

27 When Jesus had thus said he stepped aside. The Grecian masters were astonished at the wisdom of his words; they answered not.

CHAPTER 45.

Jesus teaches the Greek masters.
Goes with Apollo to Delphi and
hears the Oracle speak. It testifies
for him. He abides with Apollo,
and is recognized as the Living
Oracle of God. Explains to Apollo
the phenomenon of oracular speech.

FOR many days the Grecian masters listened to the clear incisive words that Jesus spoke, and while they could not fully comprehend the things he said, they were delighted and accepted his philosophy.

2 One day as Jesus and Apollo walked beside the sea, a Delphic courier came in haste and said, Apollo, master, come; the Oracle would speak with you.

3 Apollo said to Jesus, Sir, if you would see the Delphic Oracle, and hear it speak, you may accompany me. And Jesus did accompany him.

4 The masters went in haste; and when they came to Delphi, great excitement reigned.

5 And when Apollo stood before the Oracle it spoke and said:

6 Apollo, sage of Greece, the bell strikes twelve; the midnight of the ages now has come.

7 Within the womb of nature ages are conceived; they gestate and are born in glory with the rising sun, and when the agic sun goes down the age disintegrates and dies.

8 The Delphic age has been an age of glory and renown; the gods have spoken to the sons of men through oracles of wood, and gold, and precious stone.

9 The Delphic sun has set; the Oracle will go into decline; the time is near when men will hear its voice no more.

10 The gods will speak to man by man. The Living Oracle now stands within these sacred groves; the Logos from on high has come.

11 From henceforth will decrease my wisdom and my power; from henceforth will increase the wisdom and the power of him, Im-

12 Let all the masters stay; let every creature hear and honor him, Immanuel.

13 And then the Oracle spoke not again for forty days, and priests and people were amazed. They came from near and far to hear the Living Oracle speak forth the wisdom of the gods.

14 And Jesus and the Grecian sage returned; and in Apollo's home the Living Oracle spoke forth for forty days.

15 One day Apollo said to Jesus as they sat alone, This sacred Delphic Oracle has spoken many a helpful word for Greece.

16 Pray tell me what it is that speaks. Is it an angel, man, or living god?

17 And Jesus said, It is not angel, man, nor god that speaks. It is the matchless wisdom of the master minds of Greece, united in a master mind.

18 This giant mind has taken to itself the substances of soul, and thinks, and hears, and speaks.

19 It will remain a living soul while master minds feed it with thought, with wisdom and with faith and hope.

20 But when the master minds of Greece shall perish from the land, this giant master mind will cease to be, and then the Delphic Oracle will speak no more.

CHAPTER 46.

A storm on the sea. Jesus rescues many drowning men. The Athenians pray to idols. Jesus rebukes their idolatry and tells how God helps. His last meeting with the Greeks. Sails on the vessel Mars.

IT was a holy day and Jesus walked upon the Athens' beach.

2 A storm was on and ships were being tossed about like toys upon the bosom of the sea.

3 The sailors and the fishermen were going down to watery graves; the shores were strewn with bodies of the dead.

4 And Jesus halted not, but with a mighty power he rescued many a helpless one, oft bringing back to life the seeming dead.

5 Now, on these shores were altars sacred to the gods supposed to rule the seas.

6 And men and women, heedless of the cries of drowning men, were crowding all about these altars, calling on their gods for help.

7 At length the storm was done, and all the sea was calm, and men could think again; and Jesus said,

8 You worshippers of wooden gods, how has the fury of this storm been lessened by your frantic prayers?

9 Where is the strength of these poor, weather-beaten gods with painted swords and crowns?

10 A god that could abide in such a little house could hardly hold a frantic fly, and who could hope that he could hold at bay the Lords of winds and waves?

11 The mighty powers of worlds unseen do not give forth their help till men have done their best; they only help when man can do no more.

12 And you have agonized and prayed around these shrines, and let men sink to death who might have been, by your assistance, saved.

13 The God that saves dwells in your souls, and manifests by making use of your own feet, and legs, and arms, and hands.

14 Strength never comes through idleness; nor through a waiting for another one to bear your loads, or do the work that you are called to do.

15 But when you do your best to bear your loads, and do your work, you offer unto God a sacrifice well-pleasing in his sight.

16 And then the Holy One breathes deep upon your glowing sacrificial coals, and makes them blaze aloft to fill your souls with light, and strength and helpfulness.

17 The most efficient prayer that men can offer to a god of any kind is helpfulness to those in need of help; for what you do for other men the Holy One will do for you.

18 And thus God helps.

19 His work in Greece was done, and Jesus must go on his way to Egypt in the South. Apollo, with the highest masters of the land and many people from the varied walks of life, stood on the shore to see the Hebrew sage depart; and Jesus said,

20 The son of man has been in many lands; has stood in temples of a multitude of foreign gods; has preached the gospel of good will and peace on earth to many people, tribes and tongues;

21 Has been received with favor in a multitude of homes; but Greece is, of them all, the royal host.

22 The breadth of Grecian thought; the depth of her philosophy; the height of her unselfish aspirations have well fitted her to be the champion of the cause of human liberty and right.

23   The fates of war have subjugated Greece, because she trusted in the strength of flesh, and bone and intellect, forgetful of the spirit-life that binds a nation to its source of power,

24   But Greece will not forever sit within the darkness of the shadowland as vassal of a foreign king.

25   Lift up your heads, you men of Greece; the time will come when Greece will breathe the ethers of the Holy Breath, and be a main spring of the spirit power of earth.

26   But God must be your shield, your buckler, and your tower of strength.

27   And then he said, Farewell. Apollo raised his hand in silent benediction, and the people wept.

28   Upon the Cretan vessel, Mars, the Hebrew sage sailed from the Grecian port.

SECTION XI.
CAPH.
Life and Works of Jesus in Egypt.

CHAPTER 47.

Jesus with Elihu and Salome in Egypt. Tells the story of his journeys. Elihu and Salome praise God. Jesus goes to the temple in Heliopolis and is received as a pupil.

AND Jesus came to Egypt land, and all was well. He tarried not upon the coast; he went at once to Zoan, home of Elihu and Salome, who five and twenty years before had taught his mother in their sacred school.

2   And there was joy when met these three. When last the son of Mary saw these sacred groves he was a babe;

3   And now a man grown strong by buffetings of every kind; a teacher who had stirred the multitudes in many lands.

4   And Jesus told the aged teachers all about his life; about his journeyings in foreign lands; about the meetings with the masters and about his kind receptions by the multitudes.

5   Elihu and Salome heard his story with delight; they lifted up their eyes to heaven and said,

6   Our Father-God, let now thy servants go in peace, for we have seen the glory of the Lord;

7   And we have talked with him, the messenger of love, and of the covenant of peace on earth, good will to men.

8   Through him shall all the nations of the earth be blest; through him, Immanuel.

9   And Jesus staid in Zoan many days; and then went forth unto the city of the sun, that men call Heliopolis, and sought admission to the temple of the sacred brotherhood.

10   The council of the brotherhood convened, and Jesus stood before the hierophant; he answered all the questions that were asked with clearness and with power.

11   The hierophant exclaimed, Rabboni of the rabbinate, why come you here? Your wisdom is the wisdom of the gods; why seek for wisdom in the halls of men?

12   And Jesus said, In every way of earth-life I would walk; in every hall of learning I would sit; the heights that any man has gained, these I would gain;

13   What any man has suffered I would meet, that I may know the

griefs, the disappointments and the sore temptations of my brother man; that I may know just how to succor those in need.

14 I pray you, brothers, let me go into your dismal crypts; and I would pass the hardest of your tests.

15 The master said, Take then the vow of secret brotherhood And Jesus took the vow of secret brotherhood.

16 Again the master spoke; he said, The greatest heights are gained by those who reach the greatest depths; and you shall reach the greatest depths.

17 The guide then led the way and in the fountain Jesus bathed; and when he had been clothed in proper garb he stood again before the hierophant.

CHAPTER 48.

Jesus receives from the hierophant his mystic name and number. Passes the first brotherhood test, and receives his first degree, SIN-CERITY.

THE master took down from the wall a scroll on which was written down the number and the name of every attribute and character. He said,

2 The circle is the symbol of the perfect man, and seven is the number of the perfect man;

3 The Logos is the perfect word; that which creates; that which destroys, and that which saves.

4 This Hebrew master is the Logos of the Holy One, the Circle of the human race, the Seven of time.

5 And in the record book the scribe wrote down, The Logos-Circle-Seven; and thus was Jesus known.

6 The master said, The Logos will give heed to what I say: No man can enter into light till he has found himself. Go forth and search till you have found your soul and then return.

7 The guide led Jesus to a room in which the light was faint and mellow, like the light of early dawn.

8 The chamber walls were marked with mystic signs, with hieroglyphs and sacred texts; and in this chamber Jesus found himself alone where he remained for many days.

9 He read the sacred texts; thought out the meanings of the hieroglyphs and sought the import of the master's charge to find himself.

10 A revelation came; he got acquainted with his soul; he found himself; then he was not alone.

11 One night he slept and at the midnight hour, a door that he had not observed, was opened, and a priest in somber garb came in and said,

12 My brother, pardon me for coming in at this unseemly hour; but I have come to save your life.

13 You are the victim of a cruel plot. The priests of Heliopolis are jealous of your fame, and they have said that you shall never leave these gloomy crypts alive.

14 The higher priests do not go forth to teach the world, and you are doomed to temple servitude.

15 Now, if you would be free, you must deceive these priests; must tell them you are here to stay for life;

16 And then, when you have gained all that you wish to gain, I will return, and by a secret way will lead you forth that you may go in peace.

17 And Jesus said, My brother, man, would you come here to teach

deceit? Am I within these holy walls to learn the wiles of vile hypocrisy?

18 Nay, man, my Father scorns deceit, and I am here to do his will.

19 Deceive these priests! Not while the sun shall shine. What I have said, that I have said; I will be true to them, to God, and to myself.

20 And then the tempter left, and Jesus was again alone; but in a little time a white-robed priest appeared and said,

21 Well done! the Logos has prevailed. This is the trial chamber of hypocrisy. And then he led the way, and Jesus stood before the judgment seat.

22 And all the brothers stood; the hierophant came forth and laid his hand on Jesus' head, and placed within his hands a scroll, on which was written just one word, SINCERITY; and not a word was said.

23 The guide again appeared, and led the way, and in a spacious room replete with everything a student craves was Jesus bade to rest and wait.

CHAPTER 49.

Jesus passes the second brotherhood test, and receives the second degree, JUSTICE.

THE Logos did not care to rest; he said, Why wait in this luxurious room? I need not rest; my Father's work upon me presses hard.

2 I would go on and learn my lessons all. If there are trials, let them come, for every victory over self gives added strength.

3 And then the guide led on, and in a chamber, dark as night, was Jesus placed and left alone;

and days were spent in this deep solitude.

4 And Jesus slept, and in the dead of night a secret door was opened, and, in priest's attire, two men came in; each carried in his hand a little flickering lamp.

5 Approaching Jesus, one spoke out and said, Young man, our hearts are grieved because of what you suffer in these fearful dens, and we have come as friends to bring you light, and show the way to liberty.

6 We once, like you, were in these dens confined, and thought that through these wierd, uncanny ways we could attain to blessedness and power;

7 But in a luckful moment we were undeceived, and, making use of all our strength, we broke our chains, and then we learned that all this service is corruption in disguise. These priests are criminals just hid away.

8 They boast in sacrificial rites; they offer to their gods, and burn them while alive, poor birds, and beasts; yea, children, women, men.

9 And now they keep you here, and, at a certain time, may offer you in sacrifice.

10 We pray you, brother, break your chains; come, go with us; accept of freedom while you may.

11 And Jesus said, Your little tapers show the light you bring. Pray, who are you? The words of man are worth no more than is the man himself.

12 These temple walls are strong and high; how gained you entrance to this place?

13 The men replied, Beneath these walls are many hidden ways, and we who have been priests, spent months and years within these dens, know all of them.

14 Then you are traitors, Jesus said. A traitor is a fiend; he who betrays another man is never man to trust.

15 If one has only reached the plane of treachery, he is a lover of deceit, and will betray a friend to serve his selfish self.

16 Behold, you men, or whatsoe'er you be, your words fall lightly on my ears,

17 Could I prejudge these hundred priests, turn traitor to myself and them, because of what you say when you confess your treachery?

18 No man can judge for me; and if I judge till testimony all is in I might not judge aright.

19 Nay, men; by whatsoever way you came, return. My soul prefers the darkness of the grave to little flickering lights like these you bring.

20 My conscience rules; what these, my brothers, have to say I'll hear, and when the testimony all is in I will decide. You cannot judge for me, nor I for you,

21 Begone, you men, begone, and leave me to this charming light; for while the sun shines not, within my soul there is a light surpassing that of sun or moon.

22 Then, with an angry threat that they would do him harm, the wily tempters left, and Jesus was again alone.

23 Again the white-robed priest appeared, and led the way, and Jesus stood again before the hierophant;

24 And not a word was said, but in his hands the master placed a scroll on which the word suggestive, JUSTICE, was inscribed.

25 And Jesus was the master of the phantom forms of prejudice and of treachery.

CHAPTER 50.

Jesus passes the third brotherhood test, and receives the third degree, FAITH.

THE Logos waited seven days, and then was taken to the Hall of Fame, a chamber rich in furnishings, and lighted up with gold and silver lamps.

2 The colors of its ceilings, decorations, furnishings and walls were blue and gold.

3 Its shelves were filled with books of master minds; the paintings and the statues were the works of highest art.

4 And Jesus was entranced with all this elegance and these manifests of thought. He read the sacred books, and sought the meanings of the symbols and the hieroglyphs.

5 And when he was absorbed in deepest thought, a priest approached and said,

6 Behold the glory of this place! my brother you are highly blest. Few men of earth, so young, have reached such heights of fame.

7 Now, if you do not waste your life in search for hidden things that men can never comprehend, you may be founder of a school of thought that will insure you endless fame;

8 For your philosophy is deeper far than that of Plato, and your teachings please the common people more than those of Socrates.

9 Why seek for mystic light within these antiquated dens? Go forth and walk with men, and think with men, and they will honor you.

10 And, after all, these weird initiations may be myths, and your Messiah hopes but base illusions of the hour.

11 I would advise you to renounce uncertain things and choose

the course that leads to certain fame.

12 And thus the priest, a demon in disguise, sung syren songs of unbelief; and Jesus meditated long and well on what he said.

13 The conflict was a bitter one, for king Ambition is a sturdy foe to fight.

14 For forty days the higher wrestled with the lower self, and then the fight was won.

15 Faith rose triumphant; unbelief was not. Ambition covered up his face and fled away, and Jesus said,

16 The wealth, the honor, and the fame of earth are but the baubles of an hour.

17 When this short span of earthly life has all been measured out, man's bursting baubles will be buried with his bones.

18 Yea, what a man does for his selfish self will make no markings on the credit side of life.

19 The good that men for other men shall do becomes a ladder strong on which the soul may climb to wealth, and power and fame of God's own kind, that cannot pass away,

20 Give me the poverty of men, the consciousness of duty done in love, the approbation of my God, and I will be content.

21 And then he lifted up his eyes to heaven and said,

22 My Father-God, I thank thee for this hour. I ask not for the glory of thyself; I fain would be a keeper of thy temple gates, and serve my brother man.

23 Again was Jesus called to stand before the hierophant; again no word was said, but in his hands the master placed a scroll on which was written FAITH.

24 And Jesus bowed his head in humble thanks; then went his way.

CHAPTER 51.

Jesus passes the fourth brotherhood test, and receives the fourth degree, PHILANTHROPY.

WHEN other certain days had passed, the guide led Jesus to the Hall of Mirth, a hall most richly furnished, and replete with every thing a carnal heart could wish.

2 The choicest viands and the most delicious wines were on the boards; and maids, in gay attire, served all with grace and cheerfulness.

3 And men and women, richly clad, were there; and they were wild with joy; they sipped from every cup of mirth.

4 And Jesus watched the happy throng in silence for a time, and then a man in garb of sage came up and said, Most happy is the man who, like the bee, can gather sweets from every flower.

5 The wise man is the one who seeks for pleasure, and can find it everywhere,

6 At best man's span of life on earth is short, and then he dies and goes, he knows not where.

7 Then let us eat, and drink, and dance, and sing, and get the joys of life, for death comes on apace.

8 It is but foolishness to spend a life for other men. Behold, all die and lie together in the grave, where none can know and none can show forth gratitude.

9 But Jesus answered not; upon the tinseled guests in all their rounds of mirth he gazed in silent thought.

10 And then among the guests he saw a man whose clothes were coarse; who showed in face and hands the lines of toil and want.

11 The giddy throng found pleasure in abusing him; they jostled him against the wall, and laughed at his discomfiture.

12 And then a poor, frail woman came, who carried in her face and form the marks of sin and shame; and without mercy she was spit upon, and jeered, and driven from the hall.

13 And then a little child, with timid ways and hungry mien, came in and asked for just a morsel of their food.

14 But she was driven out uncared for and unloved; and still the merry dance went on.

15 And when the pleasure seekers urged that Jesus join them in their mirth, he said,

16 How could I seek for pleasure for myself while others are in want? How can you think that while the children cry for bread, while those in haunts of sin call out for sympathy and love that I can fill myself to full with the good things of life?

17 I tell you, nay; we all are kin, each one a part of the great human heart.

18 I cannot see myself apart from that poor man that you so scorned, and crowded to the wall;

19 Nor from the one in female garb who came up from the haunts of vice to ask for sympathy and love, who was by you so ruthlessly pushed back into her den of sin;

20 Nor from that little child that you drove from your midst to suffer in the cold, bleak winds of night.

21 I tell you, men, what you have done to these, my kindred, you have done to me.

22 You have insulted me in your own home; I cannot stay. I will go forth and find that child, that

woman and that man, and give them help until my life's blood all has ebbed away.

23 I call it pleasure when I help the helpless, feed the hungry, clothe the naked, heal the sick, and speak good words of cheer to those unloved, discouraged and depressed.

24 And this that you call mirth is but a phantom of the night; but flashes of the fire of passion, painting pictures on the walls of time.

25 And while the Logos spoke the white-robed priest came in and said to him, The council waits for you.

26 Then Jesus stood again before the bar; again no word was said; the hierophant placed in his hands a scroll, on which was writ, PHILANTHROPY.

27 And Jesus was a victor over selfish self.

CHAPTER 52.

Jesus spends forty days in the temple groves. Passes the fifth brotherhood test and receives the fifth degree, HEROISM.

THE sacred temple groves were rich in statues, monuments and shrines; here Jesus loved to walk and meditate.

2 And after he had conquered self he talked with nature in these groves for forty days.

3 And then the guide took chains and bound him hand and foot; and then cast him into a den of hungry beasts, of unclean birds, and creeping things.

4 The den was dark as night; the wild beasts howled; the birds in fury screamed; the reptiles hissed.

5 And Jesus said, Who was it that did bind me thus? Why did I meekly sit to be bound down with chains?

6 I tell you, none has power to bind a human soul. Of what are fetters made?

7 And in his might he rose, and what he thought were chains were only worthless cords that parted at his touch.

8 And then he laughed and said, The chains that bind men to the carcasses of earth are forged in fancy's shop; are made of air, and welded in illusion's fires.

9 If man will stand erect, and use the power of will, his chains will fall, like worthless rags; for will and faith are stronger than the stoutest chains that men have ever made.

10 And Jesus stood erect among the hungry beasts, and birds, and said, What is this darkness that envelops me?

11 'Tis but the absence of the light. And what is light? 'Tis but the breath of God vibrating in the rythm of rapid thought.

12 And then he said, Let there be light; and with a mighty will he stirred the ethers up, and their vibrations reached the plane of light; and there was light.

13 The darkness of that den of night became the brightness of a newborn day.

14 And then he looked to see the beasts, and birds, and creeping things; lo, they were not.

15 And Jesus said, Of what are souls afraid? Fear is the chariot in which man rides to death;

16 And when he finds himself within the chamber of the dead, he learns that he has been deceived; his chariot was a myth, and death a fancy child.

17 But some day all man's lessons will be learned, and from the den of unclean, beasts and birds, and creeping things he will arise to walk in light.

18 And Jesus saw a ladder made of gold, on which he climbed, and at the top the white-robed priest awaited him.

19 Again he stood before the council bar; again no word was said; again the hierophant reached forth his hand to bless.

20 He placed in Jesus' hand another scroll, and on this one was written, HEROISM.

21 The Logos had encountered fear and all his phantom host, and in the conflict he achieved the victory.

CHAPTER 53.

Jesus passes the sixth brotherhood test and receives the sixth degree, LOVE DIVINE.

IN all the land there was no place more grandly furnished than the Beauty Parlors of the temple of the sun.

2 Few students ever entered these rich rooms; the priests regarded them with awe, and called them Halls of Mysteries.

3 When Jesus had attained the victory over fear, he gained the right to enter here.

4 The guide led on the way, and after passing many richly furnished rooms they reached the Hall of Harmony; and here was Jesus left alone.

5 Among the instruments of music was a harpsichord, and Jesus sat in thoughtful mood inspecting it, when, quietly, a maiden of entrancing beauty came into the hall.

6 She did not seem to notice Jesus as he sat and mused, so busy with his thoughts.

7 She found her place beside the harpsichord; she touched the chords most gently, and she sung the songs of Israel.

8 And Jesus was entranced; such beauty he had never seen; such music he had never heard.

9 The maiden sung her songs; she did not seem to know that any one was near; she went her way

10 And Jesus, talking with himself, said out, What is the meaning of this incident? I did not know that such entrancing beauty and such queen-like loveliness were ever found among the sons of men.

11 I did not know that voice of angel ever graced a human form, or that seraphic music ever came from human lips.

12 For days he sat entranced; the current of his thoughts was changed; he thought of nothing but the singer and her songs.

13 He longed to see her once again; and after certain days she came; she spoke and laid her hand upon his head.

14 Her touch thrilled all his soul, and for the time, forgotten was the work that he was sent to do.

15 Few were the words the maiden said; she went her way; but then the heart of Jesus had been touched.

16 A love-flame had been kindled in his soul, and he was brought to face the sorest trial of his life.

17 He could not sleep nor eat. Thoughts of the maiden came; they would not go. His carnal nature called aloud for her companionship.

18 And then he said, Lo, I have conquered every foe that I have met, and shall I now be conquered by this carnal love?

19 My Father sent me here to show the power of love divine, that love that reaches every living thing.

20 Shall this pure, universal love be all absorbed by carnal love? Shall I forget all creatures else, and lose my life in this fair maiden, though she is the highest type of beauty, purity and love?

21 Into its very depths his soul was stirred, and long he wrestled with this angel-idol of his heart.

22 But when the day was almost lost, his higher ego rose in might; he found himself again, and then he said,

23 Although my heart shall break I will not fail in this my hardest task; I will be victor over carnal love.

24 And when again the maiden came, and offered him her hand and heart, he said,

25 Fair one, your very presence thrills me with delight; your voice is benediction to my soul; my human self would fly with you, and be contented in your love;

26 But all the world is craving for a love that I have come to manifest.

27 I must, then, bid you go; but we will meet again; our ways on earth will not be cast apart.

28 I see you in the hurrying throngs of earth as minister of love; I hear your voice in song, that wins the hearts of men to better things.

29 And then in sorrow and in tears the maiden went away, and Jesus was again alone.

30 And instantly the great bells of the temple rang; the singers sung a new, new song; the grotto blazed with light.

31 The hierophant himself appeared, and said, All hail! triumphant Logos, hail! The conqueror of carnal love stands on the heights.

32 And then he placed in Jesus' hands a scroll on which was written LOVE DIVINE.

33 Together they passed from

the grotto of the beautiful, and in the banquet hall a feast was served, and Jesus was the honored guest.

CHAPTER 54.

Jesus becomes a private pupil of the hierophant and is taught the mysteries of Egypt. In passing the seventh test, he works in the Chamber of the Dead.

THE senior course of study now was opened up and Jesus entered and became a pupil of the hierophant.

2 He learned the secrets of the mystic lore of Egypt land; the mysteries of life and death and of the worlds beyond the circle of the sun.

3 When he had finished all the studies of the senior course, he went into the Chamber of the Dead, that he might learn the ancient methods of preserving from decay the bodies of the dead; and here he wrought.

4 And carriers brought the body of a widow's only son to be embalmed; the weeping mother followed close; her grief was great.

5 And Jesus said, Good woman, dry your tears; you follow but an empty house; your son is in it not.

6 You weep because your son is dead. Death is a cruel word; your son can never die.

7 He had a task assigned to do in garb of flesh; he came; he did his work, and then he laid the flesh aside; he did not need it more.

8 Beyond your human sight he has another work to do, and he will do it well, and then pass on to other tasks, and, by and by, he will attain the crown of perfect life.

9 And what your son has done, and what he yet must do, we all must do.

10 Now, if you harbor grief, and give your sorrows vent they will grow greater every day. They will absorb your very life until at last you will be naught but grief, wet down with bitter tears.

11 Instead of helping him you grieve your son by your deep grief. He seeks your solace now as he has ever done; is glad when you are glad; is saddened when you grieve.

12 Go bury deep your woes, and smile at grief, and lose yourself in helping others dry their tears.

13 With duty done comes happiness and joy; and gladness cheers the hearts of those who have passed on.

14 The weeping woman turned, and went her way to find a happiness in helpfulness; to bury deep her sorrows in a ministry of joy.

15 Then other carriers came and brought the body of a mother to the Chamber of the Dead; and just one mourner followed; she a girl of tender years.

16 And as the cortege neared the door, the child observed a wounded bird in sore distress; a cruel hunter's dart had pierced its breast.

17 And she left following the dead, and went to help the living bird.

18 With tenderness and love she folded to her breast the wounded bird; then hurried to her place.

19 And Jesus said to her, Why did you leave your dead to save a wounded bird?

20 The maiden said, This lifeless body needs no help from me; but I can help while yet life is; my mother taught me this.

21 My mother taught that grief and selfish love, and hopes and fears are but reflexes from the lower self;

22 That what we sense are but small waves upon the rolling billows of a life.

23 These all will pass away; they are unreal.

24 Tears flow from hearts of flesh; the spirit never weeps; and I am longing for the day when I will walk in light, where tears are wiped away.

25 My mother taught that all emotions are the sprays that rise from human loves, and hopes, and fears; that perfect bliss cannot be ours till we have conquered these.

26 And in the presence of that child did Jesus bow his head in reverence. He said,

27 For days and months and years I've sought to learn this highest truth that man can learn on earth, and here a child, fresh brought to earth, has told it all in one short breath.

28 No wonder David said, O Lord, our Lord, how excellent is thy name in all the earth!

29 Out of the mouths of babes and sucklings hast thou ordained strength.

30 And then he laid his hand upon the maiden's head, and said, I'm sure the blessings of my Father-God will rest upon you, child, forevermore.

CHAPTER 55.

Jesus passes the seventh brotherhood test, and in the purple room of the temple receives the seventh, the highest degree, THE CHRIST. He leaves the temple a conqueror.

THE work of Jesus in the Chamber of the Dead was done, and in the temple purple room he stood before the hierophant.

2 And he was clothed in purple robes; and all the brothers stood. The hierophant arose and said,

3 This is a royal day for all the hosts of Israel. In honor of their chosen son we celebrate the great Passover Feast.

4 And then he said to Jesus, Brother, man, most excellent of men, in all the temple tests you have won out.

5 Six times before the bar of right you have been judged; six times you have received the highest honors man can give; and now you stand prepared to take the last degree.

6 Upon your brow I place this diadem, and in the Great Lodge of the heavens and earth you are THE CHRIST.

7 This is your great Passover rite. You are a neophyte no more; but now a master mind.

8 Now, man can do no more; but God himself will speak, and will confirm your title and degree.

9 Go on your way, for you must preach the gospel of good will to men and peace on earth; must open up the prison doors and set the captives free.

10 And while the hierophant yet spoke the temple bells rang out; a pure white dove descended from above and sat on Jesus' head.

11 And then a voice that shook the very temple said, THIS IS THE CHRIST; and every living creature said, AMEN.

12 The great doors of the temple swung ajar; the Logos journeyed on his way a conqueror.

SECTION XII.

LAMED.

The Council of the Seven Sages of the World.

CHAPTER 56.

The seven sages of the world meet in Alexandria. The purposes of the meeting. The opening addresses.

IN every age since time began have seven sages lived.

2 At first of every age these sages meet to note the course of nations, peoples, tribes and tongues;

3 To note how far toward justice, love and righteousness the race has gone;

4 To formulate the code of laws, religious postulates and plans of rule best suited to the coming age.

5 An age had passed, and, lo, another age had come; the sages must convene.

6 Now, Alexandria was the center of the world's best thought, and here in Philo's home the sages met.

7 From China came Meng-ste; from India Vidyapati came; from Persia Kaspar came; and from Assyria Ashbina came; from Greece Apollo came; Matheno was the Egyptian sage, and Philo was the chief of Hebrew thought.

8 The time was due; the council met and sat in silence seven days.

9 And then Meng-ste arose and said, The wheel of time has turned once more; the race is on a higher plane of thought.

10 The garments that our fathers wove have given out; the cherubim have woven a celestial cloth; have placed it in our hands and we must make for men new garbs.

11 The sons of men are looking up for greater light. No longer do they care for gods hewn out of wood, or made of clay. They seek a God not made with hands.

12 They see the beams of coming day, and yet they comprehend them not.

13 The time is ripe, and we must fashion well these garments for the race.

14 And let us make for men new garbs of justice, mercy, righteousness and love, that they may hide their nakedness when shines the light of coming day.

15 And Vidyapati said, Our priests have all gone mad; they saw a demon in the wilds and at him cast their lamps and they are broken up, and not a gleam of light has any priest for men.

16 The night is dark; the heart of India calls for light.

17 The priesthood cannot be reformed; it is already dead; its greatest needs are graves and funeral chants.

18 The new age calls for liberty; the kind that makes each man a priest, enables him to go alone, and lay his offerings on the shrine of God.

19 And Kaspar said, In Persia people walk in fear; they do the good for fear to do the wrong.

20 The devil is the greatest power in our land, and though a myth, he dandles on his knee both youth and age.

21 Our land is dark, and evil prospers in the dark.

22 Fear rides on every passing breeze, and lurks in every form of life.

23 The fear of evil is a myth, is an illusion and a snare; but it will

live until some mighty power shall come to raise the ethers to the plane of light.

24 When this shall come to pass the magian land will glory in the light. The soul of Persia calls for light.

CHAPTER 57.

Meeting of the sages, continued. Opening addresses. Jesus with the sages. Seven days' silence.

ASHBINA said, Assyria is the land of doubt; the chariot of my people, that in which they mostly ride, is labeled Doubt.

2 Once Faith walked forth in Babylon; and she was bright and fair; but she was clothed in such white robes that men became afraid of her.

3 And every wheel began to turn, and Doubt made war on her, and drove her from the land; and she came back no more.

4 In form men worship God, the One; in heart they are not sure that God exists.

5 Faith worships at the shrine of one not seen; but Doubt must see her God.

6 The greatest need of all Assyria is faith—a faith that seasons every thing that is, with certainty.

7 And then Apollo said, The greatest needs of Greece are true concepts of God.

8 Theogony in Greece is rudderless, for every thought may be a god, and worshipped as a god.

9 The plane of thought is broad, and full of sharp antagonists; and so the circle of the gods is filled with enmity, with wars and base intrigues.

10 Greece needs a master mind to stand above the gods; to raise the thoughts of men away from many gods to God the One.

11 We know that light is coming o'er the hills. God speed the light.

12 Matheno said, Behold this land of mystery! this Egypt of the dead!

13 Our temples long have been the tombs of all the hidden things of time; our temples, crypts and caves are dark.

14 In light there are no secret things. The sun reveals all hidden truth. There are no mysteries in God.

15 Behold the rising sun! His beams are entering every door; yea, every crevice of the mystic crypts of Mizraim.

16 We hail the light! All Egypt craves the light.

17 And Philo said, The need of Hebrew thought and life is liberty.

18 The Hebrew prophets, seers, and givers of the law, were men of power, men of holy thought, and they bequeathed to us a system of philosophy that was ideal; one strong enough and good enough to lead our people to the goal of perfectness.

19 But carnal minds repudiated holiness; a priesthood filled with selfishness arose, and purity in heart became a myth; the people were enslaved.

20 The priesthood is the curse of Israel; but when he comes, who is to come, he will proclaim emancipation for the slaves; my people will be free.

21 Behold, for God has made incarnate wisdom, love and light, which he has called Immanuel.

22 To him is given the keys to open up the dawn; and here, as man, he walks with us.

23 And then the council chamber door was opened and the Logos

stood among the sages of the world.

24 Again the sages sat in silence seven days.

CHAPTER 58.

Meeting of the sages, continued. Presentation of the seven universal postulates.

NOW, when the sages were refreshed they opened up the Book of Life and read.

2 They read the story of the life of man; of all his struggles, losses, gains; and in the light of past events and needs, they saw what would be best for him in coming years.

3 They knew the kind of laws and precepts suited best to his estate; they saw the highest God-ideal that the race could comprehend.

4 Upon the seven postulates these sages were to formulate, the great philosophy of life and worship of the coming age must rest.

5 Now Meng-ste was the oldest sage; he took the chair of chief, and said,

6 Man is not far enough advanced to live by faith; he cannot comprehend the things his eyes see not,

7 He yet is child, and during all the coming age he must be taught by pictures, symbols, rites, and forms.

8 His God must be a human God; he cannot see a God by faith.

9 And then he cannot rule himself; the king must rule; the man must serve.

10 The age that follows this will be the age of man, the age of faith.

11 In that blest age the human race will see without the aid of carnal eyes; will hear the soundless sound; will know the Spirit-God.

12 The age we enter is the Preparation age, and all the schools, and governments and worship rites must be designed in simple way that men may comprehend.

13 And man cannot originate; he builds by patterns that he sees; so in this council we must carve out pattern for the coming age.

14 And we must formulate the gnosis of the Empire of the soul, which rests on seven postulates.

15 Each sage in turn shall form a postulate; and these shall be the basis of the creeds of men until the perfect age shall come.

16 Then Meng-ste wrote the first:

17 All things are thought; all life is thought activity. The multitude of beings are but phases of the one great thought made manifest. Lo, God is Thought, and Thought is God.

18 Then Vidyapati wrote the second postulate:

19 Eternal Thought is one; in essence it is two—Intelligence and Force; and when they breathe a child is born; this child is Love.

20 And thus the Triune God stands forth, whom men call Father-Mother-Child.

21 This Triune God is one; but like the one of light, in essence he is seven.

22 And when the Triune God breathes forth, lo, seven Spirits stand before his face; these are creative attributes.

23 Men call them lesser gods, and in their image they made man.

24 And Kaspar wrote the third:

25 Man was a thought of God, formed in the image of the Septonate, clothed in the substances of soul.

26 And his desires were strong; he sought to manifest on every plane of life, and for himself he made a

body of the ethers of the earthy forms, and so descended to the plane of earth.

27 In this descent he lost his birthright; lost his harmony with God, and made discordant all the notes of life.

28 Inharmony and evil are the same; so evil is the handiwork of man.

29 Ashbina wrote the fourth:

30 Seeds do not germinate in light; they do not grow until they find the soil, and hide themselves away from light.

31 Man was evolved a seed of everlasting life; but in the ethers of the Triune God the light was far too great for seeds to grow;

32 And so man sought the soil of carnal life, and in the darksomeness of earth he found a place where he could germinate and grow.

33 The seed has taken root and grown full well.

34 The tree of human life is rising from the soil of earthy things, and, under natural law, is reaching up to perfect form.

35 There are no supernatural acts of God to lift a man from carnal life to spirit blessedness; he grows as grows the plant, and in due time is perfected.

36 The quality of soul that makes it possible for man to rise to spirit life is purity.

CHAPTER 59.

Meeting of the sages, continued. The remaining postulates. The sages bless Jesus. Seven days' silence.

APOLLO wrote the fifth:

2 The soul is drawn to perfect light by four white steeds, and these are Will, and Faith, and Helpfulness and Love.

3 That which one wills to do, he has the power to do.

4 A knowledge of that power is faith; and when faith moves, the soul begins its flight.

5 A selfish faith leads not to light. There is no lonely pilgrim on the way to light. Men only gain the heights by helping others gain the heights.

6 The steed that leads the way to spirit life is Love; is pure unselfish Love.

7 Matheno wrote the sixth:

8 The universal Love of which Apollo speaks is child of Wisdom and of Will divine, and God has sent it forth to earth in flesh that man may know.

9 The universal Love of which the sages speak, is Christ.

10 The greatest mystery of all times lies in the way that Christ lives in the heart.

11 Christ cannot live in clammy dens of carnal things. The seven battles must be fought, the seven victories won before the carnal things, like fear, and self, emotions and desire, are put away.

12 When this is done the Christ will take possession of the soul; the work is done, and man and God are one.

13 And Philo wrote the seventh:

14 A perfect man! To bring before the Triune God a being such as this was nature made.

15 This consummation is the highest revelation of the mystery of life.

16 When all the essences of carnal things have been transmuted into soul, and all the essences of soul have been returned to Holy Breath, and man is made a perfect God, the drama of Creation will conclude. And this is all.

17 And all the sages said, Amen.

18 Then Meng-ste said, The Holy One has sent to us a man illumined by the efforts of unnumbered years, to lead the thoughts of men.

19 This man, approved by all the master minds of heaven and earth, this man from Galilee, this Jesus, chief of all the sages of the world, we gladly recognize.

20 In recognition of this wisdom that he brings to men, we crown him with the Lotus wreath.

21 We send him forth with all the blessing of the seven sages of the world.

22 Then all the sages laid their hands on Jesus' head, and said with one accord, Praise God!

23 For wisdom, honor, glory, power, riches, blessing, strength, are yours, O Christ, forever more.

24 And every living creature said, Amen.

25 And then the sages sat in silence seven days.

CHAPTER 60.

Jesus addresses the seven sages. The address. Jesus goes to Galilee.

THE seven days of silence passed and Jesus, sitting with the sages said:

2 The history of life is well condensed in these immortal postulates. These are the seven hills on which the holy city shall be built.

3 These are the seven sure foundation stones on which the Universal Church shall stand.

4 In taking up the work assigned for me to do I am full conscious of the perils of the way; the cup will be a bitter one to drink and human nature well might shrink.

5 But I have lost my will in that of Holy Breath, and so I go my way to speak and act as I am moved to speak and act by Holy Breath.

6 The words I speak are not my own; they are the words of him whose will I do.

7 Man is not far enough advanced in sacred thought to comprehend the Universal Church, and so the work that God has given me to do is not the building of that Church.

8 I am a model maker, sent to make a pattern of the Church that is to be—a pattern that the age may comprehend.

9 My task as model builder lies within my native land, and there, upon the postulate that Love is son of God, that I am come to manifest that Love, the Model Church will stand.

10 And from the men of low estate I will select twelve men, who represent the twelve immortal thoughts; and these will be the Model Church.

11 The house of Judah, my own kindred in the flesh, will comprehend but little of my mission to the world.

12 And they will spurn me, scorn my work, accuse me falsely, bind me, take me to the judgment seat of carnal men who will convict and slay me on the cross.

13 But men can never slay the truth; though banished it will come again in greater power; for truth will subjugate the world.

14 The Model Church will live. Though carnal man will prostitute its sacred laws, symbolic rites and forms, for selfish ends, and make it but an outward show, the few will find through it the kingdom of the soul.

15 And when the better age shall come the Universal Church will stand upon the seven postulates, and will be built according to the pattern given.

16 The time has come; I go my way unto Jerusalem, and by the power of living faith, and by the strength that you have given,

17 And in the name of God, our Father-God, the kingdom of the soul shall be established on the seven hills,

18 And all the peoples, tribes and tongues of earth shall enter in.

19 The Prince of Peace will take his seat upon the throne of power; the Triune God will then be All in All.

20 And all the sages said, Amen.

21 And Jesus went his way, and after many days, he reached Jerusalem; and then he sought his home in Galilee.

SECTION XIII.

MEM.

The Ministry of John, the Harbinger.

CHAPTER 61.

John, the harbinger, returns to Hebron. Lives as a hermit in the wilds. Visits Jerusalem and speaks to the people.

IT came to pass when John, the son of Zacharias and Elizabeth, had finished all his studies in the Egyptian schools that he returned to Hebron, where he abode for certain days.

2 And then he sought the wilderness and made his home in David's cave where many years before, he was instructed by the Egyptian sage.

3 Some people called him Hermit of Engedi; and others said, He is the Wild Man of the hills.

4 He clothed himself with skins of beasts; his food was carobs, honey, nuts and fruits.

5 When John was thirty years of age he went into Jerusalem, and in the market place he sat in silence seven days.

6 The common people and the priests, the scribes and Pharisees came out in multitudes to see the silent hermit of the hills; but none were bold enough to ask him who he was.

7 But when his silent fast was done he stood forth in the midst of all and said,

8 Behold, the king has come; the prophets told of him; the wise men long have looked for him.

9 Prepare, O Israel, prepare to meet your king.

10 And that was all he said, and then he disappeared, and no one knew where he had gone.

11 And there was great unrest through all Jerusalem. The rulers heard the story of the hermit of the hills,

12 And they sent couriers forth to talk with him that they might know about the coming king; but they could find him not.

13 And after certain days he came again into the market place, and all the city came to hear him speak; he said,

14 Be not disturbed, you rulers of the state; the coming king is no antagonist; he seeks no place on any earthly throne.

15 He comes the Prince of Peace, the king of righteousness and love; his kingdom is within the soul.

16 The eyes of men shall see it

not and none can enter but the pure in heart.

17 Prepare, O Israel, prepare to meet your king.

18 Again the hermit disappeared; the people strove to follow him, but he had drawn a veil about his form and men could see him not.

19 A Jewish feast day came; Jerusalem was filled with Jews and proselytes from every part of Palestine, and John stood in the temple court and said,

20 Prepare, O Israel, prepare to meet your king.

21 Lo, you have lived in sin; the poor cry in your streets, and you regard them not.

22 Your neighbors, who are they? You have defrauded friend and foe alike.

23 You worship God with voice and lip; your hearts are far away, and set on gold.

24 Your priests have bound upon the people burdens far too great to bear; they live in ease upon the hard earned wages of the poor.

25 Your lawyers, doctors, scribes are useless cumberers of the ground; they are but tumors on the body of the state;

26 They toil not neither do they spin, yet they consume the profits of your marts of trade.

27 Your rulers are adulterers, extortioners and thieves, regarding not the rights of any man;

28 And robbers ply their calling in the sacred halls; the holy temple you have sold to thieves; their dens are in the sacred places set apart for prayer.

29 Hear! hear! you people of Jerusalem! Reform; turn from your evil ways or God will turn from you, and heathen from afar will come, and what is left of all your honor

and your fame will pass in one short hour.

30 Prepare, Jerusalem, prepare to meet your king.

31 He said no more; he left the court and no one saw him go.

32 The priests, the doctors and the scribes were all in rage. They sought for John intent to do him harm. They found him not.

33 The common people stood in his defense; they said, The hermit speaks the truth.

34 And then the priests, the doctors and the scribes were sore afraid; they said no more; they hid themselves away.

CHAPTER 62.

John, the harbinger, again visits Jerusalem. Speaks to the people. Promises to meet them at Gilgal in seven days. Goes to Bethany and attends a feast.

NEXT day John went again into the temple courts and said,

2 Prepare, O Israel, prepare to meet your king.

3 The chief priests and the scribes would know the meaning of his words; they said,

4 Bold man, what is the purport of this message that you bring to Israel? If you be seer and prophet, tell us plainly who has sent you here?

5 And John replied, I am the voice of one who cries out in the wilderness, Prepare the way, make straight the paths, for, lo, the Prince of Peace will come to rule in love.

6 Your prophet Malachi wrote down the words of God:

7 And I will send Elijah unto you before the retribution day shall come, to turn again the hearts of men to God and if they will not

turn, lo, I will smite them with a curse.

8 You men of Israel; you know your sins. As I passed by I saw a wounded bird prone in your streets, and men of every class were beating it with clubs; and then I saw that Justice was its name.

9 I looked again and saw that its companion had been killed; the pure white wings of Righteousness were trampled in the dust.

10 I tell you men, your awful-ness of guilt has made a cesspool of iniquity that sends a fearful stench to heaven.

11 Reform, O Israel, reform; prepare to meet your king.

12 And then John turned away and as he went he said,

13 In seven days, lo, I will stand at Gilgal, by the Jordan ford, where Israel first crossed into the prom-ised land.

14 And then he left the temple court to enter it no more; but many people followed him as far as Beth-any, and there he tarried at the home of Lazarus, his kin.

15 The anxious people gathered all about the home and would not go; then John came forth and said,

16 Reform, O Israel, reform; prepare to meet your king.

17 The sins of Israel do not all lie at the door of priest and scribe. O think you not that all the sinners of Judea are found among the rulers and the men of wealth.

18 It is no sign that man is good and pure because he lives in want.

19 The listless, shiftless vaga-bonds of earth are mostly poor and have to beg for bread.

20 I saw the very men that cheered because I told the priests and scribes of their injustice unto man, throw stones and beat poor Justice in the streets.

21 I saw them trample on the poor dead bird of Righteousness;

22 And you who follow after me, you commoners, are not one whit behind the scribes and priests in crime.

23 Reform, you men of Israel; the king has come; prepare to meet your king.

24 With Lazarus and his sisters, John remained for certain days.

25 In honor of the Nazarite a feast was spread, and all the people stood about the board.

26 And when the chief men of the town poured out the sparkling wine and offered John a cup, he took it, held it high in air, and said,

27 Wine makes glad the carnal heart, and it makes sad the human soul; it plunges deep in bitterness and gall the deathless spirit of the man.

28 I took the vow of Nazar when a child, and not a drop has ever passed my lips.

29 And if you would make glad the coming king, then shun the cup as you would shun a deadly thing.

30 And then he threw the sparkling wine out in the street.

CHAPTER 63.

John, the harbinger, visits Jericho. Meets the people at Gilgal. An-nounces his mission. Introduces the rite of baptism. Baptizes many people. Returns to Bethany and teaches. Returns to the Jordan.

AND John went down to Jericho; there he abode with Alpheus.

2 And when the people heard that he was there they came in throngs to hear him speak.

3 He spoke to none; but when the time was due he went down to the Jordan ford, and to the multi-tudes he said,

4 Reform and in the fount of purity wash all your sins away; the kingdom is at hand.

5 Come unto me and in the waters of this stream be washed, symbolic of the inner cleansing of the soul.

6 And, lo, the multitudes came down and in the Jordan they were washed, and every man confessed his sins.

7 For many months, in all the regions round about, John plead for purity and righteousness; and after many days he went again to Bethany; and there he taught.

8 At first few but the honest seekers came; but, by and by, the selfish and the vicious came with no contrition; came because the many came.

9 And when John saw the unrepentant Pharisees and Sadducees come unto him, he said,

10 You children of the vipers, stay; are you disturbed by news of coming wrath?

11 Go to, and do the things that prove repentance genuine.

12 Is it enough for you to say that you are heirs of Abraham? I tell you, no.

13 The heirs of Abraham are just as wicked in the sight of God when they do wrong as any heathen man.

14 Behold the ax! and every tree that bears not wholesome fruit is cut down at the roots and cast into the fire.

15 And then the people asked, What must we do?

16 And John replied, Accept the ministry of helpfulness for all mankind; spend not upon your selfish selves all that you have.

17 Let him who has two coats give one to him who has no coat·

give part of all the food you have to those in need.

18 And when the publicans came up and asked, What must we do? John answered them,

19 Be honest in your work; do not increase for selfish gain the tribute you collect; take nothing more than what your king demands.

20 And when the soldiers came and asked, What must we do? The harbinger replied,

21 Do violence to none; exact no wrongful thing, and be contented with the wages you receive.

22 Among the Jews were many who had been waiting for the Christ to come, and they regarded John as Christ.

23 But to their questions John replied, In water I do cleanse, symbolic of the cleansing of the soul; but when he comes who is to come, lo, he will cleanse in Holy Breath and purify in fire.

24 His fan is in his hand, and he will separate the wheat and chaff; will throw the chaff away, but garner every grain of wheat. This is the Christ.

25 Behold he comes! and he will walk with you, and you will know him not.

26 He is the king; the latchet of his shoes I am not worthy to unloose.

27 And John left Bethany and went again unto the Jordan ford.

CHAPTER 64.

Jesus comes from Galilee, and is baptized by John. The Holy Breath testifies of his messiahship.

THE news reached Galilee, and Jesus with the multitude went down to where the harbinger was preaching at the ford.

2 When Jesus saw the harbinger

he said, Behold the man of God! Behold the greatest of the seers! Behold, Elijah has returned!

3 Behold the messenger whom God has sent to open up the way! The kingdom is at hand.

4 When John saw Jesus standing with the throng he said, Behold the king who cometh in the name of God!

5 And Jesus said to John, I would be washed in water as a symbol of the cleansing of the soul.

6 And John replied, You do not need to wash, for you are pure in thought, and word, and deed. And if you need to wash I am not worthy to perform the rite.

7 And Jesus said, I come to be a pattern for the sons of men, and what I bid them do, that I must do; and all men must be washed, symbolic of the cleansing of the soul.

8 This washing we establish as a rite—baptism rite we call it now, and so it shall be called.

9 Your work, prophetic harbinger, is to prepare the way, and to reveal the hidden things.

10 The multitudes are ready for the words of life, and I have come to be made known by you to all the world, as prophet of the Triune God, and as the chosen one to manifest the Christ to men.

11 Then John led Jesus down into the river at the ford and he baptized him in the sacred name of him who sent him forth to manifest the Christ to men.

12 And as they came out of the stream, the Holy Breath, in form of dove, came down and sat on Jesus' head.

13 A voice from heaven said, This is the well-beloved son of God, the Christ, the love of God made manifest.

14 John heard the voice, and understood the message of the voice.

15 Now Jesus went his way, and John preached to the multitude.

16 As many as confessed their sins, and turned from evil ways to ways of right, the harbinger baptized, symbolic of the blotting out of sins by righteousness.

SECTION XIV.

NUN.

The Christine Ministry of Jesus—Introductory Epoch.

CHAPTER 65.

Jesus goes to the wilderness for self-examination, where he remains forty days. Is subjected to three temptations. He overcomes. Returns to the camps of John and begins teaching.

THE harbinger had paved the way; the Logos had been introduced to men as love made manifest, and he must now begin his Christine ministry.

2 And he went forth into the wilderness to be alone with God that he might look into his inner heart, and note its strength and worthiness.

3 And with himself he talked; he said, My lower self is strong; by many ties I am bound down to carnal life.

4 Have I the strength to overcome and give my life a willing sacrifice for men?

5 When I shall stand before the face of men, and they demand a

proof of my messiahship, what will I say?

6 And then the tempter came and said, If you be son of God, command these stones to turn to bread.

7 And Jesus said, Who is it that demands a test? It is no sign that one is son of God because he does a miracle; the devils can do mighty things.

8 Did not the black magicians do great things before the Pharaohs?

9 My words and deeds in all the walks of life shall be the proof of my

10 And then the tempter said, If you will go into Jerusalem, and from the temple pinnacle cast down yourself to earth, the people will believe that you are the Messiah sent from God.

11 This you can surely do; for did not David say, He gives his angels charge concerning you, and with their hands will they uphold lest you should fall?

12 And Jesus said, I may not tempt the Lord, my God.

13 And then the tempter said, Look forth upon the world; behold its honors and its fame! Behold its pleasures and its wealth!

14 If you will give your life for these they shall be yours.

15 But Jesus said, Away from me all tempting thoughts. My heart is fixed; I spurn this carnal self with all its vain ambition and its pride.

16 For forty days did Jesus wrestle with his carnal self; his higher self prevailed. He then was hungry, but his friends had found him and they ministered to him.

17 Then Jesus left the wilderness, and in the consciousness of Holy Breath, he came unto the camps of John and taught.

CHAPTER 66.

Six of John's disciples follow Jesus and become his disciples. He teaches them. They sit in the Silence.

AMONG the followers of John were many men from Galilee. The most devout were Andrew, Simon, James, and John, with Philip and his brother of Bethsaida.

2 One day as Andrew, Philip and a son of Zebedee, were talking with the harbinger, the Logos came, and John exclaimed, Behold the Christ!

3 And then the three disciples followed Jesus, and he asked, What do you seek?

4 And the disciples asked, Where do you live? And Jesus answered, Come and see.

5 And Andrew called his brother Simon, saying, Come with me, for I have found the Christ.

6 When Jesus looked in Simon's face he said, Behold a rock! and Peter is your name.

7 And Philip found Nathaniel sitting by a tree, and said, My brother, come with me, for I have found the Christ! In Nazareth he abides.

8 Nathaniel said, Can anything of good come out of Nazareth? And Philip answered, Come and see.

9 When Jesus saw Nathaniel come he said, Behold an Israelite indeed in whom there is no guile!

10 Nathaniel said, How can you speak about me thus?

11 And Jesus said, I saw you as you sat beneath the fig tree over there, before your brother called.

12 Nathaniel lifted up his hands and said, This surely is the Christ,

the king, for whom the harbinger has often testified.

13 And John went forth and found his brother James, and brought him to the Christ.

14 The six disciples went with Jesus to the place where he abode.

15 And Peter said, We long have sought for Christ. We came from Galilee to John; we thought that he was Christ, but he confessed to us that he was not;

16 That he was but the harbinger sent forth to clear the way, and make the pathway easy for the coming king; and when you came he said, Behold the Christ!

17 And we would gladly follow where you go. Lord, tell us what to do.

18 And Jesus said, The foxes of the earth have homes, the birds have nests; I have no place to lay my head.

19 He who would follow me must give up all the cravings of the self and lose his life in saving life.

20 I come to save the lost, and man is saved when he is rescued from himself. But men are slow to comprehend this doctrine of the Christ.

21 And Peter said, I cannot speak for any other man, but for myself I speak: I will leave all and follow where you lead.

22 And then the others spoke and said, You have the words of truth; you came from God, and if we follow in your footsteps we cannot miss the way.

23 Then Jesus and the six disciples sat a long, long time in silent thought.

CHAPTER 67.

Jesus visits John at the Jordan. Delivers his first Christine address to the people. The address. He goes with his disciples to Bethany.

NOW, on the morrow Jesus came again and stood with John beside the ford; and John prevailed on him to speak, and standing forth he said,

2 You men of Israel, hear! The kingdom is at hand.

3 Behold the great key-keeper of the age stands in your midst; and with the spirit of Elijah he has come.

4 Behold, for he has turned the key; the mighty gates fly wide and all who will may greet the king.

5 Behold these multitudes of women, children, men! they throng the avenues, they crowd the outer courts; each seems to be intent to be the first to meet the king.

6 Behold, the censor comes and calls, Whoever will may come; but he who comes must will to prune himself of every evil thought;

7 Must overcome desire to gratify the lower self; must give his life to save the lost.

8 The nearer to the kingdom gate you come, more spacious is the room; the multitudes have gone.

9 If men could come unto the kingdom with their carnal thoughts, their passions and desires, there scarcely would be room for all.

10 But when they cannot take these through the narrow gate they turn away; the few are ready to go in and see the king.

11 Behold, John is a mighty fisher, fishing for the souls of men. He throws his great net out into the sea of human life; he draws it in and it is full.

12 But what a medley catch! a catch of crabs, and lobsters, sharks and creeping things, with now and then a fish of better kind.

13 Behold, the thousands come

to hear the Wild Man of the hills; they come in crowds that he may wash them in the crystal flood, and with their lips they do confess their sins.

14 But when the morrow comes we find them in their haunts of vice again, reviling John, and cursing God, and heaping insults on the king.

15 But blessed are the pure in heart, for they shall see the king.

16 And blessed are the strong in heart, for they shall not be cast about by every wind that blows;

17 But while the fickle and the thoughtless have gone back to Egypt land for leeks and carnal herbs to satisfy their appetites, the pure in heart have found the king.

18 But even those whose faith is weak, and who are naught but carnal manifests, will some day come again, and enter in with joy to see the king.

19 O men of Israel, take heed to what this prophet has to say! Be strong in mind; be pure in heart; be vigilant in helpfulness; the kingdom is at hand.

20 When Jesus had thus said he went his way, and with his six disciples came to Bethany; and they abode with Lazarus many days.

CHAPTER 68.

Jesus speaks to the people in Bethany. Tells them how to become pure in heart. Goes to Jerusalem and in the temple reads from a prophetic book. Goes to Nazareth.

THE news soon spread abroad that Jesus, king of Israel, had come to Bethany, and all the people of the town came forth to greet the king.

2 And Jesus, standing in the midst of them exclaimed, Behold, indeed, the king has come, but Jesus is not king.

3 The kingdom truly is at hand; but men can see it not with carnal eyes; they cannot see the king upon the throne.

4 This is the kingdom of the soul; its throne is not an earthly throne; its king is not a man.

5 When human kings found kingdoms here, they conquer other kings by force of arms; one kingdom rises on the ruins of another one.

6 But when our Father-God sets up the kingdom of the soul, he pours his blessings forth, like rain, upon the thrones of earthly kings who rule in righteousness.

7 It is not rule that God would overthrow; his sword is raised against injustice, wantonness and crime.

8 Now, while the kings of Rome do justice, and love mercy and walk humbly with their God, the benediction of the Triune God will rest upon them all.

9 They need not fear a messenger whom God sends forth to earth.

10 I am not sent to sit upon a throne to rule as Cæsar rules; and you may tell the ruler of the Jews that I am not a claimant for his throne.

11 Men call me Christ, and God has recognized the name; but Christ is not a man. The Christ is universal love, and Love is king.

12 This Jesus is but man who has been fitted by temptations overcome, by trials multiform, to be the temple through which Christ can manifest to men.

13 Then hear, you men of Israel, hear! Look not upon the flesh; it is not king. Look to the Christ within, who shall be formed in every one of you, as he is formed in me.

14 When you have purified your hearts by faith, the king will enter in, and you will see his face.

15 And then the people asked, What must we do that we may make our bodies fit abiding places for the king?

16 And Jesus said, Whatever tends to purity in thought, and word, and deed will cleanse the temple of the flesh.

17 There are no rules that can apply to all, for men are specialists in sin; each has his own besetting sin,

18 And each must study for himself how he can best transmute his tendency to evil things to that of righteousness and love.

19 Until men reach the higher plane, and get away from selfishness, this rule will give the best results:

20 Do unto other men what you would have them do to you.

21 And many of the people said, We know that Jesus is the Christ, the king who was to come, and blessed be his name.

22 Now, Jesus and his six disciples turned their faces toward Jerusalem, and many people followed them.

23 But Mathew, son of Alpheus, ran on before, and when he reached Jerusalem, he said, Behold the Christines come! The multitudes came forth to see the king.

24 But Jesus did not speak to any one until he reached the temple court, and then he opened up a book and read:

25 Behold, I send my messenger, and he will pave the way, and Christ, for whom you wait, will come unto his temple unannounced. Behold, for he will come, says God, the Lord of hosts.

26 And then he closed the book; he said no more; he left the temple halls, and with his six disciples, went his way to Nazareth,

27 And they abode with Mary, Jesus' mother, and her sister, Miriam.

CHAPTER 69.

Jesus and the ruler of the synagogue of Nazareth. Jesus teaches not in public, and the people are amazed.

NEXT day as Peter walked about in Nazareth, he met the ruler of the synagogue who asked, Who is this Jesus lately come to Nazareth?

2 And Peter said, This Jesus is the Christ of whom our prophets wrote; he is the king of Israel. His mother, Mary, lives on Marmion Way.

3 The ruler said, Tell him to come up to the synagogue, for I would hear his plea.

4 And Peter ran and told to Jesus what the ruler said; but Jesus answered not; he went not to the synagogue.

5 Then in the evening time the ruler came up Marmion Way, and in the home of Mary found he Jesus and his mother all alone.

6 And when the ruler asked for proof of his messiahship, and why he went not to the synagogue when he was bidden, Jesus said,

7 I am not slave to any man; I am not called unto this ministry by priest. It is not mine to answer when men call. I come the Christ of God; I answer unto God alone.

8 Who gave you right to ask for proof of my messiahship? My proof lies in my words and works, and so if you will follow me you will not lack for proof.

9 And then the ruler went his way; he asked himself, What man-

ner of a man is this to disregard the ruler of the synagogue?

10 The people of the town came out in throngs to see the Christ, and hear him speak; but Jesus said,

11 A prophet has no honor in his native town, among his kin.

12 I will not speak in Nazareth until the words I speak, and works I do in other towns have won the faith of men,

13 Until men know that God has christed me to manifest eternal love.

14 Good will to you, my kin; I bless you with a boundless love, and I bespeak for you abundant joy and happiness.

15 He said no more, and all the people marveled much because he would not speak in Nazareth.

CHAPTER 70.

Jesus and his disciples at a marriage feast in Cana. Jesus speaks on marriage. He turns water into wine. The people are amazed.

IN Cana, Galilee, there was a marriage feast, and Mary and her sister Miriam, and Jesus and his six disciples were among the guests.

2 The ruler of the feast had heard that Jesus was a master sent from God, and he requested him to speak.

3 And Jesus said, There is no tie more sacred than the marriage tie.

4 The chain that binds two souls in love is made in heaven, and man can never sever it in twain,

5 The lower passions of the twain may cause a union of the twain, a union as when oil and water meet.

6 And then a priest may forge a chain, and bind the twain. This is not marriage genuine; it is a counterfeit.

7 The twain are guilty of adultery; the priest is party to the crime. And that was all that Jesus said.

8 As Jesus stood apart in silent thought his mother came and said to him, The wine has failed; what shall we do?

9 And Jesus said, Pray what is wine? It is but water with the flavoring of grapes.

10 And what are grapes? They are but certain kinds of thought made manifest, and I can manifest that thought, and water will be wine.

11 He called the servants, and he said to them, Bring in six water pots of stone, a pot for each of these, my followers, and fill them up with water to the brims,

12 The servants brought the water pots, and filled them to their brims.

13 And Jesus with a mighty thought stirred up the ethers till they reached the manifest, and, lo, the water blushed, and turned to wine.

14 The servants took the wine and gave it to the ruler of the feast who called the bridegroom in and said to him,

15 This wine is best of all; most people when they give a feast bring in the best wine at the first; but, lo, you have reserved the best until the last.

16 And when the ruler and the guests were told that Jesus, by the power of thought, had turned the water into wine, they were amazed;

17 They said, This man is more than man; he surely is the christed one who prophets of the olden times declared would come.

18 And many of the guests believed on him, and gladly would have followed him.

CHAPTER 71.

Jesus, his six disciples and his mother, go to Capernaum. Jesus teaches the people, revealing the difference between the kings of earth and the kings of heaven.

THE city of Capernaum was by the sea of Galilee, and Peter's home was there. The homes of Andrew, John and James were near,

2 These men were fishermen, and must return to tend their nets, and they prevailed on Jesus and his mother to accompany them, and soon with Philip and Nathaniel they were resting by the sea in Peter's home.

3 The news spread through the city and along the shore that Judah's king had come, and multitudes drew near to press his hand.

4 And Jesus said, I cannot show the king, unless you see with eyes of soul, because the kingdom of the king is in the soul.

5 And every soul a kingdom is. There is a king for every man.

6 This king is love, and when this love becomes the greatest power in life, it is the Christ; so Christ is king.

7 And every one may have this Christ dwell in his soul, as Christ dwells in my soul.

8 The body is the temple of the king, and men may call a holy man a king.

9 He who will cleanse his mortal form and make it pure, so pure that love and righteousness may dwell unsullied side by side within its walls, is king.

10 The kings of earth are clothed in royal robes, and sit in state that men may stand in awe of them.

11 A king of heaven may wear a fisher's garb; may sit in mart of trade; may till the soil, or be a gleaner in the field; may be a slave in mortal chains;

12 May be adjudged a criminal by men; may languish in a prison cell; may die upon a cross.

13 Men seldom see what others truly are. The human senses sense what seems to be, and that which seems to be and that which is, may be diverse in every way.

14 The carnal man beholds the outer man, which is the temple of the king, and worships at his shrine.

15 The man of God is pure in heart; he sees the king; he sees with eyes of soul;

16 And when he rises to the plane of Christine consciousness, he knows that he himself is king, is love, is Christ, and so is son of God.

17 You men of Galilee, prepare to meet your king.

18 And Jesus taught the people many lessons as he walked with them beside the sea.

SECTION XV.

SAMECH.

The First Annual Epoch of the Christine Ministry of Jesus.

CHAPTER 72.

Jesus in Jerusalem. Drives the merchants out of the temple. The priests resent, and he defends himself from the standpoint of a loyal Jew. He speaks to the people.

THE Jewish paschal feast time came and Jesus left his mother in Capernaum and journeyed to Jerusalem.

2   And he abode with one a Sadducee, whose name was Jude.

3   And when he reached the temple courts the multitudes were there to see the prophet whom the people thought had come to break the yoke of Rome, restore the kingdom of the Jews, and rule on David's throne.

4   And when the people saw him come they said, All hail! behold the king!

5   But Jesus answered not; he saw the money changers in the house of God, and he was grieved.

6   The courts had been converted into marts of trade, and men were selling lambs and doves for offerings in sacrifice.

7   And Jesus called the priests and said, Behold, for paltry gain you have sold out the temple of the Lord.

8   This house ordained for prayer is now a den of thieves. Can good and evil dwell together in the courts of God? I tell you, no.

9   And then he made a scourge of cords and drove the merchants out; he overturned their boards, and threw their money on the floor.

10   He opened up the cages of the captive birds, and cut the cords that bound the lambs, and set them free.

11   The priests and scribes rushed out, and would have done him harm, but they were driven back; the common people stood in his defense.

12   And then the rulers said, Who is this Jesus you call king?

13   The people said, He is the Christ of whom our prophets wrote; he is the king who will deliver Israel.

14   The rulers said to Jesus, Man, if you be king, or Christ, then show us signs.   Who gave you right to drive these merchants out?

15   And Jesus said, There is no loyal Jew who would not give his life to save this temple from disgrace; in this I acted simply as a loyal Jew, and you yourselves will bear me witness to this truth.

16   The signs of my messiahship will follow me in words and deeds.

17   And you may tear the temple down (and you will tear it down) and in three days it will be built again more glorious than before.

18   Now Jesus meant that they might take his life; tear down his body, temple of the Holy Breath, and he would rise again.

19   The Jews knew not the meaning of his words; they laughed his claims to scorn. They said,

20   A multitude of men were forty and six years in building up this house, and this young stranger claims that he will build it up in three score hours; his words are idle, and his claims are naught.

21   And then they took the scourge with which he drove the

merchants out, and would have driven him away; but Philo, who had come from Egypt to attend the feast, stood forth and said.

22 You men of Israel, hear! This man is more than man; take heed to what you do. I have, myself, heard Jesus speak, and all the winds were still.

23 And I have seen him touch the sick, and they were healed. He stands a sage above the sages of the world;

24 And you will see his star arise, and it will grow until it is the full-orbed Sun of Righteousness.

25 Do not be hasty, men; just wait and you will have the proofs of his messiahship.

26 And then the priests laid down the scourge, and Jesus said,

27 Prepare, O Israel, prepare to meet your king! But you can never see the king while you press sin as such a precious idol to your hearts.

28 The king is God; the pure in heart alone can see the face of God and live.

29 And then the priests cried out, This fellow claims to be the God. Is not this sacrilege! away with him!

30 But Jesus said, No man has ever heard me say, I am a king. Our Father-God is king. With every loyal Jew I worship God.

31 I am the candle of the Lord aflame to light the way; and while you have the light walk in the light.

CHAPTER 73.

Jesus again visits the temple, and is favorably received by the people Tells the parable of a king and his sons. Defines messiahship.

NEXT day the multitudes were surging through the temple courts, intent on hearing Jesus speak.

2 And when he came the people said, All hail! behold the king!

3 And Jesus spoke a parable; he said, A king had vast domains; his people all were kin, and lived in peace.

4 Now, after many years the king said to his people, Take these lands and all I have; enhance their values; rule yourselves, and live in peace.

5 And then the people formed their states; selected governors and petty kings.

6 But pride, ambition, selfish greed, and base ingratitude grew fast, and kings began to war.

7 They wrote in all their statute books that might is right; and then the strong destroyed the weak, and chaos reigned through all the vast domain.

8 A long time passed, and then the king looked out on his domain. He saw his people in their cruel wars; he saw them sick and sore distressed; he saw the strong enslave the weak,

9 And then he said, What shall I do? Shall I send forth a scourge? shall I destroy my people all?

10 And then his heart was stirred with pity and he said, I will not send a scourge; I will send forth my only son, heir to the throne, to teach the people love, and peace, and righteousness.

11 He sent his son; the people scorned him and maltreated him, and nailed him to a cross.

12 He was entombed; but death was far too weak to hold the prince, and he arose.

13 He took a form man could not kill; and then he went again to teach the people love, and peace and righteousness.

14 And thus God deals with men.

15 A lawyer came and asked, What does messiah mean? and who has right to make messiah of a man?

16 And Jesus said, Messiah is one sent from God to seek and save the lost. Messiahs are not made by men.

17 In first of every age Messiah comes to light the way; to heal up broken hearts; to set the prisoners free. Messiah and the Christ are one.

18 Because a man claims to be Christ is not a sign that he is Christ

19 A man may cause the streams to flow from flinty rocks; may bring on storms at will; may stay tempestuous winds; may heal the sick and raise the dead, and not be sent from God.

20 All nature is subservient to the will of man, and evil men, as well as good, have all the powers of mind, and may control the elements.

21 The head gives not the proof of true messiahship, for man by means of intellect, can never know of God, nor bring himself to walk in light.

22 Messiah lives not in the head, but in the heart, the seat of mercy and of love.

23 Messiah never works for selfish gains; he stands above the carnal self; his words and deeds are for the universal good.

24 Messiah never tries to be a king, to wear a crown and sit upon an earthly throne.

25 The king is earthy, of the earth; Messiah is the man from heaven.

26 And then the lawyer asked, Why do you pose as king?

27 And Jesus said, No man has ever heard me say that I am king.

I could not sit in Cæsar's place and be the Christ.

28 Give unto Cæsar what belongs to him; give unto God the treasures of your heart.

CHAPTER 74.

Jesus heals on the Sabbath, and is censured by the Pharisees. Restores a drowned child. Rescues a wounded dog. Cares for a homeless child. Speaks on the law of kindness.

IT was the Sabbath day, and Jesus stood among the surging masses of the people in the temple courts and sacred halls.

2 The blind, the deaf, the dumb, and those obsessed were there, and Jesus spoke the Word, and they were healed.

3 On some he laid his hands, and they were healed; to others he just spoke the Word, and they were full restored to health; but others had to go and wash in certain pools; and others he anointed with a holy oil.

4 A doctor asked him why he healed in divers ways, and he replied,

5 Disease is discord in the human form, and discords are produced in many ways.

6 The body is a harpsichord; sometimes the strings are too relaxed, and then inharmony results.

7 Sometimes we find the strings too tense, and then another form of discord is induced.

8 Disease is many-formed, and there are many ways to cure, to tune anew the mystic harpsichord.

9 Now when the Pharisees were told that Jesus healed the people on the Sabbath day they were enraged, and they commanded him to quit the place.

10 But Jesus said, Was man de-

signed to fit the Sabbath day, or was the Sabbath day designed to fit the man?

11 If you had fallen in a pit and, lo, the Sabbath day had come, and I should pass your way, would you cry out,

12 Let me alone; it is a sin to help me on the Sabbath day; I'll swelter in this filth until another day?

13 You Pharisees, you hypocrites! you know you would be glad to have my help upon the Sabbath day, or any other day.

14 These people all have fallen into pits, and they are calling loud for me to help them out, and man and God would curse me should I pass along and heed them not.

15 And then the Pharisees returned to say their prayers, and curse the man of God because he heeded not their words.

16 Now, in the evening Jesus stood beside a pool; a playful child had fallen in, and it was drowned, and friends were bearing it away.

17 But Jesus called the carriers to stop; and then he stretched himself upon the lifeless form, and breathed into its mouth the breath of life.

18 And then he called aloud unto the soul that had gone out, and it returned; the child revived and lived.

19 And Jesus saw a wounded dog; it could not move; it lay beside the way and groaned with pain. He took it in his arms and bore it to the home where he abode.

20 He poured the healing oil into the wounds; he cared for it as though it were a child till it was strong and well.

21 And Jesus saw a little boy who had no home, and he was hungry; when he called for bread the people turned away.

22 And Jesus took the child and gave him bread; he wrapped him in his own warm coat, and found for him a home.

23 To those who followed him the master said, If man would gain again his lost estate he must respect the brotherhood of life.

24 Whoever is not kind to every form of life—to man, to beast, to bird, and creeping thing—cannot expect the blessings of the Holy One; for as we give, so God will give to us.

CHAPTER 75.

Nicodemus visits Jesus in the night. Jesus reveals to him the meaning of the new birth and the kingdom of heaven.

NICODEMUS was a ruler of the Jews, and he was earnest, learned and devout.

2 He saw the master's signet in the face of Jesus as he talked, but was not brave enough to publicly confess his faith in him;

3 So in the night he went to talk with Jesus at the home of Jude.

4 When Jesus saw him come he said, Full blessed are the pure in heart;

5 Twice blessed are the fearless, pure in heart;

6 Thrice blessed are the fearless, pure in heart who dare to make confession of their faith before the highest courts.

7 And Nicodemus said, Hail, master, hail! I know you are a teacher come from God, for man alone could never teach as you have taught; could never do the works that you have done.

8 And Jesus said, Except a man be born again he cannot see the

king; he cannot comprehend the words I speak.

9 And Nicodemus said, How can a man be born again? Can he go back into the womb and come again to life?

10 And Jesus said, The birth of which I speak is not the birth of flesh.

11 Except a man be born of water and the Holy Breath, he cannot come into the kingdom of the Holy One.

12 That which is born of flesh is child of man; that which is born of Holy Breath is child of God.

13 The winds blow where they please; men hear their voices, and may note results; but they know not from whence they come, nor where they go; and so is every one that is born of Holy Breath.

14 The ruler said, I do not understand; pray tell me plainly what you mean.

15 And Jesus said, The kingdom of the Holy One is in the soul; men cannot see it with their carnal eyes; with all their reasoning powers they comprehend it not.

16 It is a life deep hid in God; its recognition is the work of inner consciousness.

17 The kingdoms of the world are kingdoms of the sight; the kingdom of the Holy One is that of faith; its king is love.

18 Men cannot see the love of God unmanifest, and so our Father-God has clothed this love with flesh —flesh of a son of man.

19 And that the world may see and know this love made manifest, the son of man must needs be lifted up.

20 As Moses in the wilderness raised up the serpent for the healing of the flesh, the son of man must be raised up.

21 That all men bitten by the serpent of the dust, the serpent of this carnal life, may live.

22 He who believes in him shall have eternal life.

23 For God so loved the world that he sent forth his only son to be raised up that men may see the love of God.

24 God did not send his son to judge the world; he sent him forth to save the world; to bring men to the light.

25 But men love not the light, for light reveals their wickedness; men love the dark.

26 Now, every one who loves the truth comes to the light; he does not fear to have his works made manifest.

27 The light had come, and Nicodemus went his way; he knew the meaning of the birth of Holy Breath; he felt the presence of the Spirit in his soul.

28 And Jesus tarried in Jerusalem for many days and taught and healed the sick.

29 The common people gladly listened to his words, and many left their all of carnal things and followed him.

CHAPTER 76.

Jesus in Bethlehem. Explains the Empire of Peace to the shepherds. An unusual light appears. The shepherds recognize Jesus as the Christ.

THE Logos went to Bethlehem, and many people followed him.

2 He found the shepherd's home where he was cradled when a babe; here he abode.

3 He went up to the hills where more than thirty years before the shepherds watch their flocks and

heard the messenger of peace exclaim:

4 At midnight in a cave in Bethlehem the Prince of Peace is born.

5 And shepherds still were there, and sheep still fed upon the hills.

6 And in the valley near great flocks of snow-white doves were flying to and fro.

7 And when the shepherds knew that Jesus, whom the people called the king, had come, they came from near and far to speak to him.

8 And Jesus said to them, Behold the life of innocence and peace!

9 White is the symbol of the virtuous and pure! the lamb of innocence; the dove of peace;

10 And it was meet that love should come in human form amid such scenes as these.

11 Our father Abraham walked through these vales, and on these very hills he watched his flocks and herds.

12 And here it was that one, the Prince of Peace, the king of Salim, came; the Christ in human form; a greater far than Abraham was he.

13 And here it was that Abraham gave to this king of Salim, tithes of all he had.

14 This Prince of Peace went forth in battle everywhere. He had no sword; no armor of defence; no weapons of offence;

15 And yet he conquered men, and nations trembled at his feet.

16 The hosts of Egypt quailed before this sturdy king of right; the kings of Egypt placed their crowns upon his head,

17 And gave into his hands the scepter of all Egypt land, and not a drop of blood was shed, and not a captive placed in chains;

18 But everywhere the conqueror threw wide the prison doors and set the captives free.

19 And, once again, the Prince of Peace has come, and from these blessed hills he goes again to fight.

20 And he is clothed in white; his sword is truth; his shield is faith; his helmet innocence; his breath is love; his watchword peace.

21 But this is not a carnal war; it is not man at war with man; but it is right against the wrong.

22 And love is captain, love is warrior, love is armor, love is all, and love shall win.

23 And then again the hills of Bethlehem were clothed with light; again the messenger exclaimed,

24 Peace, peace on earth, good will to men.

25 And Jesus taught the people; healed the sick; revealed the mysteries of the kingdom of the Holy One.

26 And many said, He is the Christ; the king who was to come has come; Praise God.

CHAPTER 77.

Jesus in Hebron. Goes to Bethany. Advises Ruth regarding certain family troubles.

WITH three disciples Jesus went to Hebron where he tarried seven days and taught.

2 And then he went to Bethany and in the home of Lazarus he taught.

3 The evening came; the multitudes were gone, and Jesus, Lazarus, and his sisters, Martha, Ruth and Mary, were alone.

4 And Ruth was sore distressed. Her home was down in Jericho; her husband was the keeper of an inn; his name was Asher-ben.

5 Now, Asher was a Pharisee of

strictest mien and thought, and he regarded Jesus with disdain.

6 And when his wife confessed her faith in Christ, he drove her from his home.

7 But Ruth resisted not; she said, If Jesus is the Christ he knows the way, and I am sure he is the Christ,

8 My husband may become enraged and slay my human form; he cannot kill the soul, and in the many mansions of my Fatherland I have a dwelling-place.

9 And Ruth told Jesus all; and then she said, What shall I do?

10 And Jesus said, Your husband is not willingly at fault; he is devout; he prays to God, our Father-God.

11 His zeal for his religion is intense; in this he is sincere; but it has driven him insane, and he believes it right to keep his home unsullied by the heresy of Christ.

12 He feels assured that he has done the will of God in driving you away.

13 Intolerance is ignorance matured.

14 The light will come to him some day, and then he will repay for all your heartaches, griefs and tears.

15 And Ruth, you must not think that you are free from blame.

16 If you had walked in wisdom's ways, and been content to hold your peace, this grief would not have come to you.

17 It takes a long, long time for light to break into the shell of prejudice, and patience is the lesson you have need to learn.

18 The constant dropping of the water wears away the hardest stone.

19 The sweet and holy incense of a godly life will melt intolerance

much quicker than the hottest flame, or hardest blow.

20 Just wait a little time, and then go home with sympathy and love. Talk not of Christ, nor of the kingdom of the Holy One.

21 Just live a godly life; refrain from harshness in your speech, and you will lead your husband to the light.

22 And it was so.

CHAPTER 78.

Jesus in Jericho. Heals a servant of Asher. Goes to the Jordan and speaks to the people. Establishes baptism as a pledge of discipleship. Baptizes six disciples, who in turn baptize many people.

AND Jesus went to Jericho, and at the inn of Asher he abode.

2 A servant at the inn was sick, nigh unto death; the healers could not cure.

3 And Jesus came and touched the dying girl, and said, Malone, arise! and in a moment pain was gone; the fever ceased; the maid was well.

4 And then the people brought their sick, and they were healed.

5 But Jesus did not tarry long in Jericho; he went down to the Jordan ford where John was wont to teach.

6 The multitudes were there and Jesus said to them, Behold, the time has come; the kingdom is at hand.

7 None but the pure in heart can come into the kingdom of the Holy One; but every son and daughter of the human race is called upon to turn from evil and become the pure in heart.

8 The resolution to attain and enter through the Christine gate into the kingdom of the Holy One

will constitute discipleship, and every one must make a public pledge of his discipleship.

9 John washed your bodies in the stream, symbolic of the cleansing of the soul, in preparation for the coming of the king, the opening of the Christine gate into the kingdom of the Holy One.

10 John did a mighty work; but now the Christine gate is opened up, and washing is established as the pledge of your discipleship.

11 Until this age shall close this pledge shall be a rite, and shall be called, Baptism rite; and it shall be a sign to men, and seal to God of men's discipleship.

12 You men of every nation, hear! Come unto me; the Christine gate is opened up; turn from your sins and be baptized, and you shall enter through the gate and see the king.

13 The six disciples who had followed Jesus stood a-near, and Jesus led them forth and in the Jordan he baptized them in the name of Christ; and then he said to them,

14 My friends, you are the first to enter through the Christine gate into the kingdom of the Holy One.

15 As I baptized you in the name of Christ, so you shall, in that sacred name, baptize all men and women who will confess their faith in Christ, and shall renounce their sins.

16 And, lo, the multitudes came down, renounced their sins, confessed their faith in Christ, and were baptized.

CHAPTER 79.

John, the harbinger, at Salim. A lawyer inquires about Jesus. John explains to the multitude the mission of Jesus.

NOW, John the harbinger, was at the Salim Springs where water was abundant, and there he preached and washed the bodies of the people who confessed their sins.

2 A Jewish lawyer went to John and said, Has not this man from Galilee, he whom you washed and called the Christ, become your foe?

3 They say that he is at the Jordan ford; that he is building up a church, or something else, and that he washes people, just as you have done.

4 And John replied, This Jesus is indeed the Christ whose way I came to pave. He is not foe of mine.

5 The bridegroom hath the bride; his friends are near, and when they hear his voice they all rejoice.

6 The kingdom of the Holy One is bride, and Christ the groom; and I, the harbinger, am full of joy because they prosper so abundantly.

7 I have performed the work that I was sent to do; the work of Jesus just begins.

8 Then turning to the multitudes he said, Christ is the king of righteousness; Christ is the love of God; yea, he is God; one of the holy persons of the Triune God.

9 Christ lives in every heart of purity.

10 Now, Jesus who is preaching at the Jordan ford, has been subjected to the hardest tests of human life, and he has conquered all the appetites and passions of the carnal man.

11 And by the highest court of heaven, has been declared a man of such superior purity and holiness that he can demonstrate the presence of the Christ on earth.

12 Lo, love divine, which is the Christ, abides in him, and he is pattern for the race.

13 And every man can see in him what every man will be when he has conquered all the passions of the selfish self.

14 In water I have washed the bodies of the people who have turned from sin, symbolic of the cleansing of the soul;

15 But Jesus bathes forever in the living waters of the Holy Breath.

16 And Jesus comes to bring the savior of the world to men; Love is the savior of the world.

17 And all who put their trust in Christ, and follow Jesus as a pattern and a guide, have everlasting life.

18 But they who do not trust the Christ, and will not purify their hearts so that the Christ can dwell within, can never enter life.

CHAPTER 80.

Lamaas comes from India to see Jesus. He listens to the teachings of John at Salim. John tells him of the divine mission of Jesus. Lamaas finds Jesus at the Jordan. The masters recognize each other.

LAMAAS, priest of Brahm, who was a friend of Jesus when he was in the temple Jagannath, had heard of Jesus and his mighty works in many lands; and he had left his home and come to Palestine in search of him.

2 And as he journeyed towards Jerusalem he heard of John, the harbinger, who was esteemed a prophet of the living God.

3 Lamaas found the harbinger at Salim Springs; for many days he was a silent listener to the pungent truths he taught.

4 And he was present when the Pharisee told John of Jesus and his mighty works.

5 He heard the answer of the harbinger; he heard him bless the name of Jesus, whom he called the Christ.

6 And then he spoke to John; he said, Pray, tell me more about this Jesus whom you call the Christ.

7 And John replied, this Jesus is the love of God made manifest.

8 Lo, men are living on the lower planes—the planes of greed and selfishness; for self they fight; they conquer with the sword.

9 In every land the strong enslave and kill the weak. All kingdoms rise by force of arms; for force is king.

10 This Jesus comes to overthrow this iron rule of force, and seat Love on the throne of power.

11 And Jesus fears no man. He preaches boldly in the courts of kings, and everywhere, that victories won by force of arms are crimes;

12 That every worthy end may be attained by gentleness and love, just as the Prince of Peace, Melchisedec, the priest of God, won gallant victories in war without the shedding of a drop of blood.

13 You ask where are the temples of the Christ? He ministers at shrines not made with hands; his temples are the hearts of holy men who are prepared to see the king.

14 The groves of nature are his synagogues; his forum is the world.

15 He has no priests dressed up in puppet style to be admired by men; for every son of man is priest of Love.

16 When man has purified his heart by faith, he needs no middle man to intercede.

17 He is on friendly terms with God; is not afraid of him, and he is able, and is bold enough, to lay his body on the altar of the Lord.

18 Thus every man is priest, and is himself a living sacrifice.

19 You need not seek the Christ, for when your heart is purified the Christ will come, and will abide with you forevermore.

20 And then Lamaas journeyed on; he came to Jesus as he taught beside the ford.

21 And Jesus said, Behold the Star of India!   ·

22 Lamaas said, Behold the Sun of Righteousness! And he confessed his faith in Christ, and followed him.

CHAPTER 81.

The Christines journey toward Gali-lee. They tarry for a time at Jacob's well and Jesus teaches a woman of Samaria.

THE Christine gate into the kingdom of the Holy One was opened up, and Jesus and the six disciples and Lamaas left the Jordan ford and turned their faces toward Galilee.

2 Their way lay through Samaria, and as they journeyed on they came to Sychar, which was near the plot of ground that Jacob gave to Joseph when a youth.

3 And Jacob's well was there, and Jesus sat beside the well in silent thought, and his disciples went into the town to purchase bread.

4 A woman of the town came out to fill her pitcher from the well; and Jesus was athirst, and when he asked the woman for a drink she said,

5 I am a woman of Samaria, and you a Jew; do you not know that there is enmity between Samaritans and Jews? They traffic not; then why ask me the favor of a drink?

6 And Jesus said Samaritans and Jews are all the children of one God, our Father-God, and they are kin.

7 It is but prejudice born of the carnal mind that breeds this enmity and hate.

8 While I was born a Jew I recognize the brotherhood of life. Samaritans are just as dear to me as Jew or Greek.

9 And then had you but known the blessings that our Father-God has sent to men by me, you would have asked me for a drink,

10 And I would glad have given you a cup of water from the Fount of Life, and you would never thirst again.

11 The woman said, This well is deep, and you have naught with which to draw; how could you get the water that you speak about?

12 And Jesus said, The water that I speak about comes not from Jacob's well; it flows from springs that never fail.

13 Lo, every one who drinks from Jacob's well will thirst again; but they who drink the water that I give will never thirst again;

14 For they themselves become a well, and from their inner parts the sparkling waters bubble up into eternal life.

15 The woman said, Sir, I would drink from that rich well of life. Give me to drink, that I may thirst no more.

16 And Jesus said, Go call your husband from the town that he may share with you this living cup.

17 The woman said, I have no husband, sir.

18 And Jesus answered her and said, You scarcely know what husband means; you seem to be a gilded butterfly that flits from flower to flower,

19 To you there is no sacredness in marriage ties, and you affinitize with any man.

20 And you have lived with five of them who were esteemed as husbands by your friends.

21 The woman said, Do I not speak unto a prophet and a seer? Will you not condescend to tell me who you are?

22 And Jesus said, I need not tell you who I am for you have read the Law, the Prophets and the Psalms that tell of me,

23 I am one come to break away the wall that separates the sons of men. In Holy Breath there is no Greek, nor Jew, and no Samaritan; no bond, nor free; for all are one.

24 The woman asked, Why do you say that only in Jerusalem men ought to pray, and that they should not worship in our holy mount?

25 And Jesus said, What you have said, I do not say. One place is just as sacred as another place.

26 The hour has come when men must worship God within the temple of the heart; for God is not within Jerusalem, nor in your holy mount in any way that he is not in every heart.

27 Our God is Spirit; they who worship him must worship him in spirit and in truth.

28 The woman said, We know that when Messiah comes that he will lead us in the ways of truth.

29 And Jesus said, Behold the Christ has come; Messiah speaks to you.

CHAPTER 82.

While Jesus is teaching, his disciples come and marvel because he speaks with a Samaritan. Many people from Sychar come to see Jesus. He speaks to them. With his disciples he goes to Sychar and remains for certain days.

WHILE Jesus yet was talking to the woman at the well, the six disciples came from Sychar with the food.

2 And when they saw him talking to a woman of Samaria, and one they thought a courtesan, they were amazed; yet no one asked him why he spoke with her.

3 The woman was so lost in thought and so intent on what the master said, that she forgot her errand to the well; she left her pitcher and ran quickly to the town.

4 She told the people all about the prophet she had met at Jacob's well; she said, He told me every thing I ever did.

5 And when the people would know more about the man, the woman said, Come out and see. And multitudes went out to Jacob's well.

6 When Jesus saw them come he said to those who followed him, You need not say, It is four months before the harvest time;

7 Behold, the harvest time is now. Lift up your eyes and look; the fields are golden with the ripened grain.

8 Lo, many sowers have gone forth to sow the seeds of life; the seed has grown; the plants have strengthened in the summer sun; the grain has ripened, and the master calls for men to reap.

9 And you shall go out in the fields and reap what other men have sown; but when the reckoning day shall come the sowers and the reapers all together will rejoice.

10 And Philip said to Jesus, Stay now your work a time and sit beneath this olive tree and eat a portion of this food; you must be

faint for you have eaten naught since early day.

11 But Jesus said, I am not faint, for I have food to eat you know not of.

12 Then the disciples said among themselves, Who could have brought him aught to eat?

13 They did not know that he had power to turn the very ethers into bread.

14 And Jesus said, The master of the harvest never sends his reapers forth and feeds them not.

15 My Father who has sent me forth into the harvest field of human life will never suffer me to want; and when he calls for you to serve, lo, he will give you food, will clothe and shelter you.

16 Then turning to the people of Samaria, he said, Think not it strange that I, a Jew, should speak to you, for I am one with you.

17 The universal Christ who was, and is, and evermore shall be, is manifest in me; but Christ belongs to every man.

18 God scatters forth his blessings with a lavish hand, and he is not more kind to one than to another one of all the creatures of his hand.

19 I just came up from Judah's hills, and God's same sun was shining and his flowers were blooming, and in the night his stars were just as bright as they are here.

20 God cannot cast a child away; the Jew, the Greek and the Samaritan are equal in his sight.

21 And why should men and women fret and quarrel, like children in their plays?

22 The lines that separate the sons of men are made of straw, and just a single breath of love would blow them all away.

23 The people were amazed at what the stranger said, and many said, The Christ that was to come has surely come.

24 And Jesus went with them into the town, and tarried certain days.

CHAPTER 83.

Jesus teaches the people of Sychar. Casts a wicked spirit out of one obsessed. Sends the spirit to its own place. Heals many people. The priests are disturbed by the presence of Jesus in Sychar, but he speaks to them and wins their favor.

IN Sychar Jesus taught the people in the market place.

2 A man obsessed was brought to him. The wicked spirit that possessed the man was full of violence and lust, and often threw his victim to the ground.

3 And Jesus spoke aloud and said, Base spirit, loose your hold upon the vitals of this man, and go back to your own.

4 And then the spirit begged that he might go into the body of a dog that stood near by.

5 But Jesus said, Why harm the helpless dog? Its life is just as dear to it as mine to me.

6 It is not yours to throw the burden of your sin on any living thing.

7 By your own deeds and evil thoughts you have brought all these perils on yourself. You have hard problems to be solved; but you must solve them for yourself.

8 By thus obsessing man you make your own conditions doubly sad. Go back into your own domain; refrain from harming anything, and, by and by, you will, yourself, be free.

9 The wicked spirit left the man

and went unto his own. The man looked up in thankfulness and said, Praise God.

10 And many of the people brought their sick, and Jesus spoke the Word, and they were healed.

11 The ruler of the synagogue, and all the priests were much disturbed when told that Jesus from Jerusalem was preaching in the town.

12 They thought that he had come to proselyte and stir up strife among Samaritans.

13 And so they sent an officer to bring him to the synagogue that he might give a reason for his presence in the town.

14 But Jesus said to him who came, Go back and tell the priests and ruler of the synagogue that I am not engaged in crime.

15 I come to bind up broken hearts, to heal the sick, and cast the evil spirits out of those obsessed.

16 Tell them, their prophets spoke of me; that I am come to break no law, but to fulfil the highest law.

17 The man returned and told the priests and ruler of the synagogue what Jesus said,

18 The ruler was amazed, and with the priests went to the market place where Jesus was.

19 And when he saw them, Jesus said, Behold the honored men of all Samaria! the men ordained to lead the people in the way of right.

20 And I am come to help, and not to hinder in their work.

21 There are two classes of the sons of men; they who would build the human race upon the sure foundation stones of justice, truth, equality and right,

22 And they who would destroy the holy temple where the Spirit dwells and bring their fellows down to beggary and crime.

23 The holy brotherhood of right must stand united in the stirring conflicts of the hour.

24 No matter whether they be Jews, Samaritans, Assyrians or Greeks, they must tramp down beneath their feet all strife, all discord, jealousy and hate, and demonstrate the brotherhood of man.

25 Then to the ruler of the synagogue he spoke: he said, United in the cause of right we stand; divided we will fall.

26 And then he took the ruler by the hand; a love light filled their souls; and all the people were amazed.

CHAPTER 84.

The Christines resume their journey. They tarry a while in the city of Samaria. Jesus speaks in the synagogue. Heals a woman by mental power. He disappears, but later joins his disciples as they journey toward Nazareth.

THE Christines turned their faces toward the land of Galilee; but when they reached the city of Samaria, the multitudes pressed hard about them, begging them to tarry in their city for a while.

2 And then they went up to the synagogue, and Jesus opened up the book of Moses, and he read:

3 In thee and in thy seed shall all the nations of the earth be blest.

4 And then he closed the book and said, These words were spoken by the Lord of hosts unto our father Abraham, and Israel has been blessedness to all the world.

5 We are his seed; but not a tithe of the great work that we were called to do has yet been done.

6 The Lord of hosts has set

apart the Israelites to teach the unity of God and man; but one can never teach that which he does not demonstrate in life.

7 Our God is Spirit, and in him all wisdom, love and strength abide.

8 In every man these sacred attributes are budding forth, and in due time they will unfold; the demonstration will completed be, and man will comprehend the fact of unity.

9 And you, the ruler of the synagogue, and you, these priests, are honored servants of the Lord of hosts.

10 All men are looking unto you for guidance in the ways of life; example is another name for priest; so what you would that people be, that you must be.

11 A simple godly life may win ten thousand souls to purity and right.

12 And all the people said, Amen.

13 Then Jesus left the synagogue, and at the hour of evening prayer he went up to the sacred grove, and all the people turned their faces toward their holy mount and prayed.

14 And Jesus prayed.

15 And as he sat in silent mood a voice of soul spoke to his soul imploring help.

16 And Jesus saw a woman on a couch in sore distress; for she was sick nigh unto death.

17 She could not speak, but she had heard that Jesus was a man of God, and in her heart she called on him for help.

18 And Jesus helped; he did not speak; but like a flash of light, a mighty virtue from his soul filled full the body of the dying one, and she arose, and joined her kindred while they prayed.

19 Her kindred were astonished and they said to her, How were you healed? And she replied,

20 I do not know; I simply asked the man of God in thought for healing power, and in a moment I was well.

21 The people said, The gods have surely come to earth; for man has not the power to heal by thought.

22 But Jesus said, The greatest power in heaven and earth is thought.

23 God made the universe by thought; he paints the lily and the rose with thought.

24 Why think it strange that I should send a healing thought and change the ethers of disease and death to those of health and life?

25 Lo, you shall see far greater things than this, for by the power of holy thought, my body will be changed from carnal flesh to spirit form; and so will yours.

26 When Jesus had thus said he disappeared, and no one saw him go.

27 His own disciples did not comprehend the change; they knew not where their master went, and they went on their way.

28 But as they walked and talked about the strange event, lo, Jesus came and walked with them to Nazareth of Galilee.

CHAPTER 85.

John, the harbinger, censures Herod for his wickedness. Herod sends him to prison in Machaerus. Jesus tells why God permitted the imprisonment of John.

HEROD ANTIPAS, the tetrarch of Paraca and of Galilee

was dissipated, selfish and tyrannical.

2   He drove his wife away from home that he might take as wife Herodias, the wife of one, a near of kin, a woman, like himself, immoral and unjust.

3   The city of Tiberius, upon the shores of Galilee, was Herod's home.

4   Now John, the harbinger, had left the Salim Springs to teach the people by the sea of Galilee; and he rebuked the wicked ruler and his stolen wife for all their sins.

5   Herodias was enraged because the preacher dared accuse her and her husband of their crimes;

6   And she prevailed on Herod to arrest the harbinger and cast him in a dungeon in the castle of Machaerus that stood beside the Bitter Sea.

7   And Herod did as she required; then she lived in peace in all her sins, for none were bold enough to censure her again.

8   The followers of John were warned to speak not of the trial and imprisonment of John.

9   By order of the court, they were restrained from teaching in the public halls.

10   They could not talk about this better life that Herod called, the Heresy of John.

11   When it was known that John had been imprisoned by the tetrarch court, the friends of Jesus thought it best that he should not remain in Galilee.

12   But Jesus said, I have no need of fear; my time has not yet come; no man can stay me till my work is done.

13   And when they asked why God permitted Herod to imprison John, he said,

14   Behold yon stalk of wheat! When it has brought the grain to

perfectness, it is of no more worth; it falls, becoming part of earth again from which it came.

15   John is a stalk of golden wheat; he brought unto maturity the richest grain of all the earth; his work is done.

16   If he had said another word it might have marred the symmetry of what is now a noble life.

17   And when my work is done the rulers will do unto me what they have done to John, and more.

18   All these events are part of God's own plan.   The innocent will suffer while the wicked are in power; but woe to them who cause the suffering of the innocents.

CHAPTER 86.

The Christines are in Nazareth. Jesus speaks in the synagogue. He offends the people and they attempt to kill him. He mysteriously disappears, and returns to the synagogue.

THE Christines were in Nazareth.   It was the Sabbath day, and Jesus went up to the synagogue.

2   The keeper of the books gave one to Jesus and he opened it and read:

3   The Spirit of the Lord has overshadowed me; he has anointed me to preach the gospel to the poor; to set the captives free; to open sightless eyes;

4   To bring relief to those oppressed and bruised, and to proclaim, The year of jubilee has come.

5   When he had read these words he closed the book and said, This scripture is fulfilled before your eyes this day.   The year of jubilee has come; the time when Israel shall bless the world.

6   And then he told them many

things about the kingdom of the Holy One; about the hidden way of life; about forgiveness of sins.

7   Now, many people knew not who the speaker was: And others said, Is not this Joseph's son? Does not his mother live on Marmion Way?

8   And one spoke out and said, This is the man who did such mighty works in Cana, in Capernaum and in Jerusalem.

9   And then the people said, Physician heal yourself. Do here among your kindred all the mighty works that you have done in other towns.

10   And Jesus said, No prophet is received with honor by the people of his native land; and prophets are not sent to every one.

11   Elijah was a man of God; he had the power and he closed the gates of heaven, and it did not rain for forty months; and when he spoke the Word, the rain came on, the earth brought forth again.

12   And there were many widows in the land; but this Elijah went to none but Zarephath, and she was blessed.

13   And when Elisha lived, lo, many lepers were in Israel, but none were cleansed save one—the Syrian who had faith.

14   You have no faith; you seek for signs to satisfy your curious whims; but you shall see not till you open up your eyes of faith.

15   And then the people were enraged; they rushed upon him, bound him down with cords, and took him to a precipice not far away, intent to cast him down to death;

16   But when they thought they held him fast, he disappeared; unseen he passed among the angry men, and went his way.

17   The people were confounded and they said, What manner of a man is this?

18   And when they came again to Nazareth, they found him teaching in the synagogue.

19   They troubled him no more for they were sore afraid.

CHAPTER 87.

The Christines go to Cana. Jesus heals a nobleman's child. The Christines go to Capernaum. Jesus provides a spacious home for his mother. He announces his intention to choose twelve apostles.

IN Nazareth Jesus taught no more; he went with his disciples up to Cana, where, at a marriage feast, he once turned water into wine.

2   And here he met a man of noble birth whose home was in Capernaum, whose son was sick.

3   The man had faith in Jesus' power to heal, and when he learned that he had come to Galilee he went in haste to meet him on the way.

4   The man met Jesus at the seventh hour, and he entreated him to hasten to Capernaum to save his son.

5   But Jesus did not go; he stood aside in silence for a time, and then he said, Your faith has proved a healing balm; your son is well.

6   The man believed and went his way toward Capernaum and as he went he met a servant from his home who said,

7   My lord, You need not haste; your son is well.

8   The father asked, When did my son begin to mend?

9   The servant said, On yesterday about the seventh hour the fever left.

10   And then the father knew it

was the healing balm that Jesus sent that saved his son.

11 In Cana Jesus tarried not; he went his way with his disciples to Capernaum, where he secured a spacious house where, with his mother, he could live; where his disciples might repair to hear the Word.

12 He called the men who had confessed their faith in him to meet him in his home, which his disciples called, The school of Christ; and when they came he said to them,

13 This gospel of the Christ must be proclaimed in all the world.

14 This Christine vine will be a mighty vine whose branches will comprise the peoples, tribes and tongues of all the earth.

15 I am the vine; twelve men shall be the branches of the stock, and these shall send forth branches everywhere;

16 And from among the people who have followed me, the Holy Breath will call the twelve.

17 Go now and do your work as you have done your work; but listen for the call.

18 Then the disciples went unto their daily tasks, to do their work as they had done, and Jesus went alone into the Hammoth hills to pray.

19 Three days and nights he spent communing with the Silent Brotherhood; then, in the power of Holy Breath he came to call the twelve.

CHAPTER 88.

Jesus walks by the sea. Stands in a fishing boat and speaks to the people. Under his direction the fishermen secure a great catch of fish. He selects and calls his twelve apostles.

BESIDE the sea of Galilee the Christine master walked, and multitudes of people followed him.

2 The fishing boats had just come in, and Peter and his brother waited in their boats; their helpers were ashore repairing broken nets.

3 And Jesus went into a boat and Peter pushed it out a little ways from shore; and Jesus standing in the boat spoke to the multitude. He said,

4 Isaiah, prophet of the Lord of hosts, looked forward and he saw this day; he saw the people standing by the sea, and he exclaimed,

5 The land of Zebulon and Napthali, land beyond the Jordan and toward the sea, the Gentile Galilee,

6 The people were in darkness, knowing not the way; but, lo, they saw the Day Star rise; a light streamed forth; they saw the way of life; they walked therein.

7 And you are blest beyond all people of the earth today, because you first may see the light, and may become the children of the light.

8 Then Jesus said to Peter, Bring your nets aboard, and put out in the deep,

9 And Peter did as Jesus bade him do; but in a faithless way he said, This is a useless trip; there are no fish upon this shore of Galilee today; with Andrew I have toiled all night, and taken naught.

10 But Jesus saw beneath the surface of the sea; he saw a multitude of fish. He said to Peter,

11 Cast out your net upon the right side of the boat.

12 And Peter did as Jesus said, and, lo, the net was filled; it scarce was strong enough to hold the multitude of fish.

13 And Peter called to John and James, who were near by, for help; and when the net was hauled to

boat, both boats were well nigh filled with fish.

14 When Peter saw the heavy catch, he was ashamed of what he said; ashamed because he had no faith, and he fell down at Jesus' feet and said, Lord, I believe!

15 And Jesus said, Behold the catch! from henceforth you shall fish no more for fish;

16 You shall cast forth the Christine net into the sea of human life, upon the right side of the boat; you shall ensnare the multitudes to holiness and blessedness and peace.

17 Now, when they reached the shore the Christine master called to Peter, Andrew, James and John and said,

18 You fishermen of Galilee, the masters have a mighty work for us to do; I go, and you may follow me. And they left all and followed him.

19 And Jesus walked along the shore, and seeing Philip and Nathaniel walking on the beach he said to them,

20 You teachers of Bethsaida, who long have taught the people Greek philosophy, the masters have a higher work for you and me to do; I go and you may follow me; and then they followed him.

21 A little farther on there stood a Roman tribute house, and Jesus saw the officer in charge; his name was Matthew, who once abode in Jericho;

22 The youth who once ran on before the Lord into Jerusalem and said, Behold the Christines come.

23 And Matthew was a man of wealth, and learned in wisdom of the Jews, the Syrians and the Greeks.

24 And Jesus said to him, Hail, Matthew, trusted servant of the Cæsars, hail! the masters call us to

the tribute house of souls; I go and you may follow me. And Matthew followed him.

25 Ischariot and his son, whose name was Judas, were employed by Matthew and were at the tribute house.

26 And Jesus said to Judas, Stay your work; the masters call us to a duty in the savings bank of souls; I go and you may follow me. And Judas followed him.

27 And Jesus met a lawyer who had heard about the Christine master and had come from Antioch to study in the school of Christ.

28 This man was Thomas, man of doubt, and yet a Greek philosopher of culture and of power.

29 But Jesus saw in him the lines of faith, and said to him, The masters have a need of men who can interpret law; I go, and you may follow me. And Thomas followed him.

30 And when the evening came and Jesus was at home, behold, there came his kindred, James and Jude, the sons of Alpheus and Miriam.

31 And these were men of faith, and they were carpenters of Nazareth.

32 And Jesus said to them, Behold, for you have toiled with me, and with my father Joseph, building houses for the homes of men. The masters call us now to aid in building homes for souls; homes built without the sound of hammer, ax, or saw;

33 I go, and you may follow me. And James and Jude exclaimed, Lord, we will follow you.

34 And on the morrow Jesus sent a message unto Simon, leader of the Zelotes, a strict exponent of the Jewish law.

35 And in the message Jesus said, The masters call for men to

demonstrate the faith of Abraham; I go, and you may follow me. And Simon followed him.

CHAPTER 89.

The twelve apostles are at Jesus' home and are consecrated to their work. Jesus instructs them. He goes to the synagogue on the Sabbath and teaches. He casts an unclean spirit out of one obsessed. He heals Peter's mother-in-law.

NOW, on the day before the Sabbath day, the twelve disciples who had received the call were met with one accord in Jesus' home.

2 And Jesus said to them, This is the day to consecrate yourselves unto the work of God; so let us pray.

3 Turn from the outer to the inner self; close all the doors of carnal self and wait.

4 The Holy Breath will fill this place, and you will be baptized in Holy Breath.

5 And then they prayed; a light more brilliant than the noonday sun filled all the room, and tongues of flame from every head rose high in air.

6 The atmosphere of Galilee was set astir; a sound like distant thunder rolled above Capernaum, and men heard songs, as though ten thousand angels joined in full accord.

7 And then the twelve disciples heard a voice, a still, small voice, and just one word was said, a word they dared not speak; it was the sacred name of God.

8 And Jesus said to them, By this omnific Word you may control the elements, and all the powers of air.

9 And when within your souls you speak this Word, you have the keys of life and death; of things that are; of things that were; of things that are to be.

10 Behold you are the twelve great branches of the Christine vine; the twelve foundation stones; the twelve apostles of the Christ.

11 As lambs I send you forth among wild beasts; but the omnific Word will be your buckler and your shield.

12 And then again the air was filled with song, and every living creature seemed to say, Praise God! Amen!

13 The next day was the Sabbath day; and Jesus went with his disciples to the synagogue, and there he taught.

14 The people said, He teaches not as do the scribes and Pharisees; but as a man who knows, and has authority to speak.

15 As Jesus spoke, a man obsessed came in; the evil spirits that obsessed the man were of the baser sort; they often threw their victim to the ground, or in the fire.

16 And when the spirits saw the Christine master in the synagogue they knew him, and they said,

17 You son of God, why are you here? would you destroy us by the Word before our time? we would have naught to do with you; let us alone.

18 But Jesus said to them, By the omnific Word I speak; Come out; torment this man no more; go to your place.

19 And then the unclean spirits threw the man upon the floor, and, with a fiendish cry, they went away.

20 And Jesus lifted up the man and said to him, If you will keep your mind full occupied with good,

the evil spirits cannot find a place to stay;

21 They only come to empty heads and hearts. Go on your way and sin no more.

22 The people were astonished at the words that Jesus spoke, the work he did. They asked among themselves,

23 Who is this man? From whence comes all this power that even unclean spirits fear, and flee away?

24 The Christine master left the synagogue; with Peter, Andrew, James and John, he went to Peter's house where one, a near of kin, was sick.

25 And Peter's wife came in; it was her mother who was sick.

26 And Jesus touched the woman as she lay upon her couch; he spoke the Word; the fever ceased and she arose and ministered to them.

27 The neighbors heard what had occurred, and then they brought their sick, and those obsessed, and Jesus laid his hands on them, and they were healed.

CHAPTER 90.

Jesus goes alone to a mountain to pray. His disciples find him. He calls the twelve and they journey through Galilee teaching and healing. At Tiberius Jesus heals a leper. The Christines return to Capernaum. In his own home Jesus heals a palsied man and makes known the philosophy of healing and the forgiveness of sins.

THE Christine master disappeared; no one saw him go, and Peter, James and John set forth to search for him; they found him at his trysting-place out on the Hammoth hills.

2 And Peter said, The city of Capernaum is wild; the people crowd the streets and every public place is filled.

3 The men, the women and the children everywhere are asking for the man who heals by will.

4 Your home and our homes are filled with people who are sick; they call for Jesus who is called the Christ. What will we say to them?

5 And Jesus said, A score of other cities call, and we must take the bread of life to them. Go call the other men and let us go.

6 And Jesus and the twelve went to Bethsaida where Philip and Nathaniel dwelt; and there they taught.

7 The multitudes believed on Christ, confessed their sins and were baptized, and came into the kingdom of the Holy One.

8 The Christine master and the twelve went everywhere through all the towns of Galilee, and taught, baptizing all who came in faith, and who confessed their sins.

9 They opened blinded eyes, unstopped deaf ears, drove forth the evil ones from those obsessed, and healed disease of every kind.

10 And they were in Tiberius by the sea, and as they taught a leper came a-near and said, Lord, I believe, and if you will but speak the Word I will be clean.

11 And Jesus said to him, I will; be clean. And soon the leprosy was gone; the man was clean.

12 And Jesus charged the man, Say naught to any one, but go and show yourself unto the priests and offer for your cleansing what the law demands.

13 The man was wild with joy; but then he went not to the priests, but in the marts of trade, and everywhere he told what had been done.

14 And then the sick in throngs pressed hard upon the healer and the twelve, imploring to be healed.

15 And they were so importunate that little could be done, and so the Christines left the crowded thoroughfares, and went to desert places where they taught the multitudes that followed them.

16 Now, after many days the Christines came back to Capernaum. When it was noised around that Jesus was at home, the people came; they filled the house till there was no more room, not even at the door.

17 And there were present scribes and Pharisees and doctors of the law from every part of Galilee, and from Jerusalem, and Jesus opened up for them the way of life.

18 Four men brought one, a palsied man upon a cot, and when they could not pass the door they took the sick man to the roof, and opened up a way, then let him down before the healer's face.

19 When Jesus saw their faith, he said unto the palsied man, My son, be of good cheer; your sins are all forgiven.

20 And when the scribes and Pharisees heard what he said, they said, Why does this man speak thus? who can forgive the sins of men but God?

21 And Jesus caught their thought; he knew they questioned thus among themselves; he said to them,

22 Why reason thus among yourselves? What matters it if I should say, Your sins are blotted out; or say, Arise, take up your bed and walk?

23 But just to prove that men may here forgive the sins of men, I say, (and then he spoke unto the palsied man),

24 Arise, take up your bed, and go your way.

25 And in the presence of them all the man arose, took up his bed, and went his way.

26 The people could not comprehend the things they heard and saw. They said among themselves, This is a day we never can forget; we have seen wondrous things to-day.

27 And when the multitudes had gone the twelve remained, and Jesus said to them,

28 The Jewish festival draws near; next week we will go to Jerusalem, that we may meet our brethren from afar, and open up to them the way that they may see the king.

29 The Christines sought the quiet of their homes, where they remained in prayer for certain days.

SECTION XVI.

AIN.

The Second Annual Epoch of the Christine Ministry of Jesus.

CHAPTER 91.

Jesus at the feast in Jerusalem. Heals an impotent man. Gives a practical lesson in healing. Affirms that all men are the sons of God.

THE feast time came and Jesus and the twelve went to Jerusalem.

2 Upon the day before the Sabbath day they reached Mount Olives and they tarried at an inn be-

fore Mount Olives on the north.

3　And in the early morning of the Sabbath day they went in through the sheep gate to Jerusalem.

4　The healing fountain of Bethesda, near the gate, was thronged about with people who were sick;

5　For they believed that at a certain time an angel came and poured a healing virtue in the pool, and those who entered first and bathed, would be made whole.

6　And Jesus and the twelve were standing near the pool.

7　And Jesus saw a man near by who had been stricken eight and thirty years; without a hand to help he could not move.

8　And Jesus said to him, My brother, man, would you be healed?

9　The man replied, I earnestly desire to be healed; but I am helpless and when the angel comes and pours the healing virtues in the pool,

10　Another who can walk, steps in the fountain first and I am left unhealed.

11　And Jesus said, Who sends an angel here to potentize this pool for just a favored few?

12　I know it is not God, for he deals just the same with every one.

13　One has no better chance in heaven's healing fountain than another one.

14　The fount of health is in your soul; it has a door locked fast; the key is faith;

15　And every one can have this key and may unlock the door and plunge into the healing fount and be made whole.

16　And then the man looked up in hopeful mood and said, Give me this key of faith.

17　And Jesus said, Do you believe what I have said? According to your faith it shall be done.

Arise, take up your bed and walk.

18　The man at once arose and walked away; he only said, Praise God.

19　And when the people asked, Who made you whole? the man replied, I do not know. A stranger at the pool just spoke a word and I was well.

20　The many did not see when Jesus healed the man, and with the twelve he went his way up to the temple courts.

21　And in the temple Jesus saw the man and said to him, Behold you are made whole; from henceforth guard your life aright;

22　Go on your way and sin no more, or something worse may fall on you.

23　And now the man knew who it was who made him whole.

24　He told the story to the priests and they were much enraged; they said, The law forbids a man to heal upon the Sabbath day.

25　But Jesus said, My Father works on Sabbath days and may not I? .

26　He sends his rain, his sunshine and his dew; he makes his grass to grow, his flowers to bloom; he speeds the harvests just the same on Sabbath days as on the other days.

27　If it is lawful for the grass to grow and flowers to bloom on Sabbath days it surely is not wrong to succor stricken men.

28　And then the priests were angered more and more because he claimed to be a son of God.

29　A leading priest, Abihu, said, This fellow is a menace to our nation and our laws; he makes himself to be a son of God; it is not meet that he should live.

30　But Jesus said, Abihu, Sir, you are a learned man; you surely know the law of life. Pray tell who were the sons of God we read about in Genesis, who took to wife the daughters of the sons of men?

31 Our father Adam; who was he? From whence came he? Had he a father? or did he fall from heaven as a star?

32 We read that Moses said, He came from God. If Adam came from God, pray, was he offspring, was he son?

33 We are the children of this son of God; then tell me, learned priest, Who are we if not sons of God?

34 The priest had urgent business and he went his away.

35 And Jesus said, All men are sons of God and if they live a holy life they always are at home with God.

36 They see and understand the works of God, and in his sacred name they can perform these works.

37 The lightnings and the storms are messengers of God as well as are the sunshine, rain and dew.

38 The virtues of the heavens are in God's hands, and every loyal son may use these virtues and these powers.

39 Man is the delegate of God to do his will on earth, and man can heal the sick, control the spirits of the air, and raise the dead.

40 Because I have the power to do these things is nothing strange. All men may gain the power to do these things; but they must conquer all the passions of the lower self; and they can conquer if they will.

41 So man is God on earth, and he who honors God must honor man; for God and man are one, as father and the child are one.

42 Behold, I say, The hour has come; the dead will hear the voice of man, and live, because the son of man is son of God.

43 You men of Israel, hear! you live in death; you are locked up within the tomb.

44 (There is no deeper death than ignorance and unbelief.)

45 But all will some day hear the voice of God, made plain by voice of man, and live. You all will know that you are sons of God, and by the sacred Word, may do the works of God.

46 When you have come to life, that is, have come to realize that you are sons of God, you who have lived the life of right, will open up your eyes on fields of life.

47 But you who love the ways of sin will, in this resurrection, stand before a judgment bar, and be condemned to pay the debts you owe to men and to yourselves.

48 For whatsoever you have done amiss must be performed again, and yet again, until you reach the stature of the perfect man.

49 But in due time the lowest and the highest will arise to walk in light.

50 Shall I accuse you unto God? No, for your prophet, Moses, has done that; and if you hear not Moses' words you will not hearken unto me, for Moses wrote of me.

CHAPTER 92.

The Christines at a feast in Lazarus' home. A fire rages in the town. Jesus rescues a child from the flames and stays the fire by the Word. He gives a practical lesson on how to redeem a drunken man.

NOW, Lazarus was at the feast and Jesus and the twelve went with him to his home in Bethany.

2 And Lazarus and his sisters made a feast for Jesus and the twelve; and Ruth and Asher came from Jericho; for Asher was no longer hostile to the Christ.

3 And while the guests sat at the board behold a cry, The village is a-fire! and all rushed out into the streets, and, lo, the homes of many neighbors were in flames.

4 And in an upper room an infant lay asleep, and none could pass the flames to save. The mother, wild with grief, was calling on the men to save her child.

5 Then, with a voice that made the spirits of the fire pale and tremble, Jesus said, Peace, peace, be still!

6 And then he walked through smoke and flame, climbed up the falling stair, and in a moment came again, and in his arms he brought the child. And not a trace of fire was on himself, his raiment, or the child.

7 Then Jesus raised his hand, rebuked the spirits of the fire, commanding them to cease their awful work, and be at rest.

8 And then, as though the waters of the sea were all at once poured on the flames, the fire ceased to burn.

9 And when the fury of the fire was spent the multitudes were wild to see the man who could control the fire, and Jesus said,

10 Man was not made for fire, but fire was made for man.

11 When man comes to himself and comprehends the fact that he is son of God, and knows that in himself lies all the powers of God, he is a master mind and all the elements will hear his voice and gladly do his will.

12 Two sturdy asses bind the will of man; their names are Fear and Unbelief. When these are caught and turned aside, the will of man will know no bounds; then man has but to speak and it is done.

13 And then the guests returned and sat about the board. A little child came in and stood by Jesus' side.

14 She laid her hand on Jesus' arm and said, Please, Master Jesus, hear! my father is a drunken man; my mother toils from morn till night and when she brings her wages home my father snatches them away and squanders every cent for drink, and mother and us little ones are hungry all the night.

15 Please, Master Jesus, come with me and touch my father's heart. He is so good and kind when he is just himself; I know it is the wine that makes another man of him.

16 And Jesus went out with the child; he found the wretched home; he spoke in kindness to the mother and the little ones, and then upon a bed of straw he found the drunken man.

17 He took him by the hand and raised him up and said, My brother, man, made in the image of our Father-God, will you arise and come with me?

18 Your neighbors are in sore distress; they have lost all they had in this fierce fire, and men must build their homes again and you and I must lead the way.

19 And then the man arose; the two went arm in arm to view the wrecks. .

20 They heard the mothers and the children crying in the streets; they saw their wretchedness.

21 And Jesus said, My friend, here is a work for you to do. Just lead the way in helpfulness; I'm sure the men of Bethany will furnish you the means and help.

22 The spark of hope that had so long been smouldering in the man was fanned into a flame. He threw his ragged coat aside; he was himself again.

23 And then he called for help; not for himself, but for the homeless ones; and everybody helped. The ruined homes were built again.

24 And then he saw his own poor den; his heart was stirred into its depths.

25 The pride of manhood filled his soul; he said, This wretched den shall be a home. He worked as he had never wrought before, and everybody helped.

26 And in a little while the den became a home indeed; the flowers of love bloomed everywhere.

27 The mother and the little ones were filled with joy; the father never drank again.

28 A man was saved, and no one ever said a word about neglect or drunkenness, nor urged him to reform.

CHAPTER 93.

The Christines go through a field of ripe wheat, and the disciples eat of the wheat. Jesus exonerates them. The Christines return to Capernaum. Jesus heals a withered hand on the Sabbath, and defends his deed.

ANOTHER Sabbath day had come and Jesus and the twelve walked through a field of ripened wheat.

2 And they were hungry and they took the heads of wheat and in their hands threshed out the grain and ate.

3 Among the men who followed them were Pharisees of strictest sect, and when they saw the twelve thresh out the wheat and eat, they said to Jesus,

4 Sir, why do the twelve do that which is not lawful on the Sabbath day?

5 And Jesus said, Have you not heard what David did when he and those who followed him had need of food?

6 How he went to the house of God and from the table in the Holy Place took of the presence bread and ate, and gave to those who followed him?

7 I tell you, men, the needs of man are higher than the law of rites.

8 And in our sacred books we read how priests profane the Sabbath day in many ways while they are serving in the Holy Place, and still are free from guilt.

9 The Sabbath day was made for man; man was not made to fit the Sabbath day.

10 The man is son of God and under the eternal law of right, which is the highest law, he may annul the statute laws.

11 The law of sacrifice is but the law of man, and in our law we read that God desires mercy first; and mercy stands above all statute laws.

12 The son of man is Lord of every law. Did not a prophet sum the duties of the man when in the book he wrote: In mercy follow justice and walk humbly with your God?

13 Then Jesus and the twelve returned to Galilee, and on the day before the Sabbath day they reached the home of Jesus in Capernaum.

14 And on the Sabbath day they went up to the synagogue. The multitudes were there and Jesus taught.

15 Among the worshippers was one, a man who had a withered hand. The scribes and Pharisees observed that Jesus saw the man, and then they said,

16 What will he do? Will he attempt to heal upon the Sabbath day?

17 And Jesus knew their thoughts and he called to the man who had the withered hand and said, Arise, stand forth before these men.

18 And Jesus said, You scribes and Pharisees, speak out and answer me: Is it a crime to save a life upon the Sabbath day?

19 If you had sheep and one of them fell in a pit upon the Sabbath day would you do wrong to take it out?

20 Or would it please your God to let it suffer in the mire until another day?

21 But his accusers held their peace.

22 And then he said to them, Are sheep of greater value than a man?

23 The law of God is written on the rock of Right; and Justice wrote the law, and Mercy was the pen.

24 And then he said, Man, raise your hand and stretch it forth. He raised his hand; it was restored.

25 The Pharisees were filled with rage. They called in secret council the Herodians, and they began to plot and plan how they might bring about his death.

26 They were afraid to publicly accuse, because the multitudes stood forth in his defense.

27 And Jesus and the twelve went down and walked beside the sea, and many people followed them.

CHAPTER 94.

The Sermon on the Mount. Jesus reveals to the twelve the secret of prayer. The model prayer. The law of forgiveness. The holy fast. The evil of deceit. Almsgiving.

NEXT morning e'er the sun had risen Jesus and the twelve went to a mountain near the sea to pray; and Jesus taught the twelve disciples how to pray. He said,

2 Prayer is the deep communion of the soul with God;

3 So when you pray do not deceive yourselves as do the hypocrites who love to stand upon the streets and in the synagogues and pour out many words to please the ears of men.

4 And they adorn themselves with pious airs that they may have the praise of men. They seek the praise of men and their reward is sure.

5 But when you pray, go to the closet of your soul; close all the doors, and in the holy silence, pray.

6 You need not speak a multitude of words, nor yet repeat the words again and then again, as heathen do. Just say,

7 Our Father-God who art in heaven; holy is thy name. Thy kingdom come; thy will be done on earth as it is done in heaven.

8 Give us this day our needed bread;

9 Help us forget the debts that other people owe to us, that all our debts may be discharged.

10 And shield us from the tempter's snares that are too great for us to bear;

11 And when they come give us the strength to overcome.

12 If you would be discharged from all the debts you owe to God and man, the debts you have in-

curred by wilfully transgressing law,

13 You must pass by the debts of every man; for as you deal with other men your God will deal with you.

14 And when you fast you may not advertise the deed.

15 When fast the hypocrites they paint their faces, look demure, assume a pious pose, that they may seem to men to fast.

16 A fast is deed of soul, and like a prayer, it is a function of the silence of the soul.

17 God never passes by unnoticed any prayer, or fast. He walks within the silence, and his benedictions rest on every effort of the soul.

18 Deception is hypocrisy, and you shall not assume to be what you are not.

19 You may not clothe yourselves in special garb to advertise your piety, nor yet assume the tone of voice that men conceive to be a holy voice.

20 And when you give to aid the needy ones, blow not a trumpet in the street, nor synagogue to advertise your gift.

21 He who does alms for praise of men has his reward from men; but God regardeth not.

22 In giving alms do not let the right hand know the secret of the left.

CHAPTER 95.

The Sermon on the Mount, continued. Jesus pronounces the eight beatitudes and the eight woes. Speaks words of encouragement. Emphasizes the exalted character of the apostolic work.

AND Jesus and the twelve went to the mountain top, and Jesus said,

2 Twelve pillars of the church, apostles of the Christ; light-bearers of the sun of life and ministers of God to men:

3 In just a little while you must go forth alone, and preach the gospel of the king, first to the Jews and then to all the world.

4 And you shall go, not with a scourge of cords to drive; you cannot drive men to the king;

5 But you shall go in love and helpfulness and lead the way to right and light.

6 Go forth and say, The kingdom is at hand.

7 Worthy are the strong in spirit; theirs the kingdom is.

8 Worthy are the meek; they shall possess the land.

9 Worthy they who hunger and who thirst for right; they shall be satisfied.

10 Worthy are the merciful; and mercy shall be shown to them.

11 Worthy they who gain the mastery of self; they have the key of power.

12 Worthy are the pure in heart; and they shall see the king.

13 Worthy they who are maligned and wronged because they do the right; their persecutors they shall bless.

14 Worthy is the trustful child of faith; he shall sit in the throne of power.

15 Be not discouraged when the world shall persecute and call you curst; but rather be exceeding glad.

16 The prophets and the seers, and all the good of earth, have been maligned.

17 If you are worthy of the crown of life you will be slandered, vilified and curst on earth.

18 Rejoice when evil men shall drive you from their ways and cause

your name to be a hiss and by-word in the street.

19 I say, rejoice; but deal in mercy with the doers of the wrong; they are but children at their play; they know not what they do.

20 Rejoice not over fallen foes. As you help men rise from the depth of sin, so God will help you on to greater heights.

21 Woe to the rich is gold and lands; they have temptations multi-form.

22 Woe unto men who walk at will in pleasure's paths; their ways are full of snares and dangerous pits.

23 Woe to the proud; they stand upon a precipice; destruction waits for them.

24 Woe to the man of greed; for what he has is not his own; and, lo, another comes; his wealth is gone.

25 Woe to the hypocrite; his form is fair to look upon; his heart is filled with carcasses and dead men's bones.

26 Woe to the cruel and relent-less man; he is himself the victim of his deeds.

27 The evil he would do to other men rebounds; the scourger is the scourged.

28 Woe to the libertine who preys upon the virtues of the weak. The hour comes when he will be the weak, the victim of a libertine of greater power.

29 Woe unto you when all the world shall speak in praise of you. The world speaks not in praise of men who live within the Holy Breath; it speaks in praise of proph-ets false, and of illusions base.

30 You men who walk in Holy Breath are salt, the salt of earth; but if you lose your virtue you are salt in name alone, worth nothing more than dust.

31 And you are light; are called to light the world.

32 A city on a hill cannot be hid; its lights are seen afar; and while you stand upon the hills of life men see your light and imitate your works and honor God.

33 Men do not light a lamp and hide it in a cask; they put it on a stand that it may light the house.

34 You are the lamps of God; must not stand in the shade of earth illusions, but in the open, high upon the stand.

35 ⟨I am not come to nullify the law, nor to destroy; but to fulfill.

36 The Law, the Prophets and the Psalms were written in the wis-dom of the Holy Breath and cannot fail.

37 The heavens and earth that are will change and pass away; the word of God is sure; it cannot pass until it shall accomplish that where-unto it hath been sent.

38 Whoever disregards the law of God and teaches men to do the same, becomes a debtor unto God and cannot see his face until he has returned and paid his debt by sacri-fice of life.

39 But he who hearkens unto God and keeps his law and does his will on earth, shall rule with Christ.

40 The scribes and Pharisees re-gard the letter of the law; they can-not comprehend the spirit of the law;

41 And if your righteousness does not exceed the righteousness of scribe and Pharisee you cannot come into the kingdom of the soul.

42 It is not what man does that gives him right to enter through the gates; his pass word is his character and his desire is his character.

43   The letter of the law deals with the acts of man; the spirit of the law takes note of his desires.

CHAPTER 96.

The Sermon on the Mount, continued. Jesus considers the Ten Commandments. The philosophy of Christ the spirit of the Commandments. Jesus unfolds the spiritual aspects of the first four Commandments.

GOD gave the Ten Commandments unto men; upon the mountain Moses saw the words of God; he wrote them down on solid rock; they cannot be destroyed.

2   These Ten Commandments show the justice side of God; but now the love of God made manifest brings mercy on the wings of Holy Breath.

3   Upon the unity of God the law was built. In all the world there is one force; Jehovah is Almighty God.

4   Jehovah wrote upon the heavens and Moses read,

5   I am Almighty God and you shall have no God but me.

6   There is one force, but many phases of that force; these phases men call powers.

7   All powers are of God; and they are manifests of God; they are the Spirits of the God.

8   If men could seem to find another force and worship at its shrine, they would but court illusion, vain,

9   A shadow of the One, Jehovah, God, and they who worship shadows are but shadows on the wall; for men are what they court.

10   And God would have all men to be the substance, and in mercy he commanded, You shall seek no God but me.

11   And finite man can never comprehend infinite things. Man cannot make an image of the Infinite in force.

12   And when men make a God of stone or wood or clay they make an image of a shade; and they who worship at the shrine of shades are shades.

13   So God in mercy said, You shall not carve out images of wood, or clay, or stone.

14   Such idols are ideals, abased ideals, and men can gain no higher plane than their ideals.

15   The God is Spirit, and in spirit men must worship if they would attain a consciousness of God.

16   But man can never make a picture or an image of the Holy Breath.

17   The name of God man may not speak with carnal lips; with Holy Breath alone can man pronounce the name.

18   In vanity men think they know the name of God; they speak it lightly and irreverently, and thus they are accursed.

19   If men did know the sacred name and spoke it with unholy lips, they would not live to speak it once again.

20   But God in mercy has not yet unveiled his name to those who cannot speak with Holy Breath.

21   But they who speak the substitute in idle way are guilty in the sight of God, who said,

22   You shall not take the name of God in vain.

23   The number of the Holy Breath is seven, and God holds in his hands the sevens of time.

24   In forming worlds he rested on the seventh day, and every seventh day is set apart as Sabbath day for men. God said,

25   The seventh is the Sabbath

of the Lord thy God; remember it and keep it wholly set apart for works of holiness; that is, for works not for the selfish self, but for the universal self.

26 Men may do work for self upon the six days of the week; but on the Sabbath of the Lord they must do naught for self.

27 This day is consecrated unto God; but man serves God by serving man.

CHAPTER 97.

The Sermon on the Mount, continued. Jesus unfolds to the twelve the spiritual aspects of the fifth and sixth Commandments.

GOD is not force alone; for wisdom is his counterpart.

2 When cherubim instructed man in wisdom's ways they said that wisdom is the Mother of the race, as force is Father of the race.

3 The man who honors the almighty and omniscient God is blessed, and in the tables of the law we read,

4 Pay homage to your Father and your Mother of the race, that your days may be prolonged upon the land that they have given you.

5 The letter of the law commands; You shall not kill; and he who kills must stand before the judgment seat,

6 A person may desire to kill, yet if he does not kill he is not judged by law.

7 The spirit of the law avers that he who shall desire to kill, or seeks revenge, is angry with a man without sufficient cause, must answer to the judge;

8 And he who calls his brother soulless vagabond shall answer to the council of the just;

9 And he who calls his brother a degenerate, a dog, fans into life the burning fires of hell within himself.

10 Now, in the higher law we read that if your brother is aggrieved by something you have done, before you offer unto God your gifts, go forth and find your brother and be reconciled to him.

11 It is not well to let the sun go down upon your wrath.

12 If he will not be reconciled when you have laid aside all selfish pleas, have waived all selfish rights, you will be guiltless in the sight of God; then go and offer unto God your gifts.

13 If you owe aught to any man and cannot pay; or if a man shall claim a greater sum than is his due, it is not well that you dispute his claims.

14 Resistance is the sire of anger; there is no mercy and no reason in a wrathful man.

15 I tell you it is better far to suffer loss than go to law, or call upon the courts of men to judge of right and wrong.

16 The law of carnal man would say, Eye for eye and tooth for tooth; resist encroachment on your rights.

17 But this is not the law of God. The Holy Breath would say, Resist not him who would deprive you of your goods.

18 He who would take your coat by force is still a brother man and you should gain his heart, which by resistance cannot be done;

19 Give him your coat and offer him still more and more; in time the man will rise above the brute; you will have saved him from himself.

20 Refuse not him who calls for help and give to him who asks to borrow aught.

21 And if a man shall strike you

in a fitful, or an angry way, it is not well to smite him in return.

22 Men call him coward who will not fight and thus defend his rights; but he is much the greater man who is assailed, is smitten and does not smite;

23 Who is maligned and answers not, than he who smites the smiter and reviles the one who slanders him.

24 It has been said in olden times that man shall love his friend and hate his foe; but, lo, I say,

25 Be merciful unto your foes; bless those who slander you; do good to those who do you harm and pray for those who trample on your rights.

26 Remember, you are children of the God who makes his sun to rise alike upon the evil and the good, who sends his rain upon the unjust and the just.

27 If you do unto other men as they do unto you, you are but slaves, but followers in the way to death.

28 But you, as children of the light, must lead the way.

29 Do unto others as you would have them do unto you.

30 When you do good to those who have done good to you, you do no more than other men; the publicans do that.

31 If you salute your friends and not your foes, you are like other men; the publicans have set the pace.

32 Be perfect as your Father-God in heaven is.

CHAPTER 98.

The Sermon on the Mount, continued. Jesus reveals to the twelve the spiritual aspects of the seventh, eighth and tenth Commandments.

THE law forbids adultery; but in the eyes of law adultery is an overt act, the satisfaction of the sensuous self outside the marriage bonds.

2 Now, marriage in the sight of law is but a promise made by man and woman, by the sanction of a priest, to live for aye in harmony and love.

3 No priest nor officer has power from God to bind two souls in wedded love.

4 What is the marriage tie? Is it comprised in what a priest or officer may say?

5 Is it the scroll on which the officer or priest has written the permission for the two to live in marriage bonds?

6 Is it the promise of the two that they will love each other until death?

7 Is love a passion that is subject to the will of man?

8 Can man pick up his love, as he would pick up precious gems, and lay it down, or give it out to any one?

9 Can love be bought and sold like sheep?

10 Love is the power of God that binds two souls and makes them one; there is no power on earth that can dissolve the bond.

11 The bodies may be forced apart by man or death for just a little time; but they will meet again.

12 Now, in this bond of God we find the marriage tie; all other unions are but bonds of straw, and they who live in them commit adultery,

13 The same as they who satisfy their lust without the sanction of an officer or priest.

14 But more than this; the man or woman who indulges lustful thoughts commits adultery.

15 Whom God has joined together man cannot part; whom man has joined together live in sin.

16 Upon a table of the law, the great lawgiver wrote, Thou shalt not steal.

17 Before the eyes of law a man to steal must take a thing that can be seen with eyes of flesh, without the knowledge or consent of him to whom the thing belongs.

18 But, lo, I say that he who in his heart desires to possess that which is not his own, and would deprive the owner of the thing without his knowledge or consent, is in the sight of God, a thief.

19 The things that men see not with eyes of flesh are of more worth than are the things that man can see.

20 A man's good name is worth a thousand mines of gold, and he who says a word or does a deed that injures or defames that name has taken what is not his own, and is a thief.

21 Upon a table of the law we also read: Thou shalt not covet anything.

22 To covet is an all-consuming wish to have what is not right for one to have.

23 And such a wish, within the spirit of the law, is theft.

CHAPTER 99.

The Sermon on the Mount, continued. Jesus unfolds to the twelve the spiritual aspects of the ninth Commandment.

THE law has said: Thou shalt not lie; but in the eyes of law a man to lie must tell in words what is not true.

2 Now, in the light of spirit law, deceit in any form is nothing but a lie.

3 A man may lie by look or act; yea, even by his silence may deceive, and thus be guilty in the eyes of Holy Breath.

4 It has been said in olden times: Thou shalt not swear by thine own life.

5 But, lo, I say, Swear not at all; not by the head, the heart, the eye, nor hand; not by the sun, the moon, nor stars;

6 Not by the name of God, nor by the name of any spirit, good or bad.

7 You shall not swear by anything; for in an oath there is no gain.

8 A man whose word must be propped up by oath of any kind is not trustworthy in the sight of God or man.

9 By oath you cannot make a leaf to fall, nor turn the color of a hair.

10 The man of worth just speaks, and men know that he speaks the truth.

11 The man who pours out many words to make men think he speaks the truth, is simply making smoke to hide a lie.

12 And there are many men with seeming double hearts; men who would serve two masters at a time—two masters quite adverse.

13 Men feign to worship God upon the Sabbath day and then pay court to Beelzebul on every other day.

14 No man can serve two masters at a time no more than he can ride two asses at a time that go in different ways.

15 The man who feigns to worship God and Beelzebul is foe of God, a pious devil and a curse of men.

16 And men cannot lay treasures up in heaven and earth at once.

17 Then, lo, I say, Lift up your

eyes and see the safety vaults of heaven, and there deposit every gem,

18   Where moth and rust cannot corrupt; where thieves cannot break in and steal.

19   There are no safety vaults on earth; no place secure from moth, and rust and thieves.

20   The treasures of the earth are but illusive things that pass away.

21   Be not deceived; your treasures are the anchor of the soul, and where your treasures are your heart will be.

22   Fix not your heart upon the things of earth; be anxious not about the things to eat, or drink, or wear.

23   God cares for those who trust in him and serve the race.

24   Behold the birds! They praise God in their songs; the earth is made more glorious by their ministry of joy; God keeps them in the hollow of his hand,

25   And not a sparrow falls to earth without his care; and every one that falls shall rise again.

26   Behold the flowers of earth! they trust in God and grow; they make the earth resplendent with their beauty and perfume.

27   Look at the lilies of the field, the messengers of holy love. No son of man, not even Solomon in all his excellence, was ever clothed like one of these.

28   And yet they simply trust in God; they feed from out his hand; they lay their heads to rest upon his breast.

29   If God so clothes and feeds the flowers and birds that do his will, will he not feed and clothe his children when they trust in him?

30   Seek first the kingdom of the soul, the righteousness of God, the good of men, and murmur not; God will protect, and feed, and clothe.

CHAPTER 100.

The Sermon on the Mount, continued. Jesus formulates and presents to the twelve a practical code of spiritual ethics.

THERE is a rule that carnal man has made, and which he rigidly observes:

2   Do unto other men as they do unto you. As others judge, they judge; as others give, they give.

3   Now, while you walk with men as men, judge not, and you shall not be judged.

4   For as you judge you shall be judged, and as you give it shall be given to you. If you condemn, you are condemned.

5   When you show mercy, men are merciful to you, and if you love in such a way that carnal man can comprehend your love, you will be well beloved.

6   And so the wise man of this world does unto other men as he would have them do to him.

7   The carnal man does good to other men for selfish gain, for he expects to have his blessings multiplied and then returned; he does not stop to note the end.

8   Man is himself the field; his deeds are seeds, and what he does to others grows apace; the harvest time is sure.

9   Behold the yield! If he has sown the wind, he reaps the wind; if he has sown the noxious seeds of scandal, theft and hate; of sensuality and crime,

10   The harvest is assured and he must reap what he has sown;

yea, more; the seeds produce an hundred fold.

11 The fruit of righteousness and peace and love and joy can never spring from noxious seeds; the fruit is like the seed.

12 And when you sow, sow seeds of right, because it is the right, and not in way of trade, expecting rich rewards.

13 The carnal man abhors the spirit law, because it takes away his liberty to live in sin; beneath its light he cannot satisfy his passions and desires.

14 He is at enmity with him who walks in Holy Breath. The carnal man has killed the holy men of old, the prophets and the seers.

15 And he will buffet you; will charge you falsely, scourge you and imprison you, and think he does the will of God to slay you in the streets.

16 But you may not prejudge nor censure him who does you wrong.

17 Each one has problems to¯be solved, and he must solve them for himself.

18 The man who scourges you may have a load of sin to bear; but how about your own?

19 A little sin in one who walks in Holy Breath is greater in the sight of God than monster sins in him who never knew the way.

20 How can you see the splinter in your brother's eye while you have chunks within your own?

21 First take the chunks from out your eye and then you may behold the splinter in your brother's eye and help him take it out,

22 And while your eyes are full of foreign things you cannot see the way, for you are blind,

23 And when the blind lead forth the blind, both lose the way and fall into the slough.

24 If you would lead the way to God you must be clear in sight, as well as pure in heart.

CHAPTER 101.

The Sermon on the Mount, conclu-
ded. The concluding part of the
code of ethics. The Christines re-
turn to Capernaum.

THE fruitage of the tree of life is all too fine to feed the carnal mind.

2 If you would throw a diamond to a hungry dog, lo, he would turn away, or else attack you in a rage.

3 The incense that is sweet to God is quite offensive unto Beelzebul; the bread of heaven is but chaff to men who cannot comprehend the spirit life.

4 The master must be wise and feed the soul with what it can digest.

5 If you have not the food for every man, just ask and you shall have; seek earnestly and you shall find.

6 Just speak the Word and knock; the door will fly ajar.

7 No one has ever asked in faith and did not have; none ever sought in vain; no one who ever knocked aright has failed to find an open door.

8 When men shall ask you for the bread of heaven, turn not away, nor give to them the fruit of carnal trees.

9 If one, a son, would ask you for a loaf, would you give him a stone? If he would ask you for a fish, would you give him a serpent of the dust?

10 What you would have your God give unto you, give unto men. The measure of your worth lies in your service unto men.

11 There is a way that leads unto the perfect life; few find it at a time.

12 It is a narrow way; it lies among the rocks and pitfalls of the carnal life; but in the way there are no pitfalls and no rocks.

13 There is a way that leads to wretchedness and want. It is a spacious way and many walk therein. It lies among the pleasure groves of carnal life.

14 Beware, for many claim to walk the way of life who walk the way of death.

15 But they are false in word and deed; false prophets they. They clothe themselves in skins of sheep, while they are vicious wolves.

16 They cannot long conceal themselves; men know them by their fruits;

17 You cannot gather grapes from thorns, nor from the thistles, figs.

18 The fruit is daughter of the tree and, like the parent, so the child; and every tree that bears not wholesome fruit is plucked up by the roots and cast away,

19 Because a man prays long and loud is not a sign that he is saint. The praying men are not all in the kingdom of the soul.

20 The man who lives the holy life, who does the will of God, abides within the kingdom of the soul.

21 The good man from the treasures of his heart sends blessedness and peace to all the world.

22 The evil man sends thoughts that blight and wither hope and joy and fill the world with wretchedness and woe.

23 Men think and act and speak out of the abundance of the heart.

24 And when the judgment hour shall come a host of men will enter pleadings for themselves and think to buy the favor of the judge with words.

25 And they will say, Lo, we have wrought a multitude of works in the Omnific name,

26 Have we not prophesied? Have we not cured all manner of disease? Have we not cast the evil spirits out of those obsessed?

27 And then the judge will say, I know you not. You rendered service unto God in words when in your heart you worshipped Beelzebul.

28 The evil one may use the powers of life, and do a multitude of mighty works. Depart from me, you workers of iniquity.

29 The man who hears the words of life and does them not is like the man who builds his house upon the sand, which when the floods come on, is washed away and all is lost.

30 But he who hears the words of life and in an honest, sincere heart receives and treasures them and lives the holy life,

31 Is like the man who builds his house upon the rock; the floods may come, the winds may blow, the storms may beat upon his house; it is not moved.

32 Go forth and build your life upon the solid rock of truth, and all the powers of the evil one will shake it not.

33 And Jesus finished all his sayings on the mount and then he, with the twelve, returned unto Capernaum.

CHAPTER 102.

The Christines at the home of Jesus. Jesus unfolds to them the secret doctrine. They go through all Galilee and teach and heal. Jesus brings to life the son of a widow at Nain. They return to Capernaum.

THE twelve apostles went with Jesus to his home, and there abode for certain days.

2 And Jesus told them many things about the inner life that may not now be written in a book.

3 Now, in Capernaum there lived a man of wealth, a Roman captain of a hundred men, who loved the Jews and who had built for them a synagogue.

4 A servant of this man was paralyzed, and he was sick nigh unto death.

5 The captain knew of Jesus and had heard that by the sacred Word he healed the sick, and he had faith in him.

6 He sent a message by the elders of the Jews to Jesus, and he plead for help.

7 And Jesus recognized the captain's faith and went at once to heal the sick; the captain met him on the way and said to him,

8 Lo, Lord, it is not well that you should come into my house; I am not worthy of the presence of a man of God.

9 I am a man of war; my life is spent with those who ofttimes take the lives of fellow men,

10 And surely he who comes to save would be dishonored if he came beneath my roof.

11 If you will speak the Word I know my servant will be well.

12 And Jesus turned and said to those who followed him,

13 Behold the captain's faith; I have not seen such faith, no, not in Israel.

14 Behold, the feast is spread for you; but while you doubt and wait, the alien comes in faith and takes the bread of life.

15 Then turning to the man he said, Go on your way; according to your faith so shall it be; your servant lives.

16 It came to pass that at the time that Jesus spoke the Word the palsied man arose, and he was well.

17 And then the Christines went abroad to teach. And as they came to Nain, a city on the Hermon way, they saw a multitude about the gates.

18 It was a funeral train; a widow's son was dead, and friends were bearing out the body to the tomb.

19 It was the widow's only son, and she was wild with grief. And Jesus said to her, Weep not, I am the life; your son shall live.

20 And Jesus raised his hand; the bearers of the dead stood still.

21 And Jesus touched the bier and said, Young man, return.

22 The soul returned; the body of the dead was filled with life; the man sat up and spoke.

23 The people were astonished at the scene, and every one exclaimed, Praise God.

24 A Jewish priest stood forth and said, Behold, a mighty prophet has appeared; and all the people said, Amen.

25 The Christines journeyed on; they taught, and healed the sick in many towns of Galilee, and then they came again unto Capernaum.

CHAPTER 103.

The Christines in Jesus' home. Jesus teaches the twelve and the foreign masters every morning. Jesus receives messengers from John, the harbinger, and sends him words of encouragement. He eulogizes the character of John.

THE home of Jesus was a school where in the early morning hours the twelve apostles and the foreign priests were taught the secret things of God.

2 And there were present priests from China, India and from Babylon; from Persia, Egypt and from Greece,

3 Who came to sit at Jesus' feet to learn the wisdom that he brought to men, that they might teach their people how to live the holy life.

4 And Jesus taught them how to teach; he told them of the trials of the way, and how to make these trials serve the race.

5 He taught them how to live the holy life that they might conquer death;

6 He taught them what the end of mortal life will be, when man has reached the consciousness that he and God are one.

7 The after midday hours were given to the multitudes who came to learn the way of life and to be healed; and many did believe and were baptized.

8 Now, in his prison by the Bitter Sea the harbinger had heard of all the mighty works that Jesus did.

9 His prison life was hard, and he was sore distressed, and he began to doubt.

10 And to himself he said, I wonder if this Jesus is the Christ of whom the prophets wrote!

11 Was I mistaken in my work? Was I, indeed, one sent from God to pave the way for him who shall redeem our people, Israel?

12 And then he sent some of his friends, who came to see him in his prison cell, up to Capernaum that they might learn about this man, and bring him word.

13 The men found Jesus in his home, and said, Behold the harbinger sent us to ask, Are you the Christ? or is he yet to come?

14 But Jesus answered not; he simply bade the men to tarry certain days that they might see and hear.

15 They saw him heal the sick, and cause the lame to walk, the deaf to hear, the blind to see;

16 They saw him cast the evil spirits out of those obsessed; they saw him raise the dead.

17 They heard him preach the gospel to the poor.

18 Then Jesus said to them, Go on your way; return to John and tell him all that you have seen and heard; then he will know. They went their way.

19 The multitudes were there, and Jesus said to them, Once you were crowding Jordan's fords; you filled the wilderness.

20 What did you go to see? The trees of Juda, and the flowers of Heth? Or did you go to see a man in kingly garb? Or did you go to see a prophet and a seer?

21 I tell you, men, you know not whom you saw. A prophet? Yea, and more; a messenger whom God had sent to pave the way for what you see and hear this day.

22 Among the men of earth a greater man has never lived than John.

23 Behold I say, This man whom Herod bound in chains and cast into a prison cell, is God's Elijah come again to earth.

24 Elijah, who did not pass the gates of death, whose body of this flesh was changed, and he awoke in Paradise.

25 When John came forth and preached the gospel of repentance for the cleansing of the soul, the common folks believed and were baptized.

26 The lawyers and the Pharisees accepted not the teachings of this man; were not baptized.

27 Behold, neglected opportunities will never come again.

28 Behold, the people are unstable as the waters of the sea; they seek to be excused from righteousness.

29 John came and ate no bread, and drank no wine. He lived the simplest life apart from men, and people said, He is obsessed.

30 Another comes who eats and drinks and lives in homes like other men, and people say, He is a glutton, an inebriate, a friend of publicans and those who sin.

31 Woe unto you, you cities of the vale of Galilee, where all the mighty works of God are done! Woe to Chorazan and Bethsaida!

32 If half the mighty works that have been done in you were done in Tyre and in Sidon they would have long ago repented of their sins, and sought the way of right.

33 And when the judgment day shall come, lo, Tyre and Sidon will be called more worthy than will you,

34 Because they slighted not their gifts, while you have thrown away the pearl of greatest price.

35 Woe unto you Capernaum! Behold, you are exalted now, but you shall be abased;

36 For if the mighty works that have been done in you had but been done within the cities of the plain— of Sodom and Zeboim—they would have heard and turned to God; would not have been destroyed.

37 They perished in their ignorance; they had no light; but you have heard; you have the evidence.

38 The light of life has shown above your hills and all the shores of Galilee have been ablaze with light;

39 The glory of the Lord has shown in every street and synagogue and home; but you have spurned the light.

40 And, lo, I say, The judgment day will come and God will deal in greater mercy with the cities of the plains than he will deal with you.

CHAPTER 104.

Jesus teaches the multitudes. Attends a feast in Simon's house. A wealthy courtesan anoints him with precious balm. Simon rebukes him and he preaches a sermon on false respectability.

AND Jesus looked upon the multitudes who pressed about for selfish gain.

2 The men of learning and of wealth, of reputation and of power, were there; but they knew not the Christ.

3 Their eyes were blinded by the tinseled glitter of their selfish selves; they could not see the king.

4 And though they walked within the light, they groped about in dark—a darkness like the night of death.

5 And Jesus cast his eyes to heaven and said,

6 I thank thee, Holy One of heaven and earth, that while the light is hidden from the wise and great, it is revealed to babes.

7 Then turning to the multitudes he said, I come to you not in the name of man, nor in a strength my own;

8 The wisdom and the virtue that I bring to you are from above; they are the wisdom and the virtue of the God whom we adore.

9 The words I speak are not my words; I give to you what I receive.

10 Come unto me all you who labor and pull heavy loads and I will give you aid.

11 Put on the yoke of Christ

with me; it does not chafe; it is an easy yoke.

12 Together we will pull the load of life with ease; and so rejoice.

13 A Pharisee, whose name was Simon, made a feast, and Jesus was the honored guest.

14 And as they sat about the board, a courtesan who had been cured of her desire to sin by what she had received and seen in Jesus' ministry, came uninvited to the feast.

15 She brought an alabaster box of costly balm and as the guests reclined she came to Jesus in her joy, because she had been freed from sin,

16 Her tears fell fast, she kissed his feet, and dried them with her hair, and she anointed them with balm.

17 And Simon thought, he did not speak aloud, This man is not a prophet or he would know the kind of woman that approaches him, and would drive her away.

18 But Jesus knew his thoughts, and said to him, My host, I have a word to say to you.

19 And Simon said, Say on.

20 And Jesus said, Sin is a monster of iniquity; it may be small; it may be large; it may be something done; it may be something left un-

21 Behold, one person leads a life of sin and is at last redeemed; another, in a careless mood, forgets to do the things he ought to do; but he reforms and is forgiven. Now, which of these has merited the higher praise?

22 And Simon said, The one who overcame the errors of a life.

23 And Jesus said, You speak the truth.

24 Behold, this woman who has bathed my feet with tears and dried

them with her hair and covered them with balm!

25 For years she led a life of sin, but when she heard the words of life she sought forgiveness and she found.

26 But when I came into your house as guest you gave me not a bowl of water that I might wash my hands and feet, which every loyal Jew must do before he feasts.

27 Now, tell me, Simon, which of these, this woman or yourself, is worthy of most praise?

28 But Simon answered not.

29 Then to the woman Jesus said, Your sins are all forgiven; your faith has saved you; go in peace.

30 And then the guests who sat around the board, began to say within themselves, What manner of a man is this who says, Thy sins are all forgiven?

CHAPTER 105.

Under the patronage of a number of wealthy women, the Christines make a grand missionary tour. In his teaching Jesus lauds sincerity and rebukes hypocrisy. He speaks concerning the sin against the Holy Breath.

NOW, many women who possessed much wealth, and who abode in other towns of Galilee, implored that Jesus and the twelve, together with the masters from the foreign lands, would thither go and preach and heal.

2 Among these anxious ones were Mary Magdalene, who was obsessed by seven homeless spirits of the air, which had been driven out by the Omnific Word which Jesus spoke;

3 Susanna, who owned vast estates at Cæsarea-Philippi;

4 Johanna, wife of Chuza, one of Herod's court;

5 And Rachel from the coast of Tyre;

6 And others from beyond the Jordan and the sea of Galilee.

7 And they provided ample means and three times seven men went forth.

8 They preached the gospel of the Christ, and they baptized the multitudes who made confession of their faith; they healed the sick and raised the dead.

9 And Jesus wrought and taught from early morn until the day had gone, and then into the night; he did not stop to eat.

10 His friends became alarmed lest he should fail from loss of strength, and they laid hold of him and would, by force, have taken him away to place of rest.

11 But he rebuked them not; he said, Have you not read that God will give his angels charge concerning me?

12 That they would hold me fast and suffer not that I should come to want?

13 I tell you, men, while I am giving out my strength unto these anxious, waiting throngs I find myself at rest within the arms of God,

14 Whose blessed messengers bring down to me the bread of life.

15 There is a tide just once in human life.

16 These people now are willing to receive the truth; their opportunity is now: our opportunity is now.

17 And if we do not teach them while we may, the tide will ebb;

18 They may not care again to hear the truth; then tell me, Who will bear the guilt?

19 And so he taught and healed.

20 Among the multitudes were men of every shade of thought.

They were divided in their views concerning everything that Jesus said.

21 Some saw in him a God, and would have worshipped him; and others saw in him a devil of the nether world and would have cast him in a pit.

22 And some were trying hard to lead a double life; like little lions of the ground that take upon themselves the color of the thing they rest upon.

23 These people without anchorage of any sort, are friends or foes as seemed to serve them best.

24 And Jesus said, No man can serve two masters at a time. No man can be a friend and foe at once.

25 All men are rising up, or sinking down; are building up, or tearing down.

26 If you are gathering not the precious grain, then you are throwing it away.

27 He is a coward who would feign to be a friend, or foe, to please another man.

28 You men, do not deceive yourselves in thought; your hearts are known;

29 Hypocrisy will blight a soul as surely as the breath of Beelzebul. An honest evil man is more esteemed by guardians of the soul than a dishonest pious man.

30 If you would curse the son of man, just curse him out aloud.

31 A curse is poison to the inner man, and if you hold and swallow down a curse it never will digest; lo, it will poison every atom of your soul.

32 And if you sin against a son of man, you may be pardoned and your guilt be cleansed by acts of kindness and of love;

33 But if you sin against the Holy Breath by disregarding her

when she would open up the doors of life for you;

34 By closing up the windows of the soul when she would pour the light of love into your hearts, and cleanse them with the fires of God;

35 Your guilt shall not be blotted out in this, nor in the life to come.

36 An opportunity has gone to come no more, and you must wait until the ages roll again.

37 Then will the Holy Breath again breathe on your fires of life, and fan them to a living flame.

38 Then she will open up the doors again, and you may let her in to sup with you forevermore, or you may slight her once again, and then again.

39 You men of Israel, your opportunity is now.

40 Your tree of life is an illusive tree; it has a generous crop of leaves; its boughs hang low with fruit.

41 Behold, your words are leaves; your deeds the fruit.

42 Behold, for men have plucked the apples of your tree of life, and found them full of bitterness; and worms have eaten to the core.

43 Behold that fig tree by the way so full of leaves and worthless fruit!

44 Then Jesus spoke a word that nature spirits know, and lo, the fig tree stood a mass of withered leaves.

45 And then he spoke again, Behold, for God will speak the Word, and you will stand a withered fig tree in the setting sun.

46 You men of Galilee, send forth and call the pruner in before it is too late, and let him prune away your worthless branches and illusive leaves, and let the sunshine in.

47 The sun is life, and it can change your worthlessness to worth.

48 Your tree of life is good; but you have nurtured it so long with dews of self, and mists of carnal things that you have shut the sunshine out.

49 I tell you, men, that you must give account to God for every idle word you speak and every evil deed you do.

CHAPTER 106.

The Christines are in Magdala. Jesus heals a man who was blind, dumb and obsessed. He teaches the people. While he speaks his mother, brothers and Miriam come to him. He teaches a lesson on family relationship. He introduces Miriam to the people and she sings her songs of victory.

MAGDALA is beside the sea, and here the teachers taught.

2 A man obsessed, and who was blind and dumb was brought, and Jesus spoke the Word, and lo, the evil spirits went away; the man spoke out, his eyes were opened and he saw.

3 This was the greatest work that men had seen the master do, and they were all amazed.

4 The Pharisees were there, and they were full of jealous rage; they sought a cause whereby they might condemn.

5 They said, Yes, it is true that Jesus does a multitude of mighty works; but men should know that he is leagued with Beelzebul.

6 He is a sorcerer, a black magician of the Simon Cerus type; he works as Jannes and as Jambres did in Moses' day.

7 For Satan, prince of evil spirits, is his stay by night and day, and in the name of Satan he casts the demons out, and in his name he

heals the sick and raises up the dead.

8 But Jesus knew their thoughts; he said to them, You men are masters, and you know the law; whatever is arrayed against itself must fall; a house divided cannot stand;

9 A kingdom warring with itself is brought to naught.

10 If Satan casts the devil out, how can his kingdom stand?

11 If I, by Beelzebul, cast devils out, by whom do you cast devils out?

12 But if I, in the holy name of God, cast devils out, and make the lame to walk, the deaf to hear, the blind to see, the dumb to speak, has not God's kingdom come to you?

13 The Pharisees were dumb; they answered not.

14 As Jesus spoke a messenger approached and said to him, Your mother and your brothers wish to speak with you.

15 And Jesus said, Who is my mother? and my brothers, who are they?

16 And then he spoke a word aside unto the foreign masters and the twelve; he said,

17 Behold, men recognize their mothers, fathers, sisters, brothers here in flesh; but when the veil is rent and men walk in the realms of soul,

18 The tender lines of love that bind the groups of fleshy kin in families will fade away.

19 Not that the love for anyone will be the less; but men will see in all the motherhood, the fatherhood, the sisterhood, the brotherhood of man.

20 The family groups of earth will all be lost in universal love and fellowship divine.

21 Then to the multitudes he said, Whoever lives the life and does the will of God is child of God and is my mother, father, sister, friend.

22 And then he went aside to speak to mother and his other kindred in the flesh.

23 But he saw more than these. The maiden who once thrilled his very soul with love, a love beyond the love of any fleshly kin;

24 Who was the sorest tempter in the temple Heliopolis beside the Nile, who sung for him the sacred songs, was there.

25 The recognition was of kindred souls, and Jesus said,

26 Behold, for God has brought to us a power men cannot comprehend, a power of purity and love;

27 To make more light the burdens of the hour, to be a balm for wounded souls;

28 To win the multitude to better ways by sacred song and holy life.

29 Behold, for Miriam who stood beside the sea and sung the song of victory when Moses led the way, will sing again.

30 And all the choirs of heaven will join and sing the glad refrain:

31 Peace, peace on earth; good will to men!

32 And Miriam stood before the waiting throngs and sung again the songs of victory, and all the people said, Amen.

CHAPTER 107.

A Pharisee demands of Jesus signs of his messiahship. Jesus rebukes him, because he does not recognize the signs that are being continually given. Jesus exhorts the people to receive the light that they may become the light.

A PHARISEE elated with himself stood forth among the multitudes and said to Jesus,

2 Sir, we would have you demonstrate. If you are truly Christ who was to come, then you can surely do what black magicians cannot do.

3 Lo, they can talk, and hold the multitudes with words of power; and they can heal the sick and drive the demons out of those obsessed;

4 They can control the storms; and fire and earth and air will hear and answer when they speak.

5 Now, if you will ascend and from that tower fly across the sea, we will believe that you are sent from God.

6 And Jesus said, No black magician ever lived a holy life; you have a demonstration of the Christ-life every day.

7 But lo, you evil and adulterous scribes and Pharisees, you cannot see a spirit-sign, because your spirit eyes are full of carnal self.

8 You seek a sign to please your curiosity. You walk the very lowest planes of carnal life and cry, Phenomena! show us a sign and then we will believe.

9 I was not sent to earth to buy up faith as men buy fish and fruit and rubbish in the streets.

10 Men seem to think it quite a favor done to me when they confess their faith in me and in the holy Christ.

11 What does it matter unto me as man if you believe or disbelieve?

12 Faith is not something you can buy with coin; it is not something you can sell for gold.

13 Once Mart, a beggar, followed me and cried, Give me a silver piece; then I will believe in you.

14 And you are like this beggar man; you offer to exchange your faith for signs.

15 But I will give to all the world one sign as surety that the Christ abides with me.

16 You all have read the parable of Jonah and the fish, wherein it is recorded that the prophet spent three days and nights within the stomach of the mighty fish, and then came forth.

17 The son of man will spend three days and nights within the heart of earth and then come forth again, and men will see and know.

18 Behold, the light may be so bright that men cannot see anything.

19 The Spirit light has shown so brightly over Galilee that you who hear me now are blind.

20 You may have read the words of prophet Azrael; he said, The light shall shine out brightly in the darkness of the night, and men shall comprehend it not.

21 That time has come; the light shines forth; you see it not.

22 The Queen of Sheba sat in darkest night and still she yearned for light.

23 She came to hear the words of wisdom from the lips of Solomon, and she believed;

24 And she became a living torch, and when she reached her home, lo, all Arabia was filled with light.

25 A greater far than Solomon is here; the Christ is here; the Day Star has arisen, and you reject the light.

26 And you remember Nineveh, the wicked city of Assyria, which God had marked to be destroyed by shock and flame unless the people turned and walked in ways of right.

27 And Jonah raised his voice and said, In forty days shall Nineveh be razed, and all her wealth shall be destroyed.

28 The people heard and they believed; and they reformed and turned to ways of right, and lo, their city was not razed; was not destroyed.

29 You men of Galilee, I tell you that Arabia and Nineveh will testify against you in the judgment day.

30 Behold, for every one to whom I speak has in him all the fires of God; but they are lying dead.

31 The will is bridled by the flesh desires, and it brings not the ethers of the fires to vibrate into light.

32 Look, therefore, to your soul and note, Is not the light within you dark as night?

33 There is no breath but Holy Breath that e'er can fan your fires of life into a living flame and make them light.

34 And Holy Breath can raise the ethers of the fires to light in none but hearts of purity and love.

35 Hear, then, you men of Galilee, Make pure the heart, admit the Holy Breath, and then your bodies will be full of light,

36 And like a city on a hill, your light will shine afar, and thus your light may light the way for other men.

CHAPTER 108.

Jesus rebukes the people for selfishness. The Christines attend a feast and Jesus is censured by the Pharisee because he washed not before he eat. Jesus exposes the hypocrisy of the ruling classes and pronounces upon them many woes.

THE multitudes were wild with selfish thought; none recognized the rights and needs of any other one.

2 The stronger pushed the weak aside, and trampled on them in their haste to be the first to get a blessing for himself.

3 And Jesus said, Behold the cage of beasts untamed; a den of stinging vipers, maddened by their fiendish greed of selfish gain!

4 I tell you, men, the benefits that come to men who see no further than themselves are baubles in the morning light;

5 They are unreal; they pass away. The selfish soul is fed today; the food does not assimilate; the soul grows not, and then it must be fed again, and then again.

6 Behold, a selfish man obsessed by just one spirit of the air; by the Omnific Word the spirit is cast out;

7 It wanders through dry places, seeking rest and finding none.

8 And then it comes again; the selfish man has failed to close and lock the door;

9 The unclean spirit finds the house all swept and cleaned; it enters in and takes with it full seven other spirits more unclean than is itself; and there they dwell.

10 The last state of the man is more than sevenfold more wretched than the first.

11 And so it is with you who snatch the blessings that belong to other men.

12 While Jesus spoke a certain woman who stood near exclaimed, Most blessed is the mother of this man of God!

13 And Jesus said, Yes, blest is she; but doubly blest are they who hear, receive and live the word of God.

14 A Pharisee of wealth prepared a feast, and Jesus and the twelve, together with the masters from afar, were guests.

15 And Jesus did not wash his hands according to the strictest Pharisaic rules, before he ate; when this the Pharisee observed he marveled much.

16 And Jesus said, My host, why do you marvel that I did not wash my hands?

17 The Pharisees wash well their hands and feet; they cleanse the body every day when, lo, within is every form of filth.

18 Their hearts are full of wickedness, extortions and deceit.

19 Did not the God who made the outside of the body make the inside, too?

20 And then he said, Woe unto you, you Pharisees! for you tithe mint and rue, and every herb, and pass by judgment and the love of God.

21 Woe unto you, you Pharisees! you love the highest seats in synagogues and courts, and bid for salutations in the market place.

22 Woe unto you, you tinseled gentry of the land! no man would ever think you servants of the Lord of hosts by what you do.

23 A lawyer sitting near remarked, Rabboni, your words are harsh, and then in what you say you censure us; and why?

24 And Jesus said, Woe unto you, you masters of the law! you heap great burdens on the sons of men, yea, loads by far too great for them to bear, and you will never help to bear a feather's weight yourselves.

25 Woe unto you! you build the tombs of prophets and of seers; they whom your fathers killed; and you are parties to the crimes.

26 And now behold, for God has sent again to you his holy men—apostles, prophets, seers; and you are persecuting them.

27 The time is near when you will plead against them in the courts; will spurn them on the streets; will cast them into prison cells, and kill them with a fiend's delight.

28 I tell you, men, the blood of all the holy men of God that has been shed from righteous Abel down to that of Zacharias, father of the holy John,

29 Who was struck down beside the altar in the Holy Place—

30 The blood of all these holy men has made more red the hands of this ungodly generation.

31 Woe unto you, you masters of the law! you snatch the keys of knowledge from the hands of men;

32 You close the doors; you enter not yourselves, and suffer not the willing ones to enter in.

33 His words provoked the Pharisees, the lawyers and the scribes, and they, resenting, poured upon him torrents of abuse.

34 The truths he spoke came like a thunderbolt from heaven; the rulers counseled how they might ensnare him by his words; they sought a legal way to shed his blood.

CHAPTER 109.

The Christines go to a place apart to pray. Jesus warns them against the leaven of the Pharisees and reveals the fact that all thoughts and deeds are recorded in God's Book of Remembrance. Man's responsibility and God's care.

NOW, when the feast was finished Jesus with the foreign masters and the twelve, with Mary, Miriam and a band of loyal women who believed in Christ, went to a place apart to pray.

2 And when their silence ended Jesus said, Be on your guard; the

leaven of the Pharisees is being thrown in every measure of the meal of life.

3 It is a poison that will taint whatever it may touch; and it will blight the soul as sure as fumes of the Diabolos; it is hypocrisy.

4 The Pharisees seem fair in speech, but they are diabolical in heart.

5 And then they seem to think that thought is something they can lock within themselves.

6 They do not seem to know that every thought and wish is photographed and then preserved within the Book of Life to be revealed at any time the masters will.

7 That which is thought, or wished, or done in darkest night shall be proclaimed in brightest day;

8 That which is whispered in the ear within the secret place shall be made known upon the streets.

9 And in the judgment day when all the books are opened up, these men, and every other man, shall be a-judged, not by what they've said or done,

10 But by the way in which they used the thoughts of God, and how the ethers of eternal love were made to serve;

11 For men may make these ethers serve the carnal self, or serve the holy self within.

12 Behold, these men may kill the body of this flesh; but what of that? the flesh is but a transitory thing, and soon, by natural law, will pass;

13 Their slaughter only hastens nature's work a little time.

14 And when they kill the flesh they reach their bounds of power; they cannot kill the soul.

15 But nature is the keeper of the soul as of the flesh, and in the harvest time of soul, the trees of life are all inspected by the judge;

16 And every tree that bears no fruit of good is plucked up by the roots and cast into the flames.

17 Who then shall you regard? Not him who has the power to kill the flesh, and nothing more.

18 Regard the mighty one who has the power to dissolve both soul and body in the flames of nature's fire.

19 But man is king; he may direct his thoughts, his loves, his life, and gain the prize of everlasting life.

20 And you are not abandoned in your struggle for the crown of life. Your Father lives, and you shall live.

21 God has a care for every living thing. He numbers stars, and suns, and moons;

22 He numbers angels, men, and every thing below; the birds, the flowers, the trees;

23 The very petals of the rose he knows by name, and every one is numbered in his Book of Life;

24 And every hair upon your head, and every drop of blood within your veins, he knows by number and by rythm.

25 He hears the birdling's call, the cricket's chirp, the glow worm's song; and not a sparrow falls to earth without his knowledge and consent.

26 A sparrow seems a thing of little worth; yea, five of them are worth two farthings in the market place, and yet God cares for every one of them.

27 Will he not care much more for you who bear his image in your soul?

28 Fear not to make confession of the Christ before the sons of men, and God will own you as his sons

and daughters in the presence of the host of heaven.

29 If you deny the Christ before the sons of men, then God will not receive you as his own before the hosts of heaven.

30 And more I say, Fear not when men shall bring you up before the rulers of the land to answer for your faith.

31 Behold, the Holy Breath shall teach you in your hour of need what you should say, and what is best to leave unsaid.

32 And then the Christines went again to teach the multitudes.

CHAPTER 110.

Miriam sings a song of victory. The song. Jesus reveals the symbolic character of the journey of Israel from Egypt to Canaan.

AND Miriam stood before the surging crowd, and casting up her eyes to heaven she sung anew the song of victory:

2 Bring forth the harp, the vina and the lyre; bring forth the highest sounding cymbal, all ye choirs of heaven. Join in the song, the new, new song.

3 The Lord of hosts has stooped to hear the cries of men, and lo, the citadel of Beelzebul is shaking as a leaf before the wind.

4 The sword of Gideon is again unsheathed.

5 The Lord, with his own hand has pulled far back the curtains of the night; the sun of truth is flooding heaven and earth;

6 The demons of the dark, of ignorance and death, are fleeing fast; are disappearing as the dew beneath the morning sun.

7 God is our strength and song; is our salvation and our hope, and we will build anew a house for him;

8 Will cleanse our hearts, and purify their chambers, every one. We are the temple of the Holy Breath.

9 We need no more a tent within the wilderness; no more a temple built with hands.

10 We do not seek the Holy Land, nor yet Jerusalem.

11 We are the tent of God; we are his temple built without the sound of edged tools.

12 We are the Holy Land; we are the New Jerusalem; Allelujah, praise the Lord!

13 And when the song was done the multitudes exclaimed, Praise God.

14 And Jesus said, Behold the way!

15 The sons of men have groped for ages in the darkness of Egyptian night.

16 The Pharaohs of sense have bound them with their chains.

17 But God has whispered through the mists of time and told them of a land of liberty and love.

18 And he has sent his Logos forth to light the way.

19 The Red Sea rolls between the promised land and Egypt's sands.

20 The Red Sea is the carnal mind.

21 Behold, the Logos reaches out his hand; the sea divides; the carnal mind is reft in twain; the sons of men walk through dry shod.

22 The Pharaohs of sense would stay them in their flight; the waters of the sea return; the Pharaohs of sense are lost and men are free.

23 For just a little while men tread the wilderness of Sin; the Logos leads the way;

24 And when at last men stand upon the Jordan's brink, these

waters stay, and men step forth into their own.

CHAPTER 111.

Jesus teaches. A man requests him to compel his brother to deal justly. Jesus reveals the divine law, the power of truth and the universality of possessions. Relates the parable of the rich man and his abundant harvest.

AND Jesus taught the multitudes; and while he spoke a man stood forth and said,

2 Rabboni, hear my plea: My father died and left a large estate; my brother seized it all, and now refuses me my share.

3 I pray that you will bid him do the right, and give me what is mine.

4 And Jesus said, I am not come to be a judge in such affairs; I am no henchman of the court.

5 God sent me not to force a man to do the right.

6 In every man there is a sense of right; but many men regard it not.

7 The fumes that rise from selfishness have formed a crust about their sense of right that veils their inner light, so that they cannot comprehend nor recognize the rights of other men.

8 This veil you cannot tear away by force of arms, and there is naught that can dissolve this crust but knowledge and the love of God.

9 While men are in the mire, the skies seem far away; when men are on the mountain top, the skies are near, and they can almost touch the stars.

10 Then Jesus turned and to the twelve he said, Behold the many in the mire of carnal life!

11 The leaven of truth will change the miry clay to solid rock, and men can walk and find the path that leads up to the mountain top.

12 You cannot haste; but you can scatter forth this leaven with a generous hand.

13 When men have learned the truth that bears upon its face the law of right, then they will haste to give to every man his dues.

14 Then to the people Jesus said, Take heed, and covet not. The wealth of men does not consist in what they seem to have—in lands, in silver and in gold.

15 These things are only borrowed wealth. No man can corner up the gifts of God.

16 The things of nature are the things of God, and what is God's belongs to every man alike.

17 The wealth of soul lies in the purity of life, and in the wisdom that descends from heaven.

18 Behold, a rich man's ground brought forth abundantly; his barns were far too small to hold his grain, and to himself he said,

19 What shall I do? I must not give my grain away; I must not let it go to waste; and then he said,

20 This will I do; I will tear down these little barns and build up larger ones; there I will store away my grain and I will say,

21 My soul take now your ease; you have enough for many years; eat, drink and fill yourself and be content.

22 But God looked down and saw the man; he saw his selfish heart and said,

23 You foolish man, this night your soul will quit its house of flesh; then who will have your garnered wealth?

24 You men of Galilee, lay not up treasures in the vaults of earth;

accumulated wealth will blight your soul.

25 God does not give men wealth to hoard away in secret vaults. Men are but stewards of God's wealth, and they must use it for the common good.

26 To every steward who is true to self, to other men, to every thing that is, the Lord will say, Well done.

CHAPTER 112.

The Christines in the home of Mary of Magdala. Jesus calls his disciples, "Little Flock," and charges them to place their affections on divine things. He teaches them regarding the inner life. ·

AND Jesus left the multitudes and went with his disciples up to Mary's home; and as they sat about the board to dine he said,

2 My little flock, fear not; it is your Father's will that you shall rule the kingdom of the soul.

3 A ruler in the house of God is servant of the Lord of hosts, and man cannot serve God except by serving men.

4 A servant in the house of God cannot be servant in the house of wealth; nor in the synagogue of sense.

5 If you are tied to lands, or bonds, or wealth of earth, your hearts are knit to things of earth; for where your treasures are there are your hearts.   ·

6 Dispose of all your wealth, distribute it among the poor, and put your trust in God, and you nor yours will ever come to want.

7 This is a test of faith, and God will not accept the service of the faithless one.

8 The time is ripe; your Master comes upon the clouds; the eastern sky is glowing with his presence now.

9 Put on reception robes; gird up your loins; trim up your lamps and fill them well with oil, and be prepared to meet your Lord; when you are ready, he will come.

10 Thrice blessed are the servants who are ready to receive their Lord.

11 Behold, for he will gird himself, and will prepare a sumptuous feast for every one, and he himself will serve.

12 It matters not when he shall come; it may be at the second watch; it may be at the third; but blessed are the servants who are ready to receive.

13 You cannot leave your door ajar and go to sleep, and wait in blissful ignorance of the fleeting time;

14 For thieves will surely come and take away your goods and bind and carry you away to robbers' dens.

15 And if you are not carried forth, the Master when he comes will not regard a sleeping guard as friend, but as a foe.

16 Beloved, these are times when every man must be awake and at his post, for none can tell the hour nor the day when man shall be revealed.

17 And Peter said, Lord is this parable for us, or for the multitudes?

18 And Jesus said, Why need you ask? God is not man that he should show respect for one and cast another off.

19 Whoever will may come and gird himself, and trim his lamp, and find a turret in the tower of life where he may watch, and be prepared to meet the Lord.

20 But you, as children of the light, have come, and you have learned the language of the court, and may stand forth and lead the way.

21 But you may wait, and think that you are ready to receive the Lord, and still he does not come.

22 And you may grow impatient and begin to long for carnal ways again, and may begin to exercise your rule;

23 To beat, and otherwise maltreat the servants of the house, and fill yourselves with wine and meat.

24 And what will say the Lord when he shall come?

25 Behold, for he will cast the faithless servant from his house; and many years will come and go before he can be cleansed, and be thought worthy to receive his Lord.

26 The servant who has come into the light, who knows the Master's will and does it not; the trusted guard who goes to sleep within the turret of the tower of life,

27 Shall feel the lash of justice many times, while he who does not know his Master's will and does it not, will not receive the graver punishment.

28 The man who comes and stands before the open door of opportunity and does not enter in, but goes his way,

29 Will come again and find the door made fast, and when he calls, the door will open not,

30 The guard will say, you had the pass-word once, but you threw it away and now the Master knows you not; depart.

31 And verily I say to you, To whom much has been given, much is required; to whom a little has been given, a little only is required.

CHAPTER 113.

In answer to a question of Lamaas Jesus teaches a lesson on the reign of peace and the way to it through antagonisms. The signs of the times. Guidance of the Holy Breath. The Christines go to Bethsaida.

NOW, after they had dined, the guests and Jesus all were in a spacious hall in Mary's home.

2 And then Lamaas said, Pray, tell us Lord, is this the dawn of peace?

3 Have we come forth unto the time when men will war no more?

4 Are you, indeed, the Prince of Peace that holy men have said would come?

5 And Jesus said, Peace reigns today; it is the peace of death.

6 A stagnant pool abides in peace. When waters cease to move they soon are ladened with the seeds of death; corruption dwells in every drop.

7 The living waters always leap and skip about like lambs in spring.

8 The nations are corrupt; they sleep within the arms of death and they must be aroused before it is too late.

9 In life we find antagonists at work. God sent me here to stir unto its depths the waters of the sea of life.

10 Peace follows strife; I come to slay this peace of death. The prince of peace must first be prince of strife.

11 This leaven of truth which I have brought to men will stir the demons up, and nations, cities, families will be at war within themselves.

12 The five that have been dwelling in a home of peace will be

divided now, and two shall war with three;

13 The son will stand against his sire; the mother and the daughter will contend; yea, strife will reign in every home.

14 The self and greed and doubt will rage into a fever heat, and then, because of me, the earth will be baptized in human blood.

15 But right is king; and when the smoke is cleared away the nations will learn war no more; the Prince of Peace will come to reign.

16 Behold, the signs of what I say are in the sky; but men can see them not.

17 When men behold a cloud rise in the west they say, A shower of rain will come and so it does; and when the wind blows from the south they say, The weather will be hot; and it is so.

18 Lo, men can read the signs of earth and sky, but they cannot discern the signs of Holy Breath; but you shall know.

19 The storm of wrath comes on; the carnal man will seek a cause to hale you into court, and cast you into prison cells.

20 And when these times shall come let wisdom guide; do not resent. Resentment makes more strong the wrath of evil men.

21 There is a little sense of justice and of mercy in the vilest men of earth.

22 By taking heed to what you do and say and trusting in the guidance of the Holy Breath, you may inspire this sense to grow.

23 You thus may make the wrath of men to praise the Lord.

24 The Christines went their way, and came unto Bethsaida and taught.

CHAPTER 114.

A great storm on the sea destroys many lives. Jesus makes an appeal for aid, and the people give with a generous hand. In answer to a lawyer's question, Jesus gives the philosophy of disasters.

AS Jesus taught, a man stood forth and said, Rabboni, may I speak?

2 And Jesus said, Say on. And then the man spoke out and said,

3 A storm upon the sea last night wrecked many fishing boats, and scores of men went down to death, and, lo, their wives and children are in need;

4 What can be done to help them in their sore distress?

5 And Jesus said, A worthy plea. You men of Galilee, take heed. We may not bring again to live these men, but we can succor those who looked to them for daily bread.

6 You stewards of the wealth of God, an opportunity has come; unlock your vaults; bring forth your hoarded gold; bestow it with a lavish hand.

7 This wealth was laid aside for just such times as these; when it was needed not, lo, it was yours to guard;

8 But now it is not yours, for it belongs to those who are in want, and if you give it not you simply bring upon your heads the wrath of God.

9 It is not charity to give to those who need; it is but honesty; it is but giving men their own.

10 Then Jesus turned to Judas, one of the twelve, who was the treasurer of the band, and said,

11 Bring forth our treasure box; the money is not ours now; turn

every farthing to the help of those in such distress.

12 Now, Judas did not wish to give the money all to those in want, and so he talked with Peter, James and John.

13 He said, Lo, I will save a certain part and give the rest; that surely is enough for us, for we are strangers to the ones in want; we do not even know their names.

14 But Peter said, Why, Judas, man, how do you dare to think to trifle with the strength of right.

15 The Lord has spoken true; this wealth does not belong to us in face of this distress, and to refuse to give it is to steal.

16 You need not fear; we will not come to want.

17 Then Judas opened up the treasure box and gave the money all.

18 And there was gold and silver, food, and raiment in abundance for the needs of the bereaved.

19 A lawyer said, Rabboni, if God rules the worlds and all that in them is, did he not bring about this storm? did he not slay these men?

20 Has he not brought this sore distress upon these people here? and was it done to punish them for crimes?

21 And we remember well when once a band of earnest Jews from Galilee were in Jerusalem, and at a feast and were, for fancied crimes against the Roman law,

22 Cut down within the very temple court by Pontius Pilate; and their blood became their sacrifice.

23 Did God bring on this slaughter all because these men were doubly vile?

24 And then we bring to mind that once a tower called Siloam, graced the defences of Jerusalem,

and, seemingly, without a cause it tottered and it fell to earth and eighteen men were killed.

25 Were these men vile? and were they slain as punishment for some great crime?

26 And Jesus said, We cannot look upon a single span of life and judge of anything.

27 There is a law that men must recognize: Result depends on cause.

28 Men are not motes to float about within the air of one short life, and then be lost in nothingness.

29 They are undying parts of the eternal whole that come and go, lo, many times into the air of earth and of the great beyond, just to unfold the God-like self.

30 A cause may be a part of one brief life; results may not be noted till another life.

31 The cause of your results cannot be found within my life, nor can the cause of my results be found in yours.

32 I cannot reap except I sow and I must reap whate'er I sow,

33 The law of all eternities is known to master minds:

34 Whatever men do unto other men the judge and executioner will do to them.

35 We do not note the execution of this law among the sons of men.

36 We note the weak dishonored, trampled on and slain by those men call the strong.

37 We note that men with wood-like heads are seated in the chairs of state;

38 Are kings and judges, senators and priests, while men with giant intellects are scavengers about the streets.

39 We note that women with a moiety of common sense, and not a

whit of any other kind, are painted up and dressed as queens,

40 Becoming ladies of the courts of puppet kings, because they have the form of something beautiful; while God's own daughters are their slaves, or serve as common laborers in the field.

41 The sense of justice cries aloud: This is a travesty on right.

42 So when men see no further than one little span of life it is no wonder that they say, There is no God, or if there is a God he is a tyrant and should die.

43 If you would judge aright of human life, you must arise and stand upon the crest of time and note the thoughts and deeds of men as they have come up through the ages past;

44 For we must know that man is not a creature made of clay to turn again to clay and disappear.

45 He is a part of the eternal whole. There never was a time when he was not; a time will never come when he will not exist.

46 And now we look; the men who now are slaves were tyrants once; the men who now are tyrants have been slaves.

47 The men who suffer now, once stood aloft and shouted with a fiend's delight while others suffered at their hands.

48 And men are sick, and halt, and lame, and blind because they once transgressed the laws of perfect life, and every law of God must be fulfilled.

49 Man may escape the punishment that seems but due for his misdoings in this life; but every deed and word and thought has its own metes and bounds,

50 Is cause, and has its own results, and if a wrong be done, the doer of the wrong must make it right.

51 And when the wrongs have all been righted then will man arise and be at one with God.

CHAPTER 115.

Jesus teaches by the sea. He relates the parable of the sower. Tells why he teaches in parables. Explains the parable of the sower. Relates the parable of the wheat and tares.

AND Jesus stood beside the sea and taught; the multitudes pressed close upon him and he went into a boat that was near by and put a little ways from shore, and then he spoke in parables; he said,

2 Behold, a sower took his seed and went into his field to sow.

3 With lavish hand he scattered forth the seed and some fell in the hardened paths that men had made,

4 And soon were crushed beneath the feet of other men; and birds came down and carried all the seed away.

5 Some seed fell on rocky ground where there was little soil; they grew and soon the blades appeared and promised much;

6 But then there was no depth of soil, no chance for nourishment, and in the heat of noonday sun they withered up and died.

7 Some seed fell where thistles grew, and found no earth in which to grow and they were lost;

8 But other seed found lodgment in the rich and tender soil and grew apace, and in the harvest it was found that some brought forth a hundred fold, some sixty fold, some thirty fold.

9 They who have ears to hear

may hear; they who have hearts to understand may know.

10 Now, his disciples were beside him in the boat, and Thomas asked, Why do you speak in parables?

11 And Jesus said, My words, like every master's words, are dual in their sense.

12 To you who know the language of the soul, my words have meanings far too deep for other men to comprehend.

13 The other sense of what I say is all the multitude can understand; these words are food for them; the inner thoughts are food for you.

14 Let every one reach forth and take the food that he is ready to receive.

15 And then he spoke that all might hear; he said, Hear you the meaning of the parable:

16 Men hear my words and understand them not, and then the carnal self purloins the seed, and not a sign of spirit life appears.

17 This is the seed that fell within the beaten paths of men.

18 And others hear the words of life, and with a fiery zeal receive them all; they seem to comprehend the truth and promise well;

19 But troubles come; discouragements arise; there is no depth of thought; their good intentions wither up and die.

20 These are the seeds that fell in stony ground.

21 And others hear the words of truth and seem to know their worth; but love of pleasure, reputation, wealth and fame fill all the soil; the seeds are nourished not and they are lost.

22 These are the seeds that fell among the thistles and the thorns.

23 But others hear the words of truth and comprehend them well; they sink down deep into their souls; they live the holy life and all the world is blest.

24 These are the seeds that fell in fertile soil, that brought forth fruit abundantly.

25 You men of Galilee, take heed to how you hear and how you cultivate your fields; for if you slight the offers of this day, the sower may not come to you again in this or in the age to come.

26 Then Jesus spoke another parable; he said:

27 The kingdom I may liken to a field in which a man sowed precious seed;

28 But while he slept an evil one went forth and sowed a measure full of darnel seed; then went his way.

29 The soil was good, and so the wheat and darnel grew; and when the servants saw the tares among the wheat, they found the owner of the field and said,

30 You surely sowed good seed; from whence these tares?

31 The owner said, Some evil one has sown the seed of tares.

32 The servants said, Shall we go out and pull up by the roots the tares and burn them in the fire?

33 The owner said, No, that would not be well. The wheat and tares grow close together in the soil, and while you pull the tares you would destroy the wheat.

34 So we will let them grow together till the harvest time. Then to the reapers I will say,

35 Go forth and gather up the tares and bind them up and burn them in the fire, and gather all the wheat into my barns.

36 When he had spoken thus, he left the boat and went up to the

house, and his disciples followed him.

CHAPTER 116.

The Christines are in Philip's home. Jesus interprets the parable of the wheat and tares. He explains the unfoldment of the kingdom by parables: the good seed; the growth of the tree; the leaven; the hidden treasure. He goes to a mountain to pray.

THE Christines were in Philip's home and Peter said to Jesus, Lord, will you explain to us the meaning of the parables you spoke today? The one about the wheat and tares, especially?

2 And Jesus said, God's kingdom is a dualty; it has an outer and an inner form.

3 As seen by man it is composed of men, of those who make confession of the name of Christ.

4 For various reasons various people crowd this outer kingdom of our God.

5 The inner kingdom is the kingdom of the soul, the kingdom of the pure in heart.

6 The outer kingdom I may well explain in parables. Behold, for I have seen you cast a great net out into the sea,

7 And when you hauled it in, lo, it was full of every kind of fish, some good, some bad, some great, some small; and I have seen you save the good and throw the bad away.

8 This outer kingdom is the net, and every kind of man is caught; but in the sorting day the bad will all be cast away, the good reserved.

9 Hear, then, the meaning of the parable of wheat and tares:

10 The sower is the son of man; the field, the world; the good seed are the children of the light; the tares, the children of the dark; the enemy, the carnal self; the harvest day, the closing of the age; the reapers are the messengers of God.

11 The reckoning day will come to every man; then will the tares be gathered up, and cast into the fire and be burned.

12 Then will the good shine forth as suns in the kingdom of the soul.

13 And Philip said, Must men and women suffer in the flames because they have not found the way of life?

14 And Jesus said, The fire purifies. The chemist throws into the fire the ores that hold all kinds of dross.

15 The useless metal seems to be consumed; but not a grain of gold is lost.

16 There is no man that has not in him gold that cannot be destroyed. The evil things of men are all consumed in fire; the gold survives.

17 The inner kingdom of the soul I may explain in parables:

18 The son of man goes forth and scatters seeds of truth; God waters well the soil; the seeds show life and grow; first comes the blade, and then the stalk, and then the ear, and then the full wheat in the ear.

19 The harvest comes and, lo, the reapers bear the ripened sheaves into the garner of the Lord.

20 Again, this kingdom of the soul is like a little seed that men may plant in fertile soil.

21 (A thousand of these seeds would scarcely be a shekel's weight.)

22 The tiny seed begins to grow; it pushes through the earth, and after years of growth it is a mighty

tree and birds rest in its leafy bowers and men find refuge 'neath its sheltering boughs from sun and storm.

23 Again, the truth, the spirit of the kingdom of the soul, is like a ball of leaven that a woman hid in measures, three, of flour and in a little time the whole was leavened.

24 Again, the kingdom of the soul is like a treasure hidden in a field which one has found, and straitway goes his way and sells all that he has and buys the field.

25 When Jesus had thus said he went alone into a mountain pass near by to pray.

CHAPTER 117.

A royal feast is held in Machaerus. John, the harbinger, is beheaded. His body is buried in Hebron. His disciples mourn. The Christines cross the sea in the night. Jesus calms a raging storm.

A ROYAL feast was held in honor of the birthday of the tetrarch in fortified Machaerus, east of the Bitter Sea.

2 The tetrarch, Herod, and his wife, Herodias, together with Salome were there; and all the men and women of the royal court were there.

3 And when the feast was done, lo, all the guests and courtiers were drunk with wine; they danced and leaped about like children in their play.

4 Salome, daughter of Herodias, came in and danced before the king. The beauty of her form, her grace and winning ways entranced the silly Herod, then half drunk with wine.

5 He called the maiden to his side and said, Salome, you have won my heart, and you may ask

and I will give you anything you wish.

6 The maiden ran in childish glee and told her mother what the ruler said.

7 Her mother said, Go back and say, Give me the head of John, the harbinger.

8 The maiden ran and told the ruler what she wished.

9 And Herod called his trusty executioner and said to him, Go to the tower and tell the keeper that by my authority you come to execute the prisoner known as John.

10 The man went forth and in a little while returned and on a platter bore the lifeless head of John, and Herod offered it unto the maiden in the presence of the guests.

11 The maiden stood aloof; her innocence was outraged when she saw the bloody gift, and she would touch it not.

12 Her mother, steeped and hardened well in crime, came up and took the head and held it up before the guests and said,

13 This is the fate of every man who dares to scorn, or criticize, the acts of him who reigns.

14 The drunken rabble gazed upon the grewsome sight with fiendish joy.

15 The head was taken back unto the tower. The body had been given unto holy men who had been friends of John; they placed it in a burial case and carried it away.

16 They bore it to the Jordan, which they crossed just at the ford where John first preached the word;

17 And through the passes of the Judean hills they carried it.

18 They reached the sacred grounds near Hebron, where the bodies of the parents of the harbinger lay in their tombs;

19 And there they buried it; and then they went their way.

20 Now, when the news reached Galilee that John was dead the people met to sing the sonnets of the dead.

21 And Jesus and the foreign masters and the twelve took ship to cross the sea of Galilee.

22 A scribe, a faithful friend of John, stood by the sea; he called to Jesus and he said, Rabboni, let me follow where you go.

23 And Jesus said, You seek a safe retreat from evil men. There is no safety for your life with me;

24 For evil men will take my life as they have taken John's.

25 The foxes of the earth have safe retreats; the birds have nests secure among the hidden rocks, but I have not a place where I may lay my head and rest secure.

26 Then an apostle said, Lord, suffer me to tarry here a while, that I may take my father, who is dead, and lay him in the tomb.

27 But Jesus said, The dead can care for those who die; the living wait for those who live; come, follow me.

28 The evening came; three boats put out to sea and Jesus rested in the foremost boat; he slept.

29 A storm came on; the boats were tossed about like toys upon the sea.

30 The waters swept the decks; the hardy boatmen were afraid lest all be lost.

31 And Thomas found the master fast asleep; he called, and Jesus woke.

32 And Thomas said, Behold the storm! have you no care for us? The boats are going down.

33 And Jesus stood; he raised his hand; he talked unto the spirits of the winds and waves as men would talk with men.

34 And, lo, the winds blew not; the waves came tremblingly and kissed his feet; the sea was calm.

35 And then he said, You men of faith, where is your faith? for you can speak and winds and waves will hear and will obey.

36 And the disciples were amazed. They said, Who is this man that even winds and waves obey his voice?

CHAPTER 118.

The Christines are in Gadara. Jesus casts a legion of unclean spirits out of a man. The spirits go into vicious animals which run into the sea, and are drowned. The people are in fear and request Jesus to leave their coast. With his disciples, he returns to Capernaum.

THE morning came; the Christines landed in the country of the Geracenes.

2 They went to Gadara, chief city of the Peracans, and here for certain days they tarried and they taught.

3 Now, legends hold that Gadara is sacred to the dead, and all the hills about are known as holy ground.

4 These are the burial grounds of all the regions round about; the hills are full of tombs; and many dead from Galilee are here entombed.

5 Now, spirits of the lately dead that cannot rise to higher planes, remain about the tombs that hold the flesh and bones of what was once their mortal homes.

6 They sometimes take possession of the living, whom they torture in a hundred ways.

7 And all through Gadara were men obsessed, and there was no one strong enough to bring relief.

8 That they might meet these hidden foes and learn the way to dispossess the evil ones the master took the foreign masters and the twelve into the tombs.

9 And as they neared the gates they met a man obsessed. A legion of the unclean ones were in this man, and they had made him strong;

10 And none could bind him down, no, not with chains; for he could break the stoutest chains, and go his way.

11 Now, unclean spirits cannot live in light; they revel in the dark.

12 When Jesus came he brought the light of life, and all the evil spirits were disturbed.

13 The leader of the legion in the man called out, Thou Jesus, thou Immanuel, we beg that thou wilt not consign it to the depths. Torment us not before our time.

14 And Jesus said, What is your number and your name?

15 The evil spirit said, Our name is legion, and our number is the number of the beast.

16 And Jesus spoke; and with a voice that shook the very hills, he said, Come forth; possess this man no more.

17 Now, all the hills were filled with unclean animals that fed, and carried forth and spread the plague among the people of the land.

18 And when the evil spirits begged that they might not be driven forth without a home, the master said,

19 Go forth and take possession of the unclean quadrupeds.

20 And they, and all the evil spirits of the tombs went forth and took possession of the breeders of the plague,

21 Which, wild with rage, ran down the steeps into the sea, and all were drowned.

22 And all the land was freed of the contagion, and the unclean spirits came no more.

23 But when the people saw the mighty works that Jesus did they were alarmed. They said,

24 If he can free the country of the plague, and drive the unclean spirits out, he is a man of such transcendent power that he can devastate our land at will.

25 And then they came and prayed that he would not remain in Gadara.

26 And Jesus did not tarry longer there, and with the other masters and the twelve, he went aboard the boats to go away.

27 The man who had been rescued from the unclean legion stood upon the shore and said, Lord, let me go with you.

28 But Jesus said, It is not well; go forth unto your home and tell the news that men may know what man can do when he is tuned with God.

29 And then the man went forth through all Decapolis and told the news.

30 The Christines sailed away, re-crossed the sea and came again into Capernaum.

CHAPTER 119.

The people of Capernaum welcome Jesus. Matthew gives a feast. The Pharisees rebuke Jesus for eating with sinners. He tells them that he is sent to save sinners. He gives lessons on fasting and on the philosophy of good and evil.

THE news soon spread through all the land that Jesus was at home and then the people came in throngs to welcome him.

2 And Matthew, one of the twelve, a man of wealth, whose home was in Capernaum, spread forth a sumptuous feast, and Jesus and the foreign masters and the twelve, and people of all shades of thought, were guests.

3 And when the Pharisees observed that Jesus sat and ate with publicans and those of ill repute they said,

4 For shame! This man who claims to be a man of God, consorts with publicans and courtesans and with the common herd of men, For shame!

5 When Jesus knew their thoughts he said, They who are well cannot be healed; the pure need not be saved.

6 They who are well are whole; they who are pure are saved.

7 They who love justice and do right need not repent; I came not unto them, but to the sinner I am come.

8 A band of John's disciples who had heard that John was dead were wearing badges for their dead;

9 Were fasting and were praying in their hearts, which when the Pharisees observed they came to Jesus and they said,

10 Why fast the followers of John and your disciples do not fast?

11 And Jesus said, Lo, you are masters of the law; you ought to know; perhaps you will make known your knowledge to these men.

12 What are the benefits derived from fasts? The Pharisees were mute; they answered not.

13 Then Jesus said, The vital force of men depends on what they eat and drink.

14 Is spirit-life the stronger when the vital force is weak? Is sainthood reached by starving, self imposed?

15 A glutton is a sinner in the sight of God, and he is not a saint who makes himself a weakling and unfitted for the heavy tasks of life by scorning to make use of God's own means of strength.

16 Lo, John is dead, and his devoted followers are fasting in their grief.

17 Their love for him impels them on to show respect, for they have thought, and have been taught that it is sin to lightly treat the memory of the dead.

18 To them it is a sin, and it is well that they should fast.

19 When men defy their consciences and listen not to what they say, the heart is grieved and they become unfitted for the work of life; and thus they sin.

20 The conscience may be taught. One man may do in conscience what another cannot do.

21 What is a sin for me to do may not be sin for you to do. The place you occupy upon the way of life determines what is sin.

22 There is no changeless law of good; for good and evil both are judged by other things.

23 One man may fast and in his deep sincerity of heart is blest.

24 Another man may fast and in the faithlessness of such a task imposed is cursed.

25 You cannot make a bed to fit the form of every man. If you can make a bed to fit yourself you have done well.

26 Why should these men who follow me resort to fasting, or to anything that would impair their

strength? They need it all to serve the race.

27 The time will come when God will let you have your way, and you will do to me what Herod did to John;

28 And in the awfulness of that sad hour these men will fast.

29 They who have ears to hear may hear; they who have hearts to feel may understand.

CHAPTER 120.

Nicodemus is at the feast. He asks Jesus, Cannot the Christine religion be introduced more successfully by reforming the Jewish service? Jesus answers in the negative and gives his reasons. Jesus heals a woman with hemorrhages. Heals Jairus' daughter. Disappears when the people would worship him.

NOW, Nicodemus, who once came to Jesus in the night to learn the way of life, was one among the guests.

2 And standing forth he said, Rabboni, it is true that Jewish laws and Jewish practices do not agree.

3 The priesthood needs to be reformed; the rulers should become more merciful and kind; the lawyers should become more just; the common people should not bear such loads.

4 But could we not gain these reforms and not destroy the service of the Jews?

5 Could you not harmonize your mighty work with that of Pharisee and scribe? Might not the priesthood be a benefit to your divine philosophy?

6 But Jesus said, You cannot put new wine in ancient skins, for when it purifies itself, lo, it expands; the ancient bottles cannot bear the

strain; they burst, and all the wine is lost.

7 Men do not mend a worn-out garment with a piece of cloth unworn, which cannot yield to suit the fabric, weak with age, and then a greater rent appears.

8 Old wine may be preserved in ancient skins; but new wine calls for bottles new.

9 This spirit-truth I bring is to this generation new, and if we put it in the ancient skins of Jewish forms, lo, it will all be lost.

10 It must expand; the ancient bottles cannot yield and they would burst.

11 Behold the kingdom of the Christ! it is as old as God himself, and yet it is as new as morning sun; it only can contain the truth of God.

12 And as he spoke a ruler of the synagogue, Jairus by name, came in and bowed at Jesus' feet and said,

13 My master, hear my prayer! My child is very sick, I fear that she will die; but this I know that if you will but come and speak the Word my child will live.

14 (She was an only child, a girl twelve years of age.)

15 And Jesus tarried not; he went out with the man, and many people followed them.

16 And as they went a woman who had been plagued with hemorrhage for many years, had been a subject of experiment of doctors near and far, and all had said, She cannot live, rose from her bed and rushed out in the way as Jesus passed.

17 She said within herself, If I can touch his garment, then I know I will be well.

18 She touched him, and at once the bleeding ceased and she was well.

19   And Jesus felt that healing power had gone from him, and speaking to the multitude, he said,

20   Who was it touched my coat?

21   And Peter said, No one can tell; the multitudes are pressing you; a score of people may have touched your coat.

22   But Jesus said, Some one in faith, with healing thought, did touch my coat, for healing virtues have gone forth from me.

23   And when the woman knew that what she did was known, she came and knelt at Jesus' feet and told it all.

24   And Jesus said, Your faith has made you whole, go on your way in peace.

25   Now, as he spoke, a servant from the home of Jairus came and said, My master, Jairus, trouble not the Lord to come; your child is dead.

26   But Jesus said, Jairus, man of faith, do not permit your faith to waver in this trying hour.

27   What is it that the servant said? The child is dead? Lo, what is death?

28   It is the passing of the soul out of the house of flesh.

29   Man is the master of the soul and of its house. When man has risen up from doubt and fear, lo, he can cleanse the empty house and bring the tenant back again.

30   Then taking with him Peter, James and John, Jairus and the mother of the child, he went into the chamber of the dead.

31   And when the doors were closed against the multitude, he spoke a word that souls can understand, and then he took the maiden by the hand and said,

32   Talitha cumi, child, arise! The maiden's soul returned and she arose and asked for food.

33   And all the people of the city were amazed, and many would have worshipped Jesus as a God,

34   But, like a phantom of the night, he disappeared and went his way.

CHAPTER 121.

The Christines are in Nazareth. Miriam sings a Christine song of praise. Jesus teaches in the synagogue. He heals a dumb man who is obsessed. The people do not believe in him. The Pharisees call him a tool of Beelzebul. The Christines go to Cana.

IT was a gala day in Nazareth. The people there had met with one accord to celebrate some great event.

2   And Jesus and the foreign masters and the twelve, and Mary, mother of the Lord, and Miriam were there.

3   And when the people were assembled in the great hall of the town, the graceful singer, Miriam, stood forth and sung a song of praise.

4   But few of all the multitude knew who the singer was; but instantly she won all hearts.

5   For many days she sung the songs of Israel, and then she went her way.

6   The Sabbath came and Jesus went into the synagogue. He took the book of Psalms and read:

7   Blest is the man who puts his trust in God, respecting not the proud nor such as turn aside to lies.

8   O Lord, my God, the works that thou hast done for us are wonderful; and many are thy thoughts for us; we cannot count them all,

9   Thou dost not call for sacrifice, nor offerings of blood; burnt

offerings and offerings for sin thou dost not want;

✓ 10 And lo, I come to do thy will, O God; thy law is in my heart,

11 And I have preached the word of righteousness and peace unto the thronging multitudes; I have declared the counsel of my God in full.

12 I have not hid thy righteousness within my heart; I have declared thy faithfulness and grace.

13 I have not kept thy lovingkindness and thy truth away from men; I have declared them to the multitudes.

14 O Lord, make wide my lips that I may tell thy praise; I do not bring the sacrifice of blood, nor yet burnt offerings for sin.

15 The sacrifices I would bring to thee, O God, are purity in life, a contrite heart, a spirit full of faith and love; and these thou wilt receive.

16 And when he had thus read, he gave the book back to the keeper of the books, and then he said,

17 Upon these ends of earth these messages of God have come.

18 Our people have exalted sacrificial rites and have neglected mercy, justice and the rights of men.

19 You Pharisees, you priests, you scribes, your God is surfeited with blood; God does not heed your prayers; you stand before your burning victims; but you stand in vain.

20 Turn you unto the testimonies of the law; reform and turn to God, and you shall live.

21 Let not your altars be accursed again with smoke of innocence.

22 Bring unto God as sacrifice a broken and a contrite heart.

23 Lift from your fellow men the burdens that you have imposed.

24 And if you hearken not, and if you turn not from your evil ways, lo, God will smite this nation with a curse.

25 And when he had thus said he stood aside, and all the people were astonished, and they said,

26 Where did this man get all his knowledge and his power? From whence did all this wisdom come?

27 Is not this Mary's son, whose home is out on Marmion Way?

28 Are not his brothers, Jude and James and Simon, known among our honored men? Are not his sisters with us here?

29 But they were all offended by the words he spoke.

30 And Jesus said, A prophet has no honor in his native land; he is not well received among his kin; his foes are in his home.

31 And Jesus wrought not many mighty works in Nazareth, because the people had no faith in him. He did not tarry long.

32 But as he passed from thence two blind men followed him and cried, Thou son of David, hear! Have mercy, Lord, and open up our eyes that we may see.

33 And Jesus said, Do you believe that I can open up your eyes and make you see?

34 They said, Yea, Lord, we know that if you speak the Word then we can see.

35 And Jesus touched their eyes and spoke the Word; he said, According to your faith so will it be.

36 And they were blest; they opened up their eyes and saw.

37 And Jesus said, Tell not this thing to any one.

38 But they went forth and told the news through all the land.

39 As Jesus walked along the way a man who was obsessed, and who was dumb, was brought to him.

40 And Jesus spoke the Word; the unclean spirit came out of the man; his tongue was loosed; he spoke; he said, Praise God.

41 The people were amazed; They said, This is a mighty deed; we never saw that done before.

42 The Pharisees were also much amazed; but they cried out and said,

43 You men of Israel, take heed; this Jesus is a tool of Beelzebul; he heals the sick and casts the spirits out in Satan's name.

44 But Jesus answered not; he went his way.

45 And with the foreign masters and the twelve he went up to the town where he once turned the water into wine and tarried certain days.

CHAPTER 122.

The Christines spend seven days in prayer. Jesus gives his charge to the twelve and sends them forth on their apostolic ministry, with instructions to meet him in Capernaum.

THE Christines prayed in silence seven days; then Jesus called the twelve aside and said,

2 Behold, the multitudes have thronged about us everywhere; the people are bewildered; they wander here and there like sheep without a fold.

3 They need a shepherd's care; they want a loving hand to lead them to the light.

4 The grain is ripe; the harvest is abundant, but the harvesters are few.

5 The time is also ripe, and you must go alone through all the villages and towns of Galilee and teach and heal.

6 And then he breathed upon the twelve and said, Receive the Holy Breath.

7 And then he gave them each the Word of power, and said, By this Omnific Word you shall cast spirits out, shall heal the sick and bring the dead to life again.

8 And you shall go not in the way of the Assyrians, nor Greek; you shall not go into Samaria; go only to your brethren of the scattered tribes.

9 And as you go proclaim, The kingdom of the Christ has come.

10 You have abundantly received, and freely you shall give.

11 But you must go in faith; provide yourselves no crutch to lean upon.

12 Give all your gold and silver to the poor; take not two coats, nor extra shoes; just take your wands.

13 You are God's husbandmen and he will never suffer you to want.

14 In every place you go search out the men of faith; with them abide until you go from hence.

15 You go for me; you act for me. They who receive and welcome you, receive and welcome me;

16 And they who shut their doors against your face, refuse to welcome me.

17 If you are not received in kindness in a town, bear not away an evil thought; do not resist.

18 An evil thought of any kind will do you harm; will dissipate your power.

19 When you are not received with favor, go your way, for there are multitudes of men who want the light.

20 Behold, I send you forth as sheep among a pack of wolves; and you must be as wise as serpents and as harmless as the doves.

21 In all your language be discreet, for Pharisees and scribes will

seek a cause for your arrest in what you say.

22 And they will surely find a way by charges false to bring you into court.

23 And judges will declare that you are guilty of some crime, and sentence you to scourgings and to prison cells.

24 But when you come to stand before the judge, be not afraid; be not disturbed about the way to act, the words to speak.

25 The Holy Breath will guide you in that hour, and give the words that you shall speak.

26 Of this be full assured; It is not you who speaks; it is the Holy Breath who gives the words and moves the lips.

27 The gospel that you preach will not bring peace, but it will stir the multitudes to wrath.

28 The carnal man abhors the truth, and he would give his life to crush the tender plant before the harvest time.

29 And this will bring confusion in the homes that were the homes of stagnant peace.

30 And brother will give brother up to death; the father will stand by and see men execute his child; and in the courts the child will testify against the sire, and gladly see its mother put to death.

31 And men will hate you just because you speak the name of Christ.

32 Thrice blessed is the man who shall be faithful in this coming day of wrath!

33 Go now; when you are persecuted in a place, go seek another place.

34 And when you meet a foe too great for you, behold, the son of man is at your door, and he can speak, and all the hosts of heaven will stand in your defense.

35 But do not hold your present life in great esteem.

36 The time will come when men will take my life; you need not hope to be immune, for they will slay you in the name of God.

37 Men call me Beelzebul and they will call you imps.

38 Be not afraid of what men say and do; they have no power over soul; they may abuse and may destroy the body of the flesh; but that is all.

39 They do not know the God who holds the issues of the soul within his hands, who can destroy the soul.

40 The Christ is king today, and men must recognize his power.

41 He who loves not the Christ, which is the love of God, before all else, can never gain the prize of spirit consciousness.

42 And they who love their parents or their children more than they love the Christ can never wear the name of Christ.

43 And he who loves his life more than he loves the Christ cannot please God.

44 And he who clings to life shall lose his life, while he who gives his life for Christ will save his life.

45 When Jesus had thus said he sent the twelve away by twos, and bade them meet him in Caper-

46 And they went out through all the towns of Galilee and taught and healed in spirit and in power.

CHAPTER 123.

Jesus gives his final charge to the foreign masters and sends them forth as apostles to the world. He goes alone to Tyre and abides in

Rachel's home. Heals an obsessed child. Goes to Sidon and then to the mountains of Lebanon. Visits Mount Hermon, Cæsarea-Philippi, Decapolis, Gadara and returns to Capernaum. Receives the twelve, who give an account of their work.

THE Christine master spent a time in prayer and then he called the foreign masters, and he said to them,

2 Behold, I sent the twelve apostles unto Israel, but you are sent to all the world.

3 Our God is one, is Spirit and is truth, and every man is dear to him.

4 He is the God of every child of India, and the farther east; of Persia, and the farther north; of Greece and Rome and of the farther west; of Egypt and the farther south, and of the mighty lands across the seas, and of the islands of the seas.

5 If God would send the bread of life to one and not to all who have arisen to the consciousness of life and can receive the bread of life, then he would be unjust and that would shake the very throne of heaven.

6 So he has called you from the seven centers of the world, and he has breathed the breath of wisdom and of power into your souls, and now he sends you forth as bearers of the light of life, apostles of the human race.

7 Go on your way, and as you go proclaim the gospel of the Christ.

8 And then he breathed upon the masters and he said, Receive the Holy Breath; and then he gave to each the Word of power.

9 And each went on his way, and every land was blest.

10 Then Jesus went alone across the hills of Galilee and after certain days he reached the coast of Tyre, and in the home of Rachel he abode.

11 He did not advertise his coming, for he did not come to teach; he would commune with God where he could see the waters of the Mighty Sea.

12 But Rachel told the news and multitudes of people thronged her home to see the Lord.

13 A Grecian woman of Phenecia came; her daughter was obsessed. She said,

14 O Lord, have mercy on my home! My daughter is obsessed; but this I know, if you will speak the Word she will be free. Thou son of David, hear my prayer!

15 But Rachel said, Good woman, trouble not the Lord. He did not come to Tyre to heal; he came to talk with God beside the sea.

16 And Jesus said, Lo, I was sent not to the Greek, nor to Syrophenicians; I come just to my people, Israel.

17 And then the woman fell down at his feet and said, Lord, Jesus, I implore that you will save my child.

18 And Jesus said, You know the common proverb well: It is not meet that one should give the children's bread to dogs.

19 And then the woman said, Yea, Jesus, this I know, but dogs may eat the crumbs that fall down from their master's board.

20 And Jesus said, Such faith I have not seen, no not among the Jews; she is not serf, nor dog.

21 And then he said to her, According to your faith so let it be.

22 The woman went her way and when she came unto her child, lo, she was healed.

23 And Jesus tarried many days

in Tyre; and then he went his way and dwelt a time in Sidon by the sea.

24 And then he journeyed on. In Lebanon hills and vales, and in its groves he walked in silent thought.

25 His earthly mission fast was drawing to a close; he sought for strength, and what he sought he found.

26 Mount Hermon stood beyond, and Jesus fain would kneel beside that mountain famed in Hebrew song.

27 And then he stood upon Mount Hermon's lofty peaks, and lifting up his eyes to heaven he talked with God.

28 And masters of the olden times revealed themselves and long they talked about the kingdom of the Christ;

29 About the mighty works that had been done; about the coming conquest of the cross; about the victory over death.

30 Then Jesus journeyed on; he went to Cæsarea-Philippi, and in Susanna's home he tarried certain days.

31 And then he went through all Decapolis to give encouragement to those who knew him as the Christ, and to prepare them for the day of Calvary.

32 And then he went to Gadara, and many friends were there, to welcome him.

33 And Chuzas, steward of the house of Herod Antipas, was there, and Jesus went aboard the royal ship with him and crossed the sea, and came unto Capernaum.

34 And when the people knew that Jesus was at home they came to welcome him.

35 In just a little while the twelve apostles came and told the master all about their journey over Galilee.

36 They said that by the sacred Word they had done many mighty works; and Jesus said to them, Well done.

SECTION XVII.

PE.

The Third Annual Epoch of the Christine Ministry of Jesus.

CHAPTER 124.

The Christines cross the sea. Jesus gives to his disciples lessons on secret doctrines. Teaches the people. Feeds five thousand. The disciples start to recross the sea. A storm arises. Jesus, walking on the waters, comes to them. Trial of Peter's faith. They land in Gennesaret.

THE twelve apostles now had reached the stage of spirit consciousness, and Jesus could reveal to them the deeper meanings of his mission to the world.

2 Next week the great feast of the Jews would be observed, and Matthew said, Shall we not girt ourselves and go unto Jerusalem?

3 But Jesus said, We will not go up to the feast; the time is short and I have many things to say to you; come you apart into a desert place and rest a while.

4 And then they took their boats and crossed the sea, and came into a desert place near Julius Bethsaida.

5 The people saw them go, and

in vast multitudes they followed them.

6 And Jesus had compassion on the anxious throng, and he stood forth and taught them all the day, because they sought the light and were like sheep without a fold.

7 And as the night came on the twelve were doubting what the multitudes would do, and Thomas said,

8 Lord, we are in a desert place; the multitudes have naught to eat and they are faint from lack of food; what shall we do?

9 And Jesus said, Go to and feed the multitudes.

10 And Judas said, Shall we go down and buy two hundred pennies' worth of bread for them to eat?

11 And Jesus said, Go look into our larder and see how many loaves we have.

12 And Andrew said, We have no bread, but we have found a lad who has five barley loaves and two small fish; but this would not be food enough for one in ten.

13 But Jesus said, Command these people all to sit upon the grass in companies of twelve; and they all sat down in companies of twelve.

14 Then Jesus took the loaves and fish, and looking up to heaven he spoke the sacred Word.

15 And then he broke the bread and gave it to the twelve; he also gave the fish unto the twelve, and said, Go to and feed the multitudes.

16 And all the people ate and were refreshed.

17 There were about five thousand men, a company of little ones, and women not a few.

18 And when the people all were filled the master said,

19 Let not a crumb be lost; Go to and gather up the pieces of the bread and fish for others that may want.

20 They gathered up the fragments and they filled twelve baskets full.

21 The people were bewildered by this wondrous act of power; they said, And now we know that Jesus is the prophet that our prophets said would come; and then they said, All hail the king!   .

22 When Jesus heard them say, All hail the king! he called the twelve and bade them take their boats and go before him to the other side;

23 And he went all alone into a mountain pass to pray.

24 The twelve were on the sea and hoped to reach Capernaum in just a little time, when all at once a fearful storm arose, and they were at the mercy of the waves.

25 And in the fourth watch of the night the wind became a whirling wind, and they were filled with fear.

26 And in the blinding storm they saw a form move on the waves; it seemed to be a man, and one spoke out and said, It is a ghost, a sign of evil things.

27 But John discerned the form and said, It is the Lord.

28 And then the wind blew not so hard, and Peter, standing in the midst, exclaimed,

29 My Lord! my Lord! If this be truly you, bid me to come to you upon the waves.

30 The form reached forth his hand and said, Come on.

31 And Peter stepped upon the waves and they were solid as a rock; he walked upon the waves.

32 He walked until he thought within himself, What if the waves should break beneath my feet?

33 And then the waves did break beneath his feet, and he began to sink, and in the fearfulness

of soul he cried, O save me, Lord, or I am lost!

34 And Jesus took him by the hand and said, O you of little faith! why did you doubt? And Jesus led the way unto the boat.

35 The storm had spent its force; the winds were still, and they were near the shore, and when they landed they were in the valley of Gennesaret.

CHAPTER 125.

The Christines are welcomed in Gennesaret. Many follow Jesus for the loaves and fish. He tells them of the bread of life. Speaks of his flesh and blood as symbols of the bread and water of life. The people are offended and many of his disciples follow him no more.

THE news soon spread through all the valley of Gennesaret that Jesus and the twelve had come, and many people came to see.

2 They brought their sick and laid them at the master's feet, and all the day he taught and healed.

3 The multitudes upon the other side who had been fed the day before and other multitudes, went down to see the Lord; but when they found him not they sought him in Capernaum.

4 And when they found him not at home, they went on to Gennesaret. They found him there and said, Rabboni, when came you to Gennesaret?

5 And Jesus said, Why are you come across the sea? you came not for the bread of life;

6 You came to gratify your selfish selves; you all were fed the other day across the sea, and you are after more of loaves and fish.

7 The food you ate was nourishment for flesh that soon must pass away.

8 You men of Galilee, seek not for food that perishes, but seek for food that feeds the soul; and, lo, I bring you food from heaven.

9 You ate the flesh of fish, and you were satisfied, and now I bring the flesh of Christ for you to eat that you may live forevermore.

10 Our fathers ate the manna in the wilderness; and then they ate the flesh of quail, and drank the waters of a flowing spring that Moses brought out from the rock; but all of them are dead.

11 The manna and the quail were symbols of the flesh of Christ; the waters of the rock were symbols of the blood.

12 But, lo, the Christ has come; he is the bread of life that God has given to the world.

13 Whoever eats the flesh of Christ and drinks his blood shall never die; and he will hunger nevermore; and he will thirst no more.

14 And they who eat this bread of heaven, and drink these waters from the spring of life cannot be lost; these feed the soul, and purify the life.

15 Behold, for God has said, When man has purified himself I will exalt him to the throne of power.

16 Then Jesus and the twelve went to Capernaum; and Jesus went into the synagogue and taught.

17 And when the Jews, who heard him in Gennesaret, were come they said,

18 This fellow is beside himself. We heard him say, I am the bread of life that comes from heaven; and we all know that he is but a man, the son of man, who came from Nazareth; we know his mother, and his other kin.

19 And Jesus knew their thoughts; he said to them, Why murmur you, and reason thus among yourselves?

20 The Christ is everlasting life; he came from heaven; he has the keys of heaven, and no man enters into heaven except he fills himself with Christ.

21 I came in flesh to do the will of God, and, lo, this flesh and blood are filled with Christ; and so I am the living bread that comes from heaven;

22 And when you eat this flesh and drink this blood you will have everlasting life; and if you will, you may become the bread of life.

23 And many of the people were enraged; they said, How can this man give us his flesh to eat, his blood to drink?

24 And his disciples were aggrieved because he said these things, and many turned away and followed him no more.

25 They said, This is a fearful thing for him to say, If you eat not my flesh and drink my blood, you cannot enter into life.

26 They could not comprehend the parable he spoke.

27 And Jesus said, You stumble and you fall before the truth; What will you do when you shall see this flesh and blood transmuted into higher form?

28 What will you say when you shall see the son of man ascending on the clouds of heaven?

29 What will you say when you shall see the son of man sit on the throne of God?

30 The flesh is naught; the spirit is the quickening power. The words I speak are spirit; they are life.

31 When Jesus saw the many who had been so loud in their pro-fessions of their faith in him, turn back and go away, he said unto the twelve,

32 Will you desert me in this hour and go away?

33 But Peter said, Lord, we have no place else to go; you have the words of everlasting life; we know that you are sent to us from God.

CHAPTER 126.

Scribes and Pharisees visit Jesus. They censure him for eating with unwashed hands. He defends his acts and teaches a lesson on hypocrisy. Privately explains to the twelve his public teachings.

A COMPANY of scribes and Pharisees came from Jerusalem to learn wherein the power of Jesus lay.

2 But when they learned that he and his disciples heeded not the custom of the Jews, regarding washing of the hands before they ate, they were amazed.

3 And Jesus said, Hypocrisy is queen among you scribes and Pharisees. Of you Isaiah wrote:

4 This people honor me with lips; their hearts are far away. In vain they worship me; their doctrines are the dogmas and the creeds of men.

5 You men who pose as men of God, and still reject the laws of God and teach the laws of men,

6 Stand forth and tell when God gave unto men the ceremonial laws that you observe; and tell these people how the spirit life is sullied if one washes not before he eats.

7 His critics answered not, and then he said,

8 Hear me, you men of Israel! Defilement is a creature of the heart. The carnal mind lays hold of

thought, and makes a monstrous bride; this bride is sin; sin is a creature of the mind.

9 That which defiles a man is not the food he eats.

10 The bread and fish and other things we eat, are simply cups to carry to the cells of flesh material for the building of the human house, and when their work is done as refuse they are cast away.

11 The life of plant and flesh that goes to build the human house is never food for soul. The spirit does not feed upon the carcasses of animal, or plant.

12 God feeds the soul direct from heaven; the bread of life comes from above.

13 The air we breathe is charged with Holy Breath, and he who wills may take this Holy Breath.

14 The soul discriminates, and he who wants the life of Christ may breathe it in. According to your faith so let it be.

15 Man is not a part of his abiding place; the house is not the man.

16 The lower world builds up the house of flesh, and keeps it in repair; the higher world provides the bread of spirit life.

17 The loveliest lilies grow from stagnant ponds and filthiest muck.

18 The law of flesh demands that one should keep the body clean.

19 The law of spirit calls for purity in thought and word and deed.

20 Now, when the evening came and they were in the house, the twelve had many things to say, and many questions to propound.

21 Nathaniel asked, Was what you said about the house of flesh a parable? If so, what does it mean?

22 And Jesus said, Can you not yet discriminate? Do you not yet

perceive that what a man takes in his mouth defiles him not?

23 His food goes not into his soul; it is material for flesh and bone and brawn.

24 To spirit everything is clean.

25 That which defiles a man wells up from carnal thoughts; and carnal thoughts spring from the heart, and generate a host of evil things.

26 From out the heart comes murders, thefts and foolishness. All selfish acts and sensual deeds spring from the heart.

27 To eat with unwashed hands does not defile the man.

28 And Peter said, Lord, What you said today has grievously offended scribe and Pharisee.

29 And Jesus said, These scribes and Pharisees are not the scions of the tree of life; they are not plants of God; they are the plants of men, and every foreign plant shall be plucked up.

30 Let all these men alone; they are blind guides; they lead a multitude of people who are blind.

31 The leaders and the led together walk; together they will fall into the yawning pits.

CHAPTER 127.

The Christines cross the sea to Decapolis. Jesus finds a retired place where he privately teaches the twelve. They remain three days, then go into a village by the sea.

NOW, Jesus took the twelve and with them crossed the sea at night and came unto the borders of Decapolis,

2 That he might find a secret place where, all alone, he could reveal to them the things to come.

3 They went into a mountain pass and spent three days in prayer.

4 Then Jesus said, Behold, the time is near when I will walk with you in flesh no more.

5 Lo, I have taught that he who counts his life of so much worth that he would give it not in willing sacrifice to save his brother man, is worthy not to enter into life.

6 Lo, I am come as pattern for the sons of men, and I have not refrained from helpfulness.

7 When I had passed the seven tests in Heliopolis, I consecrated life and all I had, to save the world.

8 In the Judean wilderness I fought the strongest foes of men, and there I reaffirmed my consecration to the service of my fellow man.

9 In troubles and in trials I have wavered not; when false accusers came, I answered not.

10 God gave the saving Word to me, and I have often spoken it and healed the sick, drove unclean spirits out, and raised the dead.

11 And I have shown you how to speak the Word; and I have given you the Word;

12 In just a little while we turn our faces toward Jerusalem, and one of you who hear me now will then betray me into wicked hands.

13 The scribes and Pharisees will bring false charges up and hale me into court, and, by consent of Rome, I will be crucified.

14 Then Peter said, My Lord, it shall not be. The Roman soldiers will tread on twelve dead men before they reach our Lord.

15 But Jesus said, A savior of the world cannot resist.

16 I came to save the world and I have taken up your names before the highest courts of heaven, and you have been confirmed as saviors of the world.

17 And not a name, excepting that of him who shall betray, will ever be disgraced.

18 I go my way, and though my flesh shall pass, my soul will stand beside you all the way to guide and bless.

19 And wicked men will seize you in the streets, and as you kneel in prayer; will charge you with some legal crime, and think they serve their God by putting you to death.

20 But falter not; the load will heavy be, but with the consciousness of duty done, the peace of God will lift the load, dispel the pain and light the way.

21 And we will meet where carnal executioners come not; there we will serve the cruel men, who in their ignorance had tortured us to death.

22 Can we prevent this outrage and this slaughter of our lives? If not we are but creatures of the ebb and flow of carnal things. It would not be a sacrifice of life.

23 But we are masters of the things of time. Lo, we can speak, and all the spirits of the fire, water, earth and air will stand in our de-

24 We can command and many legions of the angel world would come and strike our enemies to earth.

25 But it is best that not a power of heaven or earth should come to our relief. And it is best that even God should veil his face and seem to hear us not.

26 As I am pattern unto you, so you are patterns for the human race. We show by non-resistance that we give our lives in willing sacrifice for man.

27 But my example will not end with death. My body will be laid within a tomb in which no

flesh has lain, symbolic of the purity of life in death.

28 And in the tomb I will remain three days in sweet communion with the Christ, and with my Father-God, and Mother-God.

29 And then, symbolic of the ascent of the soul to higher life, my flesh within the tomb will disappear;

30 Will be transmuted into higher form, and, in the presence of you all, I will ascend to God.

31 Then Jesus and the twelve went to a village by the sea.

CHAPTER 128.

Jesus goes at night to a mountain to pray. His disciples and the villagers find him and he teaches them for three days. Feeds four thousand people. The Christines go to Cæsarea-Philippi. They consider the personality of Christ. Peter is chosen as apostolic leader.

NOW, in the night while the disciples slept, lo, Jesus rose and went alone into a mountain pass, six miles away, to pray.

2 And in the morning when the twelve awoke they could not find the Lord, and all the people of the village sought, and when the sun had passed its highest point they found him in the mountain pass.

3 And multitudes of people came and brought their sick, and Jesus taught and healed.

4 And when the night came on the people would not go; they slept upon the ground that they might be a-near the Lord.

5 Three days and nights the multitudes remained, and none had aught to eat.

6 And Jesus had compassion and he said, If I should send the multitudes away they might not reach their homes, for they are faint, for some have journeyed many miles.

7 And his disciples said, Where shall we get enough of food to feed them all? There are four thousand men, besides the women and the little ones.

8 And Jesus said, How many loaves have you?

9 They answered, Seven, and some little fish.

10 And Jesus said, Go to, and seat the people as you seated them the other day when all the multitudes were fed, in companies of twelve.

11 And when the people were sat down in companies of twelve the loaves and fish were brought.

12 And Jesus looked to heaven and spoke the Word; and then he broke the seven loaves in little bits, and likewise cut the fish.

13 And every bit of bread became a loaf, and every piece of fish became a fish.

14 The twelve went forth and gave to every one; the people ate and they were filled; and all the fragments that were left were gathered up, and there were seven baskets full.

15 And then the people went their ways, and Jesus and the twelve took boats and came to Dalmanatha by the sea.

16 Here they remained for many days, and Jesus told the twelve about the inner light that cannot fail;

17 About the kingdom of the Christ within the soul; about the power of faith; about the secret of the resurrection of the dead; about immortal life, and how the living may go forth and help the dead.

18 And then they went into their boats, and came unto the northern coast of Galilee, and in

Chorazin where the kin of Thomas lived, they left their boats and journeyed on.

19 They came to Merom, where the crystal waters seem to catch the images of heaven and to reflect the glory of the Lord of hosts.

20 And here they tarried certain days in silent thought.

21 And then they journeyed on, and came into the land of Cæsarea-Philippi

22 And as they walked and talked among themselves, the master said, What do the people say about the son of man? who do they think I am?

23 And Matthew said, Some say that you are David come again; some say that you are Enoch, Solomon, or Seth.

24 And Andrew said, I heard a ruler of the synagogue exclaim, This man is Jeremiah, for he speaks like Jeremiah wrote.

25 Nathaniel said, The foreign masters who were with us for a time, declared that Jesus is Gautama come again.

26 James said, I think that most the master Jews believe you are the reappearence of Elijah on the earth.

27 And John spoke out and said, When we were in Jerusalem I heard a seer exclaim, This Jesus is none other than Melchizedek, the king of peace, who lived about two thousand years ago, and said that he would come again.

28 And Thomas said, The Tetrarch Herod thinks that you are John arisen from the dead;

29 But then his conscience troubles him; the spirit of the murdered John looms up before him in his dreams, and haunts him as a specter of the night.

30 And Jesus asked, Who do you think I am?

31 And Peter said, You are the Christ, the love of God made manifest to men.

32 And Jesus said, Thrice blessed are you, Simon, Jonas' son. You have declared a truth that God has given you.

33 You are a rock, and you shall be a pillar in the temple of the Lord of hosts.

34 And your confession is the cornerstone of faith, a rock of strength, and on this rock the Church of Christ is built.

35 Against it all the powers of hades and of death cannot prevail.

36 Behold, I give to you the keys to open up the doors of safety for the sons of men.

37 The Holy Breath will come upon you and the ten, and in Jerusalem you shall stand before the nations of the earth, and there proclaim the covenant of God with men.

38 And you shall speak the words of Holy Breath, and whatsoever God requires of men as earnest of their faith in Christ, you shall make known.

39 Then turning to the twelve he said, What you have heard this day tell not to any man.

40 Then Jesus and the twelve went up and were Susanna's guests for many days.

CHAPTER 129.

Jesus teaches the people. He takes Peter, James and John and goes to a high mountain and is transfigured before them.

THE news soon spread that Jesus and the twelve were come, and many people came to see.

2 And Jesus said, Behold, you come to see, but that means naught. If you would have the benedictions

of the Christ, take up your cross and follow me.

3   If you would give your life for selfish self, then you will lose your life.

4   If you will give your life in service of your fellow men, then you will save your life.

5   This life is but a span, a bauble of today.   There is a life that passes not.

6   Where is your profit if you gain the world and lose your soul? What would you take in payment for your soul?

7   If you would find the spirit life, the life of man in God, then you must walk a narrow way and enter through a narrow gate.

8   The way is Christ, the gate is Christ, and you must come up by the way of Christ.   No man comes unto God but by the Christ.

9   The kingdom of the Christ will come; yea, some of you who hear me now will not pass through the gates of death until you see the kingdom come in power.

10   For seven days the master and the twelve remained in Cæsarea-Philippi.

11   Then Jesus, taking Peter, James and John, went forth unto a mountain top to pray.

12   And as he prayed a brilliant light appeared; his form became as radiant as a precious stone;

13   His face shone like the sun; his garments seemed as white as snow; the son of man became the son of God.

14   He was transfigured that the men of earth might see the possibilities of man.

15   When first the glory came the three disciples were alseep; a master touched their eyes and said, Awake and see the glory of the Lord.

16   And they awoke, and saw the glory of the Lord; and more, they saw the glory of the heavenly world, for they beheld two men from thence stand forth beside the Lord.

17   And Peter asked the master who awakened them, Who are these men who stand beside the Lord?

18   The master said, These men are Moses and Elijah, who are come that you may know that heaven and earth are one; that masters there and masters here are one.

19   The veil that separates the worlds is but an ether veil.   For those who purify their hearts by faith the veil is rolled aside, and they can see and know that death is an illusive thing.

20   And Peter said, Praise God! And then he called to Jesus and he said, My master and my Lord, this is the gate of heaven, and it is well that we remain.

21   May we go down and bring three tents; a tent for you, a tent for Moses, and for Elijah one?   But Jesus answered not.

22   And Moses and Elijah talked with Jesus on the mount.   They talked about the coming trial of the Lord;

23   About his death, his rest within the tomb; about the wonders of the resurrection morn; the transmutation of his flesh, and his ascension on the clouds of light;

24   And all symbolic of the path that every man must tread; symbolic of the way the sons of men become the sons of God.

25   The three disciples were amazed, and suddenly the ethers were surcharged with song, and forms as light as air, moved all about the mountain top.

26   And then from out the glory

of the upper world they heard a voice that said,

27 This is the son of man, my chosen one to manifest the Christ to men. Let all the earth hear him.

28 When the disciples heard the voice they were afraid; they fell upon the ground and prayed.

29 And Jesus came; he touched them and he said, Arise, fear not; lo, I am here.

30 Then they arose, and as they looked about they saw no one; the men had gone. The master only stood with them.

31 As Jesus and the three came from the mountain top they talked about the meaning of the scene, and Jesus told them all; and then he said,

32 Till I have risen from the dead tell not to any one what you have seen.

33 But the disciples could not comprehend the meaning of the words, Till I have risen from the dead.

34 And Jesus told them once again about his death, and rising from the grave; about the kingdom of the soul that was to come in glory and in power.

35 But Peter said, The scribes have taught that e'er the king shall come Elijah must appear.

36 And Jesus said, Elijah has already come; but scribes and Pharisees received him not;

37 And men reviled him, bound him, cast him in a prison cell, and shouted with a fiend's delight to see him die.

38 What men have done to him, that they will do to me.

39 Then the disciples understood that Jesus spoke of John whom Herod slew.

CHAPTER 130.

Jesus and the three disciples return to Cæsarea-Philippi. The nine had failed to cure an epileptic child. Jesus heals it and rebukes his disciples for their lack of trust in God. The Christines return to Capernaum.

WHEN Jesus, Peter, James and John were come unto the city's gates a multitude of people thronged the way.

2 The nine apostles who went not with Jesus to the mount, had tried to heal an epileptic child who was obsessed, and they had failed; the people waited for the coming of the Lord.

3 When Jesus came the father of the child knelt down before him and implored his help.

4 He said, My master, I beseech that you will look in pity on my son, my only child; he is an epileptic child and suffers grievously.

5 Sometimes he falls into the fire and is burned; again he falls into the water and is like to drown; and many times a day he falls, he grinds his teeth, the foam pours from his mouth.

6 I took my child to your disciples, and they failed to give relief.

7 And as he spoke a servant brought the child before the Lord (the child spoke not, for he was dumb), and instantly he fell upon the ground, he foamed, he writhed in agony.

8 And Jesus said, How long has he been troubled thus?

9 The father said, From infancy; and we have sought in many lands for help, but found it not; but I believe that you can speak the Word and heal my son.

10 And Jesus said, Faith is the power of God. All things are pos-

sible for him who in his heart believes.

11 The father cried, in tears, Lord, I believe; help thou mine unbelief.

12 And Jesus spoke the Word of power; the epileptic child lay in a swoon; he did not breathe, and all the people said, The child is dead.

13 But Jesus took him by the hand and said: Arise; and he arose and spoke.

14 The people were amazed, and many said, This surely is a man of God, for no such power was ever given to man.

15 Then Jesus and the twelve went to the house, and after they had taken food and been refreshed, the nine disciples said,

16 Lord, why could we not heal this child? We spoke the Word; but even that was powerless.

17 And Jesus said, Your great success in all your former work has made you careless, and you forgot to recognize the power of God.

18 Without the spirit of the Word, the Word is like an idle tale; and you forgot to pray.

19 There is no faith without the prayer of faith. Faith is the wings of prayer; but wings alone fly not.

20 By prayer and faith you can bring down the mountain peaks, and cast them in the sea; the little hills will skip about like lambs at your command.

21 This failure may be well for you. The greatest lessons that are learned in life come through the failures that are made.

22 As the disciples sat in thoughtful meditation Jesus said, Let these words sink into your hearts:

23 The time has nearly come when you must bear your load alone;

that is, without my presence in the flesh.

24 For I will fall into the hands of wicked men, and they will slay me on a mount beyond Bezetha wall.

25 And men will lay my body in a tomb where, by the sacred Word, it will be guarded and preserved three days; then I will rise again.

26 The twelve were sad; they did not understand, and yet they feared to ask him to reveal the meaning of his word.

27 Next day the Christine master and the twelve began their journey of return, and soon were in Capernaum.

CHAPTER 131.

Jesus and Peter pay the half-shekel tax. The disciples contend for the supremacy. Jesus rebukes them. Teaches them many practical lessons. The parable of the good shepherd.

AS Jesus and the twelve were resting in the house, the tax collector came to Peter saying, Man, do Jesus and yourself pay this half-shekel tax?

2 And Peter said, We pay whatever is assessed.

3 And Jesus said, From whom do publicans collect this special tax? from strangers or from native sons?

4 And Peter said, The strangers only are supposed to pay this tax.

5 Then Jesus said, We all are native sons and we are free; but lest we cause contention we will pay the tax; but neither had the shekel wherewithal to pay.

6 And Jesus said, Go to the sea; cast in a hook and catch a fish and you will find within its inner parts

a shekel, which take up and pay the tax for you and me.

7 And Peter did as Jesus said; he found the shekel and he paid the tax.

8 Now Jesus heard the twelve dispute among themselves. The spirit of the carnal self was moving in their hearts, and they were questioning among themselves who was the greatest in the sight of God and man.

9 And Jesus said, You men, for shame! the greatest is the servant of the rest. And then he called to him a little child; he took it in his arms and said,

10 The greatest is the little child, and if you would be great at all you must become as is this child in innocence, in truth, in purity in life.

11 Great men scorn not the little things of earth; he who regards and honors such a child, regards and honors me, and he who scorns a child, scorn me.

12 If you would enter through the kingdom gate you must be humble as this little child.

13 Hear me, you men, This child, as every other child, has one to plead its cause before the throne of God.

14 You scorn it at your peril, men, for lo, I say, its counterpart beholds the face of God at every moment, every day.

15 And hear me once again, He who shall cause a little one to stumble and to fall is marked, accursed; and it were better far if he had drowned himself.

16 Behold, offenses everywhere! Men find occasions for to sin and fall, and they grow strong by rising when they fall;

17 But woe to him who causes other men to stumble and to fall.

18 Be on your guard, you men of God, lest you constrain another man to fall; beware lest you fall into sinful ways yourselves.

19 Now, if your hands cause you to sin, you better cut them off; for it is better far to have no hands and not be guilty in the sight of God and men, than to be perfect in your form and lose your soul.

20 And if your feet should cause offense, you better cut them off; for it is better far to enter into life without your feet than fall beneath the curse.

21 And if your eyes, or ears, cause you to sin, you better lose them all than lose your soul.

22 Your thoughts and words and deeds will all be tried by fire.

23 Remember that you are the salt of earth; but if you lose the virtues of the salt, you are but refuse in the sight of God.

24 Retain the virtues of the salt of life and be at peace among yourselves.

25 The world is full of men who have not in themselves the salt of life, and they are lost. I come to seek and save the lost.

26 How think you? if a shepherd has a hundred sheep, and one of them has gone astray, will he not leave the ninety and the nine,

27 And go out in the desert ways and mounain tops to seek the one that went astray?

28 Yes, this you know; and if he finds the one that went astray, lo, he is glad, and he rejoices over it far more than over all the ninety and the nine that did not go astray.

29 And so there is rejoicing in the courts of heaven when one of human birth who has gone forth into the ways of sin is found and brought back to the fold;

30 Yea, there is joy, more joy

than over all the righteous men who never went astray.

31 And John said, Master, who may seek and save the lost? and who may heal the sick, and cast the demons out of those obsessed?

32 When we were on the way we saw a man who was not one of us, cast demons out and heal the sick.

33 He did it by the sacred Word and in the name of Christ; but we forbade him, for he did not walk with us.

34 And Jesus said, You sons of men, do you imagine that you own the powers of God?

35 And do you think that all the world must wait for you to do the works of God?

36 God is not man that he should have a special care for any man, and give him special gifts.

37 Forbid not any man to do the works of God.

38 There is no man who can pronounce the sacred Word, and in the name of Christ restore the sick, and cast the unclean spirits out, who is not child of God.

39 The man of whom you speak is one with us. Whoever gathers in the grain of heaven is one with us.

40 Whoever gives a cup of water in the name of Christ is one with us; so God shall judge.

CHAPTER 132.

Jesus defends a man who has been convicted of stealing bread. The verdict is reversed. The man goes free, and the people supply the needs of his starving family.

A MULTITUDE of people thronged the streets. The officers were on the way to court

with one, a man accused of stealing bread.

2 And in a little while the man was brought before the judge to answer to the charge.

3 And Jesus and the twelve were there. The man showed in his face and hands the hard drawn lines of toil and want.

4 A woman richly clad, the accuser of the man, stood forth and said, I caught this man myself; I know him well, for yesterday he came to beg for bread,

5 And when I drove him from my door, he should have known that I would harbor not a man like him; and then today he came and took the bread.

6 He is a thief and I demand that he be sent to jail.

7 The servants also testified against the man; he was adjudged a thief, and officers were leading him away.

8 But Jesus standing forth exclaimed, You officers and judge, be not in haste to lead this man away.

9 Is this a land of justice and of right? can you accuse and sentence men to punishment for any crime until they testify themselves?

10 The Roman law will not permit such travesty on right, and I demand that you permit this man to speak.

11 And then the judge recalled the man and said, If you have any tale to tell, say on.

12 In tears the man stood forth and said, I have a wife and little ones and they are perishing for bread, and I have told my story oft, and begged for bread; but none would hear.

13 This morning when I left our cheerless hut in search of work my children cried for bread, and I resolved to feed them or to die.

14 I took the bread, and I appeal to God, Was it a crime?

15 This woman snatched the loaf away and threw it to the dogs, and called the officers and I am here.

16 Good people, do with me whate'er you will, but save my wife and little ones from death.

17 Then Jesus said, Who is the culprit in this case?

18 I charge this woman as a felon in the sight of God.

19 I charge this judge as criminal before the bar of human rights.

20 I charge these servants and these officers as parties to the crime.

21 I charge the people of Capernaum with cruelty and theft, because they heeded not the cries of poverty and want, and have withheld from helpless ones that which is theirs by every law of right;

22 And I appeal unto these people here, and ask, Are not my charges based on righteousness and truth?

23 And every man said, Yes.

24 The accusing woman blushed for shame; the judge shrank back in fear; the officers threw off the shackles from the man and ran away.

25 Then Jesus said, Give this man what he needs and let him go and feed his wife and little ones.

26 The people gave abundantly; the man went on his way.

27 And Jesus said, There is no standard law to judge of crime. The facts must all be stated e'er a judgment can be rendered in a case.

28 You men with hearts; go forth and stand where stood this man and answer me, What would you do?

29 The thief thinks every other man a thief and judges him accordingly.

30 The man who judges harshly is the man whose heart is full of crime.

31 The courtesan who keeps her wickedness concealed by what she calls respectability, has not a word of pity for the honest courtesan who claims to be just what she is.

32 I tell you, men, if you would censure not till you are free from sin, the world would soon forget the meaning of the word, accused.

CHAPTER 133.

The twelve go to the feast in Jerusalem, but Jesus remains in Capernaum. He selects seventy disciples, and sends them out to teach and heal. He goes alone to the feast and on his way he heals ten lepers. He teaches in the temple.

THE harvest feast drew near; the twelve went to Jerusalem, but Jesus did not go with them; he tarried in Capernaum.

2 Among the multitudes that followed him were many who went not up to the feast; they were not Jews.

3 And Jesus called three-score-and-ten of these disciples unto him and said, The kingdom of the Christ is not for Jews alone; it is for every man.

4 Lo, I have chosen twelve to preach the gospel, first unto the Jews; and they are Jews.

5 Twelve is the number of the Jew and seven the number of the all, including every man.

6 God is the ten, the holy Jod.

7 When God and man are multiplied we have three-score-and-ten, the number of the brotherhood of man.

8 And now I send you forth by twos and twos; not to the Jews alone, but unto every nation under heaven; to Greek and to Assyrian; to the

Samaritan; to those beyond the seas; to every man.

9 You need not go afar, for men of every land are here and in Samaria.

10 Arise and go your way; but go in faith; and take no gold nor silver in your purse; no extra coat or shoes.

11 Go in the sacred name; trust God and you will never come to want.

12 And let this be your salutation everywhere, Peace be to all; good will to all.

13 And if the son of peace be in the house, the door will open wide and you will enter in; and then the holy peace will rest upon that house.

14 The seventy in twos went forth; they went into Samaria, and as they went they said, Peace be to all; good will to all!

15 Repent and turn from sin, and set your house in order, for a son of man who bears the image of the Christ, will come, and you may see his face.

16 They entered every village of Samaria; they preached in Tyre and in Sidon by the sea. Some went to Crete, and others into Greece, and others went to Gilead and taught.

17 And Jesus, all alone, went to the feast by the Samaria way; and as he went through Sychar on the way, the lepers saw him and a company of ten called from afar and said,

18 Lord Jesus, stay and speak the Word for us that we may be made clean.

19 And Jesus said, Go forth and show yourselves unto the priests.

20 They went, and as they went their leprosy was healed. One of the ten, a native of Samaria, re-turned to thank the master and to praise the Lord.

21 And Jesus said to him, Lo, ten were cleansed; where are the nine? Arise, and go your way; your faith has made you whole.

22 You have revealed your heart and shown that you are worthy of the power; behold the nine will find again their leprous hands and feet.

23 And Jesus went his way, and while the feast was on he came into Jerusalem, and went into the temple courts.

24 And he rebuked the scribes and Pharisees, the priests and doctors of the law for their hypocrisy and selfishness.

25 The common people were amazed; they said, From whence has come the wisdom of this man? he speaks as speaks a sage.

26 And Jesus said, I did not learn the wisdom of the Holy One within the schools of men; my teaching is not mine; I speak the words of him who sent me here to do his will.

27 If any man would know whereof I speak, lo, he must do the will of God. No man can know except he enters into life and does the will of God.

28 Now, Moses gave the law; but none of you have kept the law; how can you judge the worthiness of any man?

29 Once in these courts I healed a man upon a Sabbath day, and in a rage you sought to take my life; and now because I tell the truth you seek again to take my life.

30 A scribe spoke out and said, You foolish man, you are obsessed; who wants to take your life?

31 The common people said, Is this not Jesus whom the rulers long have sought to kill? and now

he comes and teaches in the temple courts.

32 If he is guilty of such monstrous crimes, why do they not take him away in chains?

33 And Jesus said, You all know me, and know from whence I came; but you know not the God who sent me here, whose words I speak.

34 The multitudes again stood forth in his defense; they said, If this is not the Christ whom God has promised to reveal to men, will he do greater works when he shall come than does this man?

35 The Pharisees and ruling priests were angered and they sent their officers to take him e'er he went away. The officers were filled with fear; they seized him not.

36 And Jesus said, Lo, I am here but for a little time and then I go my way to him who sent me here to do his will.

37 You seek me now and you can find me now; the time will come when you will seek and will not find, for where I go you cannot come.

38 The people said, Where will he go that men can find him not? Will he go forth to Greece and teach the Greeks? or will he go to Egypt or Assyria to teach?

39 But Jesus answered not; unnoticed by the multitudes he left the temple courts and went his way.

CHAPTER 134.

Jesus teaches in the temple. His words enrage the rulers. Nicodemus defends him. He spends the night in prayer on Mount Olives. Next day he again teaches in the temple. An adultress is brought before him for judgment.

NOW, on the last day of the feast when multitudes were in the courtways, Jesus said,

2 Whoever is athirst may come to me and drink.

3 He who believes in me and in the Christ whom God has sent, may drink the cup of life, and from his inner parts shall streams of living waters flow.

4 The Holy Breath will overshadow him, and he will breathe the Breath, and speak the words, and live the life.

5 The people were divided in their views concerning him. Some said, This man is prophet of the living God.

6 And others said, He is Messiah whom our prophets said would come.

7 And others said, He cannot be the Christ, for he came down from Galilee; the Christ must come from Bethlehem where David lived.

8 Again the priests and Pharisees sent officers to bring him into court to answer for his life; but when the officers returned and brought him not,

9 The rulers were enraged and said, Why did you not arrest this man and hale him into court?

10 The officers replied, We never heard a man speak like this man speaks.

11 In rage the Pharisees stood forth and said, Have you gone mad? Have you been led astray? Are you disciples of this man?

12 Have any of the rulers, or the Pharisees believed on him? The common people! yes, they may believe; they are accursed; they know not anything.

13 But Nicodemus came before the rulers and he said, Can Jewish judges judge a man and sentence him until they hear his plea? Let Jesus stand before this bar and testify himself.

14 The rulers said, This Jesus is a wily man, and if we suffer him to speak, he will rebuke us face to face, and then the multitudes will laugh and stand in his defense.

15 And then you know, as well as we, that prophets do not come from Galilee.

16 The rulers felt the force of what the officers and Nicodemus said, and they said nothing more.

17 And then the people went their way, each to his home; but Jesus went unto Mount Olives where he spent the night in prayer.

18 But in the morning when the sun had scarcely risen, Jesus came again, and many people came to see him in the temple courts, and he sat down and taught the multitudes.

19 The Pharisees and scribes were still alert to find a cause whereby they might condemn him by the words he spoke.

20 The officers had taken in the very act of crime, a courtesan. As Jesus taught, they brought this woman in and set her in the midst and said,

21 Rabboni, this vile woman has been taken in adultery. The law of Moses says that such as she shall die, be stoned to death; what do you say should be her punish-

22 And Jesus stooped and made a figure on the ground and in it placed the number of a soul, and then he sat in silent thought.

23 And when the priests demanded that he speak, he said, Let him who has no sin stand forth and be the first to cast a stone at her.

24 And then he closed his eyes, and not a word was said. When he arose and saw the woman all alone he said,

25 Where are the men who brought you here? they who accused?

26 The woman said, They all are gone; no one was here who could condemn.

27 And Jesus said, And I condemn you not; go on your way in peace, and sin no more.

CHAPTER 135.

Jesus teaches in the temple. He reveals some of the deeper meanings of the Christine ministry. The rulers are greatly enraged and attempt to stone him, but he disappears.

THE feast was done and Jesus, Peter, James and John were sitting in the temple treasury.

2 The nine had gone back to Capernaum.

3 The people thronged the temple courts and Jesus said,

4 I am the lamp; Christ is the oil of life; the Holy Breath the fire. Behold the light! and he who follows me shall not walk in the dark, but he shall have the light of life.

5 A lawyer said, You witness for yourself, your witness is not true.

6 And Jesus said, If I do witness for myself I speak that which is true, for I know whence I came and where I go.

7 And no one else in flesh can testify for me, for none know whence I came, nor where I go.

8 My works bear witness to the truth I speak. As man I could not speak the words I speak; they are the words of Holy Breath; and then my Father testifies for me.

9 The lawyer said, Where does your father live?

10 And Jesus said, You know me not or you would know my Father, and if you knew the Father

you would know the son, because the Father and the son are one.

11 I go my way and you shall find me not; for where I go you cannot come, because you do not know the way.

12 You cannot find the way because your hearts are gross, your ears are dull, your eyes are closed.

13 The light of life cannot shine through the murky veil that you have drawn about your hearts. ·

14 You do not know the Christ and if the Christ be not within the heart there is no light.

15 I come to manifest the Christ to men and you receive me not, and you will dwell in darkness and in the shadow of the grave till you believe the words I speak.

16 But you will vilify the son of man, and lift him up and laugh to see him die.

17 But then a little light will come and you will know that I am what I am.

18 The people did not comprehend the meaning of the words he spoke.

19 And then he spoke unto the people who believed in him and said, If you abide in Christ, and Christ abide in you, and if you keep my words within your heart,

20 You are the way, you are disciples in the way, and you shall know what is the truth, and truth shall make you free.

21 And still the people did not understand; they said, We are the seed of Abraham and are already free; we never were the slaves of any man; why do you say, We shall be free?

22 And Jesus said, Do you not know that every one committing sin is slave of sin? abides in bondage unto sin?

23 If you sin not then you are free; but if you sin in thought, or word, or deed, then you are slaves, and naught but truth can set you free; if you are free through Christ, then you are free indeed.

24 You are the seed of Abraham, and yet you seek to kill me just because I speak the truth of Abraham.

25 You are the children of the flesh of Abraham; but, lo, I say, There is a spiritual Abraham whom you know not.

26 In spirit you are children of your father, and your father is Diabolus; you hang upon his words and do his will.

27 He was a murderer from the first; he cannot tell the truth, and when he tells a lie he speaks his own; he is himself a lie, and he is father of himself.

28 If you were children of my Father-God, then you could hear the words of God; I speak the words of God, but you can hear them not.

29 A Pharisee stood forth and said, This fellow is not one of us; he is a curst Samaritan and is obsessed.

30 But Jesus heeded not the words of Pharisee or scribe; he knew that all the people knew he was a Jew.

31 And then he said, Whoever keeps my words shall never die.

32 A lawyer said, And now we know he is obsessed. Our father Abraham is dead; the prophets all are dead, and yet this fellow says, Whoever keeps my words shall never die.

33 Is this man greater than our father Abraham? Is he above the prophets? and all of them are dead.

34 And Jesus said, Your father Abraham rejoiced to see my day; he saw it and was glad.

35 The lawyer said, You sim-

ple man; you are not fifty years of age; have you seen Abraham?

36 And Jesus said, Before the days of Abraham I am.

37 Again the scribes and Pharisees were in a rage; they took up stones to cast at him, but, like a phantom of the night, he disappeared; the people knew not where he went.

CHAPTER 136.

Jesus teaches in the temple. Relates the parable of the good Samaritan. Goes to Bethany. Teaches in Lazarus' home. Rebukes Martha for her anxiety about the things of this life.

AND Jesus stood again within the temple courts and taught.

2 A master of the law was sent to question him that he might find a cause to censure and accuse him of a crime.

3 He said, Lord, tell me what to do that I may have eternal life?

4 And Jesus said, You know the law; what does it say?

5 The lawyer answered, You shall love the Lord your God with all your heart, with all your soul, with all your strength, with all your mind, and you shall love your neighbor as yourself.

6 And Jesus said, Lo, you have answered well; this do and you shall live.

7 The lawyer said, My neighbor, who is he?

8 And Jesus said, A man was going from Jerusalem to Jericho, and lo, he met with robbers on the way, who beat him, robbed him of his goods, and left him bleeding by the way.

9 A Pharisee was going down that way; he saw the wounded man;

but then he had no time to lose; he passed by on the other side.

10 A Levite came and saw the man; but he was loath to soil his sacerdotal robes, and he passed by.

11 A lawyer on his way to Jericho observed the dying man, and then he said, If I could make a shekel I might help the man; but he has nothing left to give, I have no time for charity; and he passed on.

12 And then a stranger from Samaria came that way; he saw the wounded man; his heart was touched with pity and he stopped, dismounted from his horse,

13 Revived the man, and placed him on his horse and took him to an inn and charged the keeper of the inn to nurse him back to strength.

14 He gave the keeper all the money that he had and said, Your charges may be more than this, but care for this unfortunate, and when I come again I will pay all; and then he went his way.

15 Now, master of the law, which of these four was neighbor unto him who fell among the thieves?

16 The lawyer said, The man who showed him mercy; he who cared for him.

17 And Jesus said, Go on your way and likewise do, and you shall live.

18 Now, Jesus, Peter, James and John went out to Bethany where Lazarus lived.

19 And Mary sat at Jesus' feet and heard him speak the words of life while Martha served.

20 And Martha called, but Mary would not leave the Lord to help her serve.

21 And Martha said to Jesus, Do you not care that Mary makes me bear the burdens of the serving

all the day? I beg that you will bid her help.

22 And Jesus said, You are too anxious, Martha, for your guests; you need not trouble so about the things of life.

23 You grow a-weary by your care for little things and slight the one thing needed most of all.

24 Your sister here has chosen far the better part, a part that none can take away.

CHAPTER 137.

Jesus and his disciples go into a retired place to pray. Jesus teaches Lazarus how to pray. The model prayer. The value of importunate prayer Parable of the importunate housewife.

NOW, in the evening Jesus, Peter, James and John, with Lazarus, went out beyond the village gates to pray. And Lazarus said, Teach me to pray.

2 And Jesus said, The prayer I taught the twelve to pray while we were up in Galilee is one acceptable to God; and when you pray just say,

3 Our Father-God who art in heaven; holy is thy name; thy kingdom come; thy will be done on earth as it is done in heaven;

4 Give us this day our needed bread;

5 Help us forget the debts that other people owe to us, that all our debts may be discharged;

6 And shield us from the tempter's snares that are too great for us to bear;

7 And when they come give us the strength to overcome.

8 And Jesus said, The answer to your prayer may not appear in fulness in a little time.

9 Be not discouraged; pray again and then again, for God will hear.

10 And then he spoke a parable; he said, A housewife was alone at night and, lo, some guests arrived, and they were hungry, having had no food for all the day.

11 The housewife had no bread, and so at midnight she went forth and called a friend and said, Loan me three loaves of bread, for guests have come, and I have naught for them to eat.

12 The friend replied, Why do you trouble me at midnight hour? My door is shut; my children are with me in bed; I cannot rise to give you bread; tomorrow you can be supplied.

13 The housewife asked again, and then again, and then because she plead, and would not be refused, the friend arose and gave her bread.

14 Behold, I say to you, Ask firmly and you shall receive; seek trustingly and you shall find; knock earnestly, the door will open up.

15 All things are yours, and when you ask, not as a begging man would ask, but as a child, you shall be satisfied.

16 A son may ask his father for a loaf of bread; the father will not give to him a stone;

17 Or he may ask him for a fish; he will not give a crab; or he may ask him for an egg; the father will not give a pebble from the brook.

18 Behold, if men of flesh know how to give abundantly to children of the flesh, will not your heavenly Father give abundantly to you when you shall pray?

CHAPTER 138.

The Christines in Jerusalem. They meet a man blind from birth. Jesus teaches a lesson on the cause of disease and disasters. He heals the blind man.

THE Lord with Peter, James and John were in Jerusalem; it was the Sabbath day.

2 And as they walked along the way they saw a man who could not see; he had been blind from birth.

3 And Peter said, Lord, if disease and imperfections all are caused by sin, who was the sinner in this case? the parents or the man himself?

4 And Jesus said, Afflictions all are partial payments on a debt, or debts, that have been made.

5 There is a law of recompense that never fails, and it is summarized in that true rule of life:

6 Whatsoever man shall do to any other man some other man will do to him.

7 In this we find the meaning of the Jewish law, expressed concisely in the words, Tooth for a tooth; life for a life.

8 He who shall injure any one in thought, or word, or deed, is judged a debtor to the law, and some one else shall, likewise, injure him in thought, or word or deed.

9 And he who sheds the blood of any man will come upon the time when his blood shall be shed by man.

10 Affliction is a prison cell in which a man must stay until he pays his debts unless a master sets him free that he may have a better chance to pay his debts.

11 Affliction is a certain sign that one has debts to pay.

12 Behold this man! Once in another life he was a cruel man, and in a cruel way destroyed the eyes of one, a fellow man.

13 The parents of this man once turned their faces on a blind and helpless man, and drove him from their door.

14 Then Peter asked, Do we pay off the debts of other men when by the Word we heal them, drive the unclean spirits out, or rescue them from any form of sore distress?

15 And Jesus said, We cannot pay the debts of any man, but by the Word we may release a man from his afflictions and distress,

16 And make him free, that he may pay the debts he owes, by giving up his life in willing sacrifice for men, or other living things.

17 Behold, we may make free this man that he may better serve the race and pay his debts.

18 Then Jesus called the man and said, Would you be free? would you receive your sight?

19 The man replied, All that I have would I most freely give if I could see.

20 And Jesus took saliva and a bit of clay and made a salve, and put it on the blind man's eyes.

21 He spoke the Word and then he said, Go to Siloam and wash, and as you wash say, *Jahhevahe.* This do for seven times and you shall see.

22 The man was led unto Siloam; he washed his eyes and spoke the word, and instantly his eyes were opened and he saw.

23 The people who had seen the man for many years sit by the way and beg, were much surprised to see him see.

24 They said, Is not this man the Job that was born blind, who sat beside the way and begged?

25 He heard them talk among themselves; he said, Yes, I am he.

26 The people asked, How were you healed? who opened up your eyes?

27 He said, A man whom men call Jesus, made a salve of clay and put it on my eyes, and bade me say a word and wash in Siloam seven times; I did as he commanded me, and now I see.

28 A certain scribe was passing, and he saw the man and heard him say that Jesus, by the Word, had opened up his eyes.

29 He therefore took the man up to the synagogue, and told the story to the priests, who asked the man about the miracle.

30 The man replied, I never saw the light until today, for I was blind from birth.

31 This morning as I sat beside Siloam, a man I never knew put on my eyes a salve that people say he made of clay; he bade me say a word and bathe my eyes in water seven times; I did as he commanded and I saw.

32 A lawyer asked the man, Who was it opened up your eyes?

33 The man replied, Some people say, His name is Jesus and that he came from Galilee; but others say, He is the son of God.

34 A Pharisee came up and said, This is the Sabbath day; a man who does a work like this, regarding not the Sabbath day, is not from God.

35 Some of the priests were much amazed and said, A wicked man could never do a miracle like this; he must possess the power of God. And so they strove among themselves.

36 They asked the man, What do you think about this man from Galilee?

37 He said, He is a prophet sent from God.

38 Now, many of the Jews did not believe the man was blind from birth; they said, There is no power to open up the eyes of one born blind.

39 And then they brought the parents of the man before the Pharisees that they might testify.

40 They said, This is our son who was born blind; we do not know how he received his sight; he is of age and he can tell; ask him.

41 They were afraid to say what they believed, that Jesus is the Christ who came to manifest the power of God, lest they offend the priests and be cast from the synagogue.

42 Again the rulers said, This Jesus is a wicked man. The man who had been healed stood forth again and said,

43 This Jesus may be sinner or be saint, I do not know; but this one thing I know; I once was blind, but now I see.

44 And then the scribes and Pharisees reviled the man and said, You are a follower of this man from Galilee. We follow Moses, but this man, we know him not, and know not whence he is.

45 The man replied, It is a marvel that you know not whence he is, and yet he opened up my eyes.

46 You know that nothing but the power of God can do such things.

47 God hears not sinners pray, and you must know that he is not a wicked man who can employ the power of God.

48 The Pharisees replied, You wretch! you were begotten and were born in sin, and now you try to teach the law to us. And then they cast him from the synagogue.

CHAPTER 139.

Jesus meets and instructs the man who was blind. Unfolds the mysteries of the kingdom. The sheepfold. Declares himself the shepherd. Goes to the home of Massalian, where he abides certain days.

WHEN Jesus heard what had been done and how the priests had cast the man whom he had healed, out of the synagogue, he round the man and said to him,

2   Do you believe in God and in the son of God?

3   The man replied, I do believe in God; but who is he, the son of God, of whom you speak?

4   And Jesus said, The son of God is he who speaks to you.

5   The man inquired then, Why do you say, The son of God? Is there but one?

6   And Jesus said, All men are sons of God by birth; God is the Father of the race; but all are not the sons of God by faith.

7   He who attains the victory over self is son of God by faith, and he who speaks to you has overcome, and he is called the son of God, because he is the pattern for the sons of men.

8   He who believes and does the will of God is son of God by faith.

9   The man in joy exclaimed, Lord, I believe in God, and in the son of God.

10   And Jesus said, I came to open prison doors, to make the blind to see; but, lo, the Pharisees are blind from birth.

11   And when I put the salve of truth upon their eyes, and bid them go and wash, and speak the sacred Word they will not go; they love the dark.

12   A multitude of people pressed about the Lord, and he stood forth and said,

13   You men of Israel, I say to you, The fold of God is large; its walls are strong, it has a gateway in the east, and he who does not enter by the gate into the fold, but climbs into the fold some other way, is thief and comes to rob.

14   The shepherd of the sheep stands by the gate; he gives the se-cret sign; he knocks; the watchman opens up the gate.

15   And then the shepherd calls his sheep by name; they hear his voice and follow him; they enter through the gate into the fold.

16   The sheep know not a stranger's voice; they will not follow him; they flee away.

17   The people did not understand the parable that Jesus spoke; and then he said,

18   Christ is the gateway of the fold; I am the shepherd of the sheep, and he who follows me through Christ shall come into the fold where living waters flow, and where rich pastures are.

19   False prophets come and go; they claim to be the shepherds of the sheep; they claim to know the way, but they know not the word of power; the watchman opens not the gate; the sheep heed not their call.

20   The shepherd of the sheep will give his life to save the sheep.

21   A hireling flees to save his life when wolves infest the fold; and then the tender lambs are snatched away, the sheep are scattered everywhere.

22   I am the shepherd of the sheep; I know the sheep of God; they know my voice, as God knows me and I know him.

23   The Father loves me with a deathless love, because I lay my life down for the sheep.

24   I lay my life down when I will, but I may take it up again; for every son of God by faith has power to lay his mortal flesh aside and take it up again.   These words I have received from God.

25   Again the people strove among themselves; they were divided in their views concerning

Christ. They could not comprehend the words that Jesus spoke.

26 Some said again, He is obsessed, or he is mad; why listen to his words?

27 And others said, His words are not the words of one obsessed. Can unclean spirits open up the eyes of one born blind?

28 Then Jesus left Jerusalem and with Massalian he tarried certain days.

CHAPTER 140.

Jesus and the three disciples return to Capernaum. Jesus receives the report of the seventy. With his disciples he goes through all Galilee encouraging the believers. He heals a woman. Relates the parable of the little seed and the great tree.

THE time had come for the return of the three score and ten whom Jesus sent abroad to preach.

2 And Jesus, Peter, James and John began their journey back to Galilee.

3 They went up through Samaria; they passed through many villages and towns, and everywhere the people thronged the ways to see the man the seventy had told about; and Jesus taught and healed the sick.

4 And when they reached Capernaum the seventy were there; and they were filled with joy; they said,

5 The Spirit of the Lord of hosts was with us all the way, and we were filled.

6 The power of the sacred Word was manifest in us; we healed the sick; we caused the lame to walk, the deaf to hear, the blind to see.

7 The very devils trembled when we spoke the Word, and they were subject unto us.

8 And Jesus said, As you were going on your way, the heavens were bright with light, the earth was bright, they seemed to meet and be at one; and I beheld, and Satan fell as lightning from the heavens.

9 Behold, for you have power to tread on serpents and on scorpions, and these are symbols of the enemies of men. You are protected in the way of right, and naught can harm.

10 And as you went I heard a master say, Well done.

11 But you may not rejoice because you have the power to heal the sick and make the devils tremble by the Word; for such rejoicing is from carnal self.

12 You may rejoice because the nations of the earth have ears to hear the Word, and eyes to see the glory of the Lord, and hearts to feel the inner breathing of the Holy Breath.

13 And you may well be glad because your names are written in the Book of Life.

14 Then Jesus looked to heaven and said, I thank thee, Father, Lord of heaven and earth, because thou hast revealed thyself to babes, and taught them how to light the path and lead the wise to thee.

15 What thou hast given to me, lo, I have given to them, and through the sacred Word I have bestowed on them the understanding heart,

16 That they might know and honor thee through Christ, who was, and is, and evermore shall be.

17 And then he said aside, unto the seventy and twelve, Most blessed are your eyes because you see the things you see;

18 And blessed are your ears because they hear the things they hear;

19 And blessed are your hearts because you understand.

20 In ages that are gone the wise of earth, the prophets, seers and kings, desired to hear and see and know what you have heard and seen and known; but they had not attained and could not hear, and see and know.

21 And Jesus said again, Lo, I have gone before you many moons, and I have given to you the bread of heaven and the cup of life;

22 Have been your buckler and your stay; but now that you have learned the way, and have the strength to stand alone, behold, I lay my body down and go to him who is the All.

23 In forty days then we will turn our faces toward Jerusalem where I will find the altar of the Lord and give my life in willing sacrifice for men.

24 Let us arise and go through all the coasts of Galilee, and give a salutation of good cheer to all the sons of God by faith.

25 And they arose and went; they entered every town and village on the coast, and everywhere they said, The benedictions of the Christ abide with you forevermore.

26 Now, in a certain town they went up to the synagogue upon the Sabbath day, and Jesus taught.

27 And as he spoke, two men brought on a cot a woman bent near double with disease; she had not risen from her bed for eighteen years without a helping hand.

28 And Jesus laid his hand upon the woman, and he said, Arise, be free from your infirmity.

29 And as he spoke the Word the woman found that she was straight and strong, and she arose and walked and said, Praise God.

30 The ruler of the synagogue was filled with wrath because the healer healed upon the Sabbath day.

31 He did not censure Jesus face to face, but turning to the multitudes he said,

32 You men of Galilee, why do you break the laws of God? There are six days in every week when you may work, and then you may bring the afflicted to be healed.

33 This is the day that God has blessed, the Sabbath day in which men may not work.

· 34 And Jesus said, You inconsistent scribes and Pharisees! Upon the Sabbath day you take your beasts of burden from their stalls, and lead them forth to eat and drink; is this not work?

35 This daughter of your father Abraham, who has been bound for eighteen years, has come in faith to be made free.

36 Now, tell me, men, is it a crime to break her bonds and set her free upon the Sabbath day?

37 The ruler said no more; the people all rejoiced and said, Behold the Christ!

38 And Jesus spoke a parable; he said, The kingdom of the Christ is like a little seed that one put in the ground;

39 It grew and after many years became a mighty tree, and many people rested in its shade, and birds built nests and reared their young among its leafy boughs.

CHAPTER 141.

Jesus speaks words of encouragement. Rebukes an officious Pharisee. Attends a wedding feast. Heals a dropsical man. Rebukes guests who seek chief seats. Relates a parable of a wedding feast.

AND Jesus went into another town upon the coast and spoke good words of cheer to those who followed him.

2 And one stood forth and said, Lord, are there few that enter into life?

3 And Jesus said, The way is rough that leads to life; the gate is narrow and is guarded well; but every one who seeks in faith shall find the way, and they who know the Word may enter in.

4 But many seek the way for selfish gain; they pound upon the gate of life; but it is fast.

5 The watchman from the turret says, I know you not; your speech is that of Ashdod, and your robes are those of sin; depart and go your way.

6 And they will go their way with weeping and with gnashing of the teeth.

7 And they will be enraged when they see their father Abraham with Isaac, Jacob and the prophets, resting in the kingdom of the Christ, and they themselves debarred.

8 And, lo, I say that men will come from lands afar, from east, from west, from north, from south and sit with me in consciousness of life.

9 Behold, I say, the last shall be the first, the first shall be the last.

10 All men are called unto the kingdom of the Christ; but few are chosen, for the pure in heart alone can see the king.

11 And as he spoke a Pharisee came up and said, You man of Galilee, if you would save your life remain not here; flee instantly, for Herod swears that he will take your life, and even now his officers are seeking you.

12 And Jesus said, Why is it that the Pharisees are so concerned about my life? And then he said unto the man who spoke,

13 Go forth and say to that sly fox, Behold, I heal the sick and cast the unclean spirits out today, tomorrow, and the days to come, and then I will attain.

14 Go say to him, I need not fear in Galilee, for I must meet the cruel wrath of men within Jerusalem.

15 And while they tarried in the place a man, a Pharisee, invited Jesus and a few of those who followed him, to dine with him upon the Sabbath day, to celebrate the marriage of his son.

16 Among the guests was one afflicted with a dropsical disease.

17 And Jesus said to those who had been sent to get from his own lips some words by which they might accuse him of a crime,

18 You lawyers and you Pharisees, what do you say about the lawlessness of healing on the Sabbath day? Here is a man, one of your own, and he is sore distressed.

19 Shall I, in God's own strength, say out the healing Word and heal this man?

20 The lawyers and the Pharisees were dumb; they answered not.

21 Then Jesus spoke the healing Word and healed the man and he, rejoicing, went his way.

22 Then Jesus said again unto the lawyers and the Pharisees, Which one of you who has a horse or cow, if it would fall into a pit upon the Sabbath day would not call in his friends to help to draw it out?

23 And not a man could answer, Here am I.

24 As Jesus looked upon the guests who had been bidden to the

feast and saw them crowding in to get the highest seats, he said to them,

25 You selfish men why do you strive to take the highest seats when you are but invited guests? You do not show our host the courtesies of life.

26 When men are bidden to a marriage feast they should sit in the lower seats until the host shall place them where he wills.

27 You may, unbidden, take the highest seat; but then a man more honorable may come and when the host shall bid you rise and take a lower seat that he may honor his more worthy guest, you cannot help but blush for very shame in your humility.

28 But if you take the lowest seat and then are honored by your host and asked to take a higher seat, you are esteemed an honored guest.

29 In this event we note a principle in life, That he who would exalt himself shall be abased, and he who humbles low himself shall be exalted in the sight of men.

30 Then Jesus spoke to all the guests; he said, When any one of you would make a feast it should not be for friends, or kindred, or the rich;

31 For they consider such a courtesy loaned out, and they feel called upon to make a greater feast for you, just in the payment of a debt.

32 But when you make a feast invite the poor, the lame, the blind; in this a blessing waits for you, for well you know that you will get naught in return; but in the consciousness of helping those who need, you will be recompensed.

33 And then he spoke a parable:

he said, A wealthy man prepared a feast; he sent his servants forth to bid his chosen ones to come; but they desired not to go, and they formed such excuses as they thought would satisfy the would-be host.

34 One said, I have just bought a piece of land, and I must go and prove my title to the land; I pray to be excused.

35 Another said, I must go down and prove my ownership in sheep that I have bought; I pray to be excused.

36 Another said, I have been married but a little time and so I cannot go; I beg to be excused.

37 Now, when the servants came and told the man who had prepared the feast that those he had invited would not come,

38 The man was grieved in heart; and then he sent his servants forth into the streets and alleys of the town to bring up to the feast the poor, the lame, the blind.

39 The servants went abroad and found the poor, the lame, the blind, and brought them in; but there was room for more.

40 The host then sent his men of arms to bring by force the people to his feast; and then the house was full.

41 And God has made a feast for men. Long years ago he sent his servants forth unto the favored sons of men. They would not hear his call; they came not to the feast.

42 He then sent forth his servants to the strangers and the multitudes; they came, but there is room for more.

43 Behold, for he will send his angels forth with mighty trumpet blast, and men will be compelled to come up to the feast.

CHAPTER 142.

The path of discipleship, its difficulties. The cross and its meaning. The danger of wealth. The young man who loved wealth more than he loved Christ. Parable of the rich man and Lazarus.

NOW, Jesus and the twelve went to another town, and as they entered it they said, Peace be to all; good will to all.

2 A multitude of people followed and the master said to them, Behold, for you are followers for selfish gain.

3 If you would follow me in love, and be disciples of the Holy Breath, and gain at last the crown of life, you must leave all there is of carnal life behind.

4 Be not deceived; stay, men, and count the cost.

5 If one would build a tower, or a home, he first sits down and counts the cost to be assured that he has gold enough to finish it.

6 For well he knows that if he makes a failure of his enterprise he may lose all his wealth, and be the butt of ridicule.

7 And if a king desires to take the kingdom of another king, he calls his trusted men and they consider well their strength; he will not measure arms with one of matchless power.

8 Count well the cost before you start to follow me; it means the giving up of life, and all you have.

9 If you love father, mother, wife, or child, more than you love the Christ, you cannot follow me.

10 If you love wealth or honor more than you love the Christ, you cannot follow me.

11 The paths of carnal life do not run up the mountain side towards the top; they run around the mount of life, and if you go straight to the upper gate of consciousness you cross the paths of carnal life; tread in them not.

12 And this is how men bear the cross; no man can bear another's cross.

13 Take up your cross and follow me through Christ into the path of true discipleship; this is the path that leads to life.

14 This way of life is called the pearl of greatest price, and he who finds it must put all he has beneath his feet.

15 Behold, a man found in a certain field the croppings of a wondrous mine of gold, and he went forth and sold his home and all he had and bought the field; then he rejoiced in wealth.

16 Now, there were present, scribes and Pharisees of wealth who loved their money, and their bonds and lands, and they laughed loud to scorn what Jesus said.

17 Then Jesus spoke to them and said, You are the men who justify yourselves in sight of men; God knows your wickedness of heart;

18 And you must know, O men, that whatsoever is revered and is exalted by the carnal mind, is an abomination in the sight of God.

19 And Jesus went his way, and as he went a young man ran and knelt down at his feet and said, Good master, tell me what to do that I may have eternal life.

20 And Jesus said, Why do you call me good? No one is truly good but God himself.

21 And God has said, If you would enter into life, keep the Commandments of the law.

22 The young man asked, To which commands did he refer?

23 And Jesus said, You shall

not kill; you shall not steal; you shall not do adulterous things; you shall not falsely testify;

24 And you shall love your God with all your heart, and you shall love your neighbor as yourself.

25 The man replied, These things I have observed from youth; what lack I yet?

26 And Jesus said, One thing you lack; your heart is fixed on things of earth; you are not free.

27 Go forth and sell all that you have, and give your money to the poor, and come and follow me, and you shall have eternal life.

28 The man was grieved at what the master said; for he was rich; he hid his face and went in sorrow on his way.

29 And Jesus looked upon the sorrowing man and said, It is so hard for men with hoarded wealth to enter through the door into the kingdom of the soul.

30 And his disciples were amazed at what he said.

31 He answered them and said, I tell you, men, that they who trust in riches cannot trust in God and cannot come into the kingdom of the soul;

32 Yea, it is easier for a camel to go through a needle's eye than for a man with hoarded wealth to find the way of life. And his disciples said, Who then can find the way? Who can be saved?

33 And Jesus said, The rich may give his gold away; the high may kiss the dust, and God will save.

34 Then Jesus spoke this parable to them:

35 A rich man lived in splendid state; he wore the finest garments men could make; his boards were loaded with the costliest viands of the land.

36 A beggar, blind and lame, whose name was Lazarus, was wont to sit beside the waste gate of this home that he might share with dogs the refuse from the rich man's boards.

37 It came to pass that Lazarus died, and angels carried him away unto the bosom of our father Abraham.

38 The rich man also died, and he was buried in a costly tomb; but in the purifying fires he opened up his eyes dissatisfied.

39 He looked and saw the beggar resting peacefully in the bosom of his father Abraham, and in the bitterness of his soul he cried,

40 My father Abraham, look down in mercy on your son; I am tormented in these flames.

41 Send Lazarus, I beseech, that he may give me just a sup of water to cool my parched tongue.

42 But Abraham replied, My son, in mortal life, you had the best things of the earth and Lazarus had the worst, and you would not give him a cup of water there, but drove him from your door.

43 The law must be fulfilled, and Lazarus now is comforted, and you are paying what you owe.

44 Besides, there is a great gulf fixed between your zone and us, and if I would I could not send Lazarus to you, and you cannot come up to us till you have paid your debts.

45 Again the man in anguish said, O father Abraham, I pray, send Lazarus back to earth, and to my father's house, that he may tell my brothers who are yet in life, for I have five of them, about the horrors of this place, lest they come down to me and not to you.

46 And Abraham replied, They

have the words of Moses and the seers, let them hear them.

47 The man replied, They will not hearken to the written word; but if a man would go up from the grave they might believe.

48 But Abraham replied, If they hear not the words of Moses and the seers they would not be persuaded even though one from the dead stood in their midst.

49 And Peter said, Lord, we have left our all to follow you; and what is our reward?

50 And Jesus said, Most verily I say to you, that you who have left all to follow me shall come into a newness of a life hid deep with Christ in God.

51 And you shall sit with me upon the throne of power, and judge with me the tribes of Israel.

52 And he who conquers carnal self, and follows me through Christ shall have a hundred fold of that which is the wealth of life on earth, and in the world to come, eternal life.

CHAPTER 143.

Righteousness in rewards. Jesus relates the parable of the husbandman and the laborers. Makes known the divine law of divorce. The mystery of marriage.

THE Lord was standing by the sea; the multitudes were there and one stood forth and said,

2 Does God bestow rewards as men bestow rewards, for what is done?

3 And Jesus said, Men never know what other men have done, this life is such a seeming life.

4 One man may seem to do a mighty work, and be adjudged by men as worthy of a great reward.

5 Another man may seem to be a failure in the harvest fields of life, and be dishonored in the face of men.

6 Men do not know the hearts of men; God only knows the hearts of men, and when the day is done he may reward with life the man who fell beneath the burdens of the day, and turn away the man who was the idol of the hearts of men.

7 And then he spoke a parable; he said, The kingdom of the soul is like a man who had a vast estate,

8 And in the morning time he went down to the market place to search for men to gather in his grain.

9 He found three men, and he agreed to give to each a penny for his service for the day, and sent them to his field.

10 Again he went down to the market place the third hour of the day and found five men in waiting, and he said, Go down into my field and serve, and I will pay you what is right; and they went down and served.

11 He went again; it was the sixth hour of the day, and seven men were waiting at the stand; he sent them to the field to serve.

12 And at the eleventh hour he went again; twelve men stood there in seeming idleness; he said to them, Why stand you here in idleness all day?

13 They said, Because we have no work to do; no man has hired us.

14 And then he sent them to his field to serve.

15 Now, when the evening came the man said to his steward, Call the laborers from the field, and pay them for his services. And all were paid, and each received a penny for his hire.

16 Now, when the twelve, who served but from the eleventh hour,

received each one a penny for his hire, the three were sore aggrieved; they said,

17 These twelve have served but one short hour, and now they have an equal share with us who have toiled through the scorching hours of day; should we not have at least two pennies for our hire?

18 The man replied, My friends, I do no wrong to you. Did we not have a fast agreement when you went to work? have I not paid in full?

19 What is it unto you if I should pay these men a smaller or a larger sum? Take that which is your own and go your way, for I will give unto the twelve what I will give unto the three, the five, the seven.

20 They did their best and you could do no more than do your best.

21 The hire of man is based upon the intent of the heart.

22 As Jesus taught, a Pharisee came up and said, Lord, is it lawful for a man to put away his wife?

23 And Jesus said, You ought to know; what says the law?

24 The Pharisee replied, The law provides that man may be divorced, may put away his wife.

25 And Jesus said, The hardness of the hearts of men induced the giver of the law to make provisions such as these; but from the first it was not so.

26 God made a woman for a man, and they were one; and afterwards he said, A man shall leave his father and his mother and shall cleave unto his wife; they are no more divided; they are one, one flesh.

27 What God has joined no man can part.

28 Now, when they went up to the house, a man made free to ask again about this matter of divorce.

29 And Jesus said again what to the Pharisee he said; and then he gave the higher law of marriage life:

30 Whoever puts away his wife, except she be a courtesan, and then shall take another wife commits adultery.

31 The woman who shall leave a man, unless he be a libertine and an adulterer, and then becomes the wife of any other man, commits adultery.

32 And Thomas asked, What is adultery?

33 And Jesus said, The man who harbors lustful thoughts, who covets any woman not his wife, is an adulterer.

34 The wife who harbors lustful thoughts, and covets any man who is not wed to her, is not her husband, is a courtesan.

35 Men cannot make a law to bind two hearts.

36 When two are bound in love they have no thought of lust. The woman cannot leave the man; the man has no desire to send his wife away.

37 When men and women harbor lustful thoughts, and covet any other flesh, they are not one, not joined by God.

38 And Philip said, Lord, are there few that God has joined in holy marriage bonds?

39 And Jesus said, God knows the pure in heart; the lustful men and women are but creatures of the lustful self; they cannot be at one; nor can they be at one with God.

40 Nathaniel said, Is it not well that all men should refrain from taking on themselves the marriage vow?

41 And Jesus said, Men are not

pure because they are unmarried men. The man who lusts is an adulterer if he has wife or not.

42 And then he said to all, Some things men know by being told, while other things they know not till the gate of consciousness shall open up for them.

43 I speak a mystery that now you cannot understand; but you shall some day understand.

44 A eunuch is a man who does not lust; some men are eunuchs born, some men are eunuchs by the power of men, and some are eunuchs by the Holy Breath, who makes them free in God through Christ.

45 He who is able to receive the truth I speak, let him receive.

CHAPTER 144.

The Christines at Tiberius. Jesus speaks on the inner life. Relates the parable of the prodigal son. The resentment of the elder brother.

WHEN they had journeyed through the towns and cities of the land of Galilee, the Lord with his disciples came to Tiberius, and here they met a few who loved the name of Christ.

2 And Jesus told them many things about the inner life; but when the multitudes came up, he spoke a parable; he said,

3 A certain man with great possessions had two sons. The youngest son grew tired of life at home and said,

4 My father, pray divide your wealth and give the portion that is mine to me, and I will seek my fortune in another land.

5 The father did as he desired, and with his wealth the young man went into a foreign land.

6 He was a profligate and soon had squandered all his wealth in ways of sin.

7 When nothing else remained for him to do he found employment in the fields to care for swine.

8 And he was hungry and no one gave him aught to eat, and so he ate the carob pods that he was feeding to the swine.

9 And after many days he found himself and said unto himself, My father is a man of wealth; he has a score of servants who are bountifully fed while I, his son, am starving in the fields among the swine.

10 I do not hope to be received again as son, but I will rise and go straight to my father's house, and I will make confession of my waywardness;

11 And I will say, My father, I am come again; I am a profligate, and I have lost my wealth in ways of sin; I am not worthy to be called your son.

12 I do not ask to be received again as son, but let me have a place among your servants, where I may have a shelter from the storms and have enough to eat.

13 And he arose and sought his father's house, and as he came his mother saw him while yet a great way off.

14 (A mother's heart can feel the first faint yearning of a wandering child.)

15 The father came, and hand in hand they walked a-down the way to meet the boy, and there was joy, great joy.

16 The boy tried hard to plead for mercy and a servant's place; but love was all too great to listen to the plea.

17 The door was opened wide; he found a welcome in the mother's heart, and in the father's heart.

18 The father called the serv-

ants in, and bade them bring the finest robe for him; the choicest sandals for his feet; a ring of purest gold for him to wear.

19 And then the father said, My servants, go and kill the fatted calf; prepare a feast, for we are glad;

20 Our son we thought was dead is here alive; a treasure that we thought was lost is found.

21 The feast was soon prepared and all were merry, when the eldest son who had been serving in a distant field and knew not that his brother had returned, came home.

22 And when he learned the cause of all the merriment he was offended, and would not go into the house.

23 His father and his mother both besought him tearfully to disregard the waywardness and folly of their son; but he would not; he said,

24 Lo, all these years I have remained at home, have served you every day, have never yet transgressed your most severe commands;

25 And yet you never killed for me a kid, nor made for me a simple feast that I might make merry with my friends;

26 But when your son, this profligate, who has gone forth and squandered half your wealth in ways of sin, comes home, because he could do nothing else, you kill for him the fatted calf and make a wondrous feast.

27 His father said, My son, all that I have is yours and you are ever with us in our joys;

28 And it is well to show our gladness when your brother, who is near and dear to us, and who we thought was dead, returns to us alive.

29 He may have been a profligate; may have consorted with gay courtesans and thieves, yet he is still your brother and our son.

30 Then Jesus said so all might hear: He who has ears to hear, and hearts to understand will comprehend the meaning of this parable.

31 Then Jesus and the twelve came to Capernaum.

CHAPTER 145.

Jesus speaks on the establishment of the Christine kingdom and the future coming of the Lord in power. Exhorts to faithfulness. Parable of the unjust judge. Parable of the Pharisee and the publican.

A COMPANY of Pharisees came up to speak with Jesus and they said, Rabboni, we have heard you say, The kingdom is at hand.

2 We read in Daniel that the God of heaven will form a kingdom, and we ask, Is this the kingdom of the God you speak about? If so, when will it come?

3 And Jesus said, The prophets all have told about this kingdom of the God, and it is just at hand; but men can never see it come.

4 It never can be seen with carnal eyes; it is within.

5 Lo, I have said, and now I say again, None but the pure in heart can see the king, and all the pure in heart are subjects of the king.

6 Reform, and turn away from sin; prepare you, O prepare! the kingdom is at hand.

7 And then he spoke to his disciples and he said, The seasons of the son of man are past.

8 The time will come when you will wish above all else to see again one of these days; but you can see it not.

9 And many men will say, Lo, here is Christ; lo, there is Christ. Be not deceived; go not into their ways.

10 For when the son of man will come again no man need point the way; for as the lightning lights the heavens, so will the son of man light up the heavens and earth.

11 But, lo, I say, that many generations will have come and gone before the son of man shall come in power; but when he comes no one will say, Lo, here is Christ; lo, there.

12 But as it was before the flood in Noah's day, so shall it be. The people ate, they drank, were filled with merriment and sung for joy,

13 And did not know their doom until the ark was done and Noah entered in; but then the flood came on and swept them all away.

14 So, also, in the days of Lot; the people ate and drank; they bought, they sold, they planted and they reaped, they went their ways in sin, and they cared not;

15 But when the righteous Lot went from their city's gates the earth beneath the city shook, and brimstone fires fell from heaven;

16 The gapping jaws of earth flew wide, and swallowed up their homes, their wealth, and they went down to rise no more.

17 So shall it be when comes the son of man in power.

18 I charge you men, as I will charge men then, Seek not to save your wealth, or you will lose your lives. Go forth, and look not back upon the crumbling walls of sin. Do not forget Lot's wife.

19 Whoever tries to save his life will lose his life; whoever freely gives his life in serving life will save his life.

20 Then comes the sifting time. Two men will be in bed; one will be called, the other left; two women will be working side by side; one will be snatched away, the other left.

21 And his disciples said, Explain to us this parable; or is it not a parable?

22 And Jesus said, The wise will understand, for where the bread of heaven is, there you will find the pure in heart; and where the carcass lies will gather all the birds of prey.

23 But, lo, I say, before these days will come, the son of man will be betrayed by one of you into the hands of wicked men, and he will give his life for you and all the world.

24 Yea, more; the Holy Breath will come in power and fill you with the wisdom of the just.

25 And you will tell the wondrous story in Judea and in Samaria and in the farther lands of earth.

26 And then to teach that men should pray and never faint, he told this parable:

27 There was a judge who feared not God, nor yet regarded man.

28 There was a widow who oft implored the judge to right her wrongs and to avenge her foes.

29 At first the judge would hear her not, but after many days he said,

30 I fear not God, and I regard not man, yet, lest this widow wear me out by pleading every day I will avenge her on her foes.

31 When the disciples asked the meaning of this parable, the Lord replied, The wise can understand; the foolish have no need to know.

32 And then to teach a lesson unto certain of his followers who trusted in themselves and thought

that they were holier than other men, he told this parable:

33 Two men went to the synagogue to pray; one was a Pharisee, the other was a publican.

34 The Pharisee stood forth and prayed thus with himself, O God, I thank thee that I am not like other men, who are extortioners, unjust, adulterers;

35 Not even like this publican. I fast two times a week, and I give tithes of all I get.

36 The publican came not a-near; he would not lift his eyes to heaven, but smote his breast and said,

37 O Lord, be merciful to me; I am a sinner in thy sight; I am undone.

38 And now, you men, I say to you, The publican knew how to pray, and he was justified.

39 The Pharisee knew how to talk, but still he went away condemned.

40 Lo, every one who lauds himself shall be abased, and he who does not praise himself shall be exalted in the sight of God.

CHAPTER 146.

Last meeting of Jesus with his disciples in Galilee. Miriam sings a song of praise. The song. The Christines begin their journey to Jerusalem. They rest at Enon Springs. The selfish request of the mother of James and John. The Christines reach Jerusalem.

THE work of Jesus in the land of Galilee was done, and he sent forth a message, and the many came from many towns of Galilee; came to receive a benediction from his hand.

2 Among the multitudes who came was Luke, a Syrian from Anti-och, a learned physician and a just and upright man.

3 Theophilus, a Grecian senator, a minister of Cæsar's court, was also there; and many other men of honor and renown.

4 And Miriam sung: All hail the Day Star from on high!

5 All hail the Christ who ever was, and is and evermore shall be!

6 All hail the darkness of the shadowland! All hail the dawn of peace on earth; good will to men!

7 All hail triumphant king, who grapples with the tyrant Death, who conquers in the fight, and brings to light immortal life for men!

8 All hail the broken cross, the mutilated spear!

9 All hail the triumph of the soul! All hail the empty tomb!

10 All hail to him despised by men, rejected by the multitudes; for he is seated on the throne of power!

11 All hail! for he has called the pure in heart of every clime to sit with him upon the throne of power!

12 All hail, the rending veil! The way into the highest courts of God is open for the sons of men!

13 Rejoice, O men of earth, rejoice, and be exceeding glad!

14 Bring forth the harp and touch its highest strings; bring forth the lute, and sound its sweetest notes!

15 For men who were made low, are high exalted now, and they who walked in darkness and in the vale of death, are risen up and God and man are one forevermore,

16 Allelujah! praise the Lord forevermore. Amen.

17 And Jesus lifted up his eyes to heaven and said,

18 My Father-God, let now the

benediction of thy love, thy mercy and thy truth rest on these men.

19 The lamp is taken from their midst, and if the inner light be not aflame, lo, they must tread the ways of darkness and of death.

20 And then he said to all, Farewell.

21 Then Jesus and his mother, and the twelve, and Miriam and Mary, mother of the two disciples, James and John,

22 And many other loyal souls who loved the Christ, went to Jerusalem, that they might celebrate the Jewish feast.

23 And as they journeyed on their way they came to Enon Springs, near unto Salim where the harbinger once taught.

24 And as they rested by the fountain, Mary, wife of Zebedee, and mother of the two disciples, James and John, came to the master and she said,

25 My Lord, I know the kingdom is about to come, and I would ask this boon: Command that these my sons shall sit with you upon the throne, the one upon the right, the other on the left.

26 And Jesus said to her, You know not what you ask.

27 And then he turned to James and John and said, Are you prepared and are you strong enough to drink the cup that I will drink?

28 They said, Yes, master, we are strong enough to follow where you go.

29 Then Jesus said, You shall indeed drink of my cup; but I am not the judge of who will sit upon my right hand or my left.

30 The men who live the life and keep the faith will sit upon the throne of power.

31 Now, when the apostles heard the pleadings of the mother for her sons, and knew that James and John were seeking special favors from the Lord, they were indignant and they said,

32 We surely thought that James and John had risen above the selfish self. Who can we trust among the sons of men?

33 And Jesus called the ten apart and said to them, How hard for men to comprehend the nature of the kingdom of the soul!

34 These two disciples do not seem to know that rulership in heaven is not akin to rulership on earth.

35 In all the kingdoms of the world, the men of power, they who exalt themselves, show their authority, and rule with iron rule;

36 But you must know that they who rule the sons of light are they who seek no earthly power, but give their lives in willing sacrifice for men.

37 Whoever would be great must be the minister of all. The highest seat in heaven is at the feet of him who is the lowest man of earth.

38 I had a glory with our Father-God before the worlds were made, and still I come to serve the race of men; to be the minister of men; to give my life for men.

39 And then the Christines journeyed on and came unto Jerusalem.

CHAPTER 147.

Jesus speaks to the people in the temple regarding the messiahship. Rebukes the Jews for treachery. The Jews attempt to stone him, but are prevented by Joseph. The Christines go to Jericho, and later to Bethabara.

NOW, many Jews from Galilee, Judea and Samaria were in Jerusalem and at the feast.

2 The porch of Solomon was filled with scribes and Pharisees and doctors of the law, and Jesus walked with them.

3 A scribe approaching Jesus said, Rabboni, why do you keep the people waiting in suspense? If you are the Messiah that the prophets said would come, will you not tell us now?

4 And Jesus said, Lo, I have told you many times, but you believed me not.

5 No man can do the work that I have done and bring to men the truth as I have brought the truth who did not come from God.

6 What I have done and said are witnesses for me.

7 God calls, and they whose ears have been attuned to hear the heavenly voice have heard the call and have believed in me; because God testifies for me.

8 You cannot hear the voice of God, because your ears are closed. You cannot comprehend the works of God, because your hearts are full of self.

9 And you are busy-bodies, mischief-makers, hypocrites. You take these men whom God has given me into your haunts and try to poison them with sophistries and lies, and think that you will snatch them from the fold of God.

10 I tell you, men, these men are tried and you can snatch not one of them away.

11 My Father who has given them to me is greater than you all, and he and I are one.

12 And then the Jews took stones to throw at him and cried, Now we have heard enough; away with him; let him be stoned.

13 But Joseph, member of the great Sanhedrim of the Jews, was in the porch and he came forth and said,

14 You men of Israel, do nothing rash; throw down those stones; your reason is a better guide than passion in such times as these.

15 You do not know your accusations to be true, and if this man should prove himself to be the Christ, and you should take his life, the wrath of God would rest upon you evermore.

16 And Jesus said to them, Lo, I have healed your sick, have caused your blind to see your deaf to hear, your lame to walk, and cast out unclean spirits from your friends;

17 For which of these great works would you desire to take my life?

18 The Jews replied, We would not stone you for your works of grace, but for your vile, blasphemous words. You are but man and still you say that you are God.

19 And Jesus said, A prophet of your own said to the sons of men, Lo, you are gods!

20 Now, hark, you men, if he could say that to the men who simply heard the word of God, why should you think that I blaspheme the name of God because I say, I am a son of God?

21 If you believe not what I say you must have faith in what I do, and you should see the Father in these works, and know that I dwell in the Father-God, and that the Father dwells in me.

22 And then again the Jews took stones and would have stoned him in the temple court; but he withdrew himself from sight and left the porch and court and went his way;

23 And with the twelve he went

to Jericho, and after certain days they crossed the Jordan and in Bethabara abode for many days.

CHAPTER 148.

Lazarus dies and Jesus and the twelve return to Bethany. The resurrection of Lazarus, which greatly excites the rulers in Jerusalem. The Christines go to the hills of Ephriam, and there abide.

ONE day as Jesus and the twelve were in the silence in a home in Araba a messenger came and said,

2 Lord, Jesus, hear! your friend in Bethany is sick, nigh unto death; his sisters urge that you arise and come in haste.

3 Then turning to the twelve the master said, Lo, Lazarus has gone to sleep, and I must go and waken him.

4 And his disciples said, What need to go if he has gone to sleep; he will awaken by and by?

5 Then Jesus said, It is the sleep of death; for Lazarus is dead.

6 But Jesus did not haste to go; he stayed two days in Araba; and then he said, The hour has come and we must go to Bethany.

7 But his disciples urged him not to go; they said, The Jews are waiting your return that they may take your life.

8 And Jesus said, Men cannot take my life till I have handed unto them my life.

9 And when the time shall come I will myself lay down my life; that time is near, and God knows best; I must arise and go.

10 And Thomas said, Then we will also go; yes, we will offer up our lives and die with him. And they arose and went.

11 Now, Mary, Martha, Ruth and many friends were weeping in their home when one approached and said, The Lord has come; but Mary did not hear the words.

12 But Ruth and Martha heard, and they arose and went to meet the Lord; he waited at the village gate.

13 And when they met the master Martha said, You are too late, for Lazarus is dead; if you had only been with us I know that he would not have died.

14 But even now I know that you have power over death; that by the sacred Word you may cause life to rise from death.

15 And Jesus said, Behold, for Lazarus shall live again.

16 And Martha said, I know that he will rise and live again when all the dead shall rise.

17 And Jesus said, I am the resurrection and the life; he who has faith in me, though he be dead, yet shall he live;

18 And he who is alive, and has a living faith in me, shall never die. Do you believe what I have said?

19 And Martha said, Lord, I believe that you are come to manifest the Christ of God.

20 Then Jesus said, Go back and call aside your sister, and my mother and the prophetess and say that I have come; and I will stay here by the gate till they have come to me.

21 And Ruth and Martha did as Jesus bade them do, and in a little while the Marys and the prophetess had met the Lord.

22 And Mary said, Why did you tarry thus? If you had been with us our brother, dear, would not have died.

23 Then Jesus went up to the house and when he saw the heavy grief of all, he was himself stirred

up with grief, and said, Where is the tomb in which he lies?

24 They said, Lord, come and see. And Jesus wept.

25 The people said, Behold how Jesus loved this man!

26 And others said, Could not this Lord who opened up the eyes of one born blind, have saved this man from death?

27 But soon the mourners stood beside the tomb, a sepulcher hewn out of solid rock; a massive stone closed up the door.

28 And Jesus said, Take you away the stone.

29 But Martha said, Lord, is it well? Behold our brother has been dead four days; the body must be in decay, and is it well that we should see it now?

30 The Lord replied, Have you forgotten, Martha, what I said while we were at the village gate? Did I not say that you should see the glory of the Lord?

31 And then they rolled the stone away; the flesh had not decayed; and Jesus lifted up his eyes to heaven and said,

32 My Father-God, thou who hast ever heard my prayers, I thank thee now, and that these multitudes may know that thou hast sent me forth, that I am thine and thou art mine, make strong the Word of power.

33 And then he spoke the Word, and in a voice that souls can comprehend, he said, O Lazarus, awake!

34 And Lazarus arose and came out of the tomb. The grave clothes were about him fast, and Jesus said,

35 Loose him and let him go.

36 The people were amazed and multitudes confessed their faith in him.

37 And some went to Jerusalem and told the Pharisees about this resurrection of the dead.

38 The chief priests were confounded, and they said, What shall we do? This man is doing many mighty deeds, and if we do not stay him in his work, all men will look on him as king, and through the Romans he may take the throne, and we will lose our place and power.

39 And then the chief priests and the Pharisees in council met and sought a plan by which they might put him to death.

40 Caiaphas was the high priest then, and he came forth and said, You men of Israel, do you not know the law?

41 Do you not know that in such times as these we may give up one life to save our nation and our laws?

42 Caiaphas did not know that he was prophet, speaking out the words of truth.

43 He did not know the time had come for Jesus to be offered up a sacrifice for every man, for Jew and Greek, and all the world.

44 From that day forth the Jews conferred together every day, maturing plans to put the Lord to death.

45 Now, Jesus and the twelve did not remain in Bethany; but in the hills of Ephriam, upon the borders of Samaria, they found a home, and there abode for many days.

CHAPTER 149.

The Jews gather in Jerusalem to attend the feast. The Christines go to Jericho. Jesus dines with Zaccheus. He relates the parable of the ten talents.

THE great passover of the Jews, the feast of spring, was calling every loyal Jew up to Jerusalem.

2 Ten days before the feast the Lord and his disciples left the Ephriam hills and, by the Jordan way, went down to Jericho.

3 And as they entered Jericho a wealthy publican came out to see the Lord; but he was small in stature and the throng was great and he could see him not.

4 A tree, a sycamore, stood by the way and he climbed up the tree and found a seat among its boughs.

5 When Jesus came, he saw the man and said, O Zaccheus, make haste, come down; I would abide with you today.

6 And Zaccheus came down and joyfully received the Lord; but many of the stricter sect called out and said,

7 For shame! he goes to lodge with Zaccheus, the sinner and the publican.

8 But Jesus did not care for what they said; he went his way with Zaccheus, who was a man of faith, and as they talked together Zaccheus said,

9 Lord, I have ever tried to do the right; I give unto the poor half of my goods, and if by any means I wrong a man, I right the wrong by paying him four fold.

10 And Jesus said to him, Your life and faith are known to God, and lo, the benedictions of the Lord of hosts abide with you and all your house.

11 Then Jesus spoke a parable to all; he said, A vassal of an emperor was made a king, and he went to the foreign land to claim his rights and take the kingdom to himself.

12 Before he went he called ten trusted servants and to each he gave a pound and said,

13 Go forth and use these pounds as you have opportunity,

that you may gain for me more wealth. And then he went his way.

14 And after many days he came again, and called the ten, demanding a report.

15 The first one came and said, Lord, I have gained for you nine pounds; you gave me one and here are ten.

16 The king replied, Well done, you faithful man; because you have been faithful in a little thing I judge that you will be a faithful servant in a greater thing;

17 Behold, I make you ruler over nine important cities of my realm.

18 The second came and said, Lord, I have gained for you four pounds; you gave me one, and here are five.

19 The king replied, and you have proven up your faithfulness. Behold, I make you ruler over four important cities of my realm.

20 Another came and said, Lord, I have doubled what you gave to me. You gave one pound to me and here are two.

21 The ruler said, And you have proved your faithfulness; Behold, I make you ruler over one important city of my realm.

22 Another came and said, Lord, here is what you gave to me. I knew you were an austere man, oft reaping where you did not sow and I was sore afraid, and so I took the pound you gave to me and hid it in a secret place; and here it is.

23 The king exclaimed, You slothful man! you knew what I required, that I expected every man to do his best.

24 If you were timid and afraid to trust your judgment in the marts of trade, why did you not go forth and put my money out for gain, that I could have my own with interest?

25 Then turning to the steward of his wealth the ruler said, Take you this pound and give it unto him who has by diligence earned nine.

26 For lo, I say, that every one who uses what he has and gains, shall have abundantly; but he who hides away his talent in the earth shall forfeit what he has.

CHAPTER 150.

Jesus heals blind Bartimœus. With the twelve he goes to Bethany. The multitudes come to welcome him and to speak with Lazarus.

THE Christines started on their way to Bethany, and as they went, while yet in Jericho, they passed a beggar sitting by the way; and he was blind Bartimæus.

2 And when the beggar heard the multitude pass by he said, What is it that I hear?

3 The people said to him, Jesus of Nazareth is passing by.

4 And instantly the man cried out, Lord Jesus, son of David, stay! have mercy on poor blind Bartimæus!

5 The people said to him, Be quiet; hold your peace.

6 But blind Bartimæus called again, Thou son of David, hear! have mercy on poor blind Bartimæus!

7 And Jesus stopped and said, Bring him to me.

8 And then the people brought the blind man to the Lord, and as they brought him up they said, Be cheerful now, Bartimæus, the Lord is calling you.

9 And then he threw his cloak aside, and ran to Jesus as he waited by the way.

10 And Jesus said, What will you have, Bartimæus?

11 The blind man said, Rab-

boni, open up mine eyes that I may see.

12 And Jesus said, Bartimæus, look up; receive your sight; your faith has made you whole.

13 And he at once received his sight, and from the fullness of his heart he said, Praise God.

14 And all the people said, Praise God.

15 Then Jesus and the twelve went on to Bethany. It was six days before the feast.

16 And when the people knew that Jesus was in Bethany they came from near and far to see him and to hear him speak.

17 And they were anxious all to talk with Lazarus, whom Jesus had awakened from the dead.

18 Now in Jerusalem the priests and Pharisees were all alert; they said, This Jesus will be at the feast, and we must not permit that he shall slip away again.

19 And they commanded every man to be alert and help to apprehend the Lord that they might take his life.

CHAPTER 151.

Jesus teaches in the synagogue. Makes his triumphal entry into Jerusalem. The multitudes, with the children, sing his praises, and say, Hosanna to the king! The Christines return to Bethany.

IT was the day before the Sabbath day, the eighth day of the Jewish Nasan month, that Jesus came to Bethany.

2 And on the Sabbath day he went up to the synagogue and taught.

3 And on the morning of the first day of the week, the Sunday of the week, he called his twelve apostles unto him and said,

4   This day we go up to Jerusalem; be not afraid; my time has not yet come.

5   Now, two of you may go unto the village of Bethphage, and you will find an ass tied to a tree, and you will see a little colt near by.

6   Untie the ass and bring her here to me. If any one inquires why you take the ass, just say, The master has a need of her; and then the owner will come on with you.

7   And the disciples went as Jesus bade them go; they found the ass and colt a-near an open door; and when they would untie the ass the owner said, Why would you take the ass away?

8   And the disciples said, The master has a need of her; and then the owner said, 'Tis well.

9   And then they brought the animal, and on her put their coats, and Jesus sat upon the ass and rode into Jerusalem.

10   And multitudes of people came and filled the way, and his disciples praised the Lord and said,

11   Thrice blessed is the king who in the name of God is come! All glory be to God, and peace on earth; good will to men!

12   And many spread their garments in the way, and some tore branches from the trees, and cast them in the way.

13   And many children came with garlands of sweet flowers and placed them on the Lord, or strewed them in the way, and said, All hail the king! Long live the king!

14   The throne of David shall be built again. Hosanna to the Lord of hosts!

15   Among the throng were Pharisees, who said to Jesus as he passed, Rebuke this noisy throng; it is a shame for them to cry thus in the street.

16   The Lord replied, I tell you, men, if these should hold their peace the very stones would cry aloud.

17   And then the Pharisees conferred among themselves; they said, Our threats are idle words. Behold, for all the world is following him.

18   As Jesus drew a-near Jerusalem he paused and wept, and said, Jerusalem, Jerusalem, the holy city of the Jews! yours was the glory of the Lord; but you have cast the Lord away.

19   Your eyes are closed, you cannot see the king; the kingdom of the Lord of heaven and earth has come; you comprehend it not.

20   Behold, the day will come when armies from afar will cast a bank about your way; will compass you about, and hem you in on every side;

21   Will dash you to the ground and slay you and your children in the streets.

22   And of your holy temple, and of your palaces and walls, they will not leave a stone upon a stone, because today you spurn the offers of the God of heaven.

23   When Jesus and the multitude had come into Jerusalem, excitement reigned, and people asked, Who is this man?

24   The multitude replied, This is the king, the prophet, priest of God; this is the man from Galilee.

25   But Jesus tarried not; he went directly to the temple porch, and it was filled with people pressing hard to see the king.

26   The sick, the halt, the lame, the blind were there, and Jesus paused, and laid his hands on them and healed them by the sacred Word.

27   The temple and the temple courts were filled with children

praising God. They said, Hosanna to the king! The son of David is the king! All hail the king! Praise God!

28 The Pharisees were filled with anger when they heard the children sing. They said to Jesus, Hear you what the children say?

29 And Jesus said, I hear; but have you never read the words of our own bard who said,

30 Out of the mouths of babes and sucklings thou hast perfected praise!

31 And when the evening came the Lord and his disciples went again to Bethany.

CHAPTER 152.

Jesus rebukes a barren fig tree. Drives the merchants out of the temple. Teaches the people. Returns to Bethany.

NEXT day, the Monday of the week, the master with the twelve, went to Jerusalem.

2 And as they passed along the way they saw a fig tree full of leaves without a sign of fruit.

3 And Jesus spoke unto the tree; he said, You useless cumberer of the ground; you fig tree fair to look upon, but a delusive thing.

4 You take from earth and air the food that fruitful trees should have.

5 Go back to earth and be yourself the food for other trees to eat.

6 When Jesus had thus spoken to the tree he went his way.

7 And when he reached the temple, lo, the rooms were filled with petty merchants selling doves and animals, and other things, for sacrifice; the temple was a mart of trade.

8 And Jesus was indignant at the sight, and said, You men of Israel, for shame! This is supposed to be the house of prayer; but it is now a den of thieves. Remove this plunder from this holy place.

9 The merchants only laughed and said, We are protected in our trade by those who bear the rule; we will not go.

10 Then Jesus made a scourge of cords, as he did once before, and rushed among the merchantmen, threw all their money on the floor;

11 Threw wide the cages of the doves, and cut the cords that held the bleating lambs and set them free.

12 And then he drove the merchants from the place, and with a clean, new broom he swept the floors.

13 Chief priests and scribes were filled with wrath, but feared to touch or even to rebuke the Lord, for all the people stood in his defense.

14 And Jesus taught the people all day long and healed a multitude of those diseased,

15 And when the evening came he went again to Bethany.

CHAPTER 153.

The Christines go to Jerusalem. They note the withered fig tree; its symbolic meaning. Jesus teaches in the temple. Is censured by the priests. Relates a parable of a rich man's feast.

ON Tuesday, early in the day, the master and the twelve went to Jerusalem.

2 And as they went the twelve observed the tree to which the Lord had talked the day before, and lo, the leaves were withered, just as if they had been scorched with fire.

3 And Peter said, Lord, see the

tree! Its leaves are withered and the tree seems dead.

4 And Jesus said, So shall it be with those who bear no fruit. When God shall call them up to give account, lo, he will breathe upon them, and their leaves, their empty words, will wither and decay.

5 God will not let the fruitless trees of life encumber ground, and he will pluck them up and cast them all away.

6 Now, you can demonstrate the power of God. Have faith in God, and you can bid the mountains to depart, and they will crumble at your feet;

7 And you may talk to wind and wave, and they will hear, and will obey what you command.

8 God hears the prayer of faith and when you ask in faith you shall receive.

9 You must not ask amiss; God will not hear the prayer of any man who comes to him with blood of other men upon his hands.

10 And he who harbors envious thoughts, and does not love his fellow men, may pray forever unto God, and he will hear him not.

11 God can do nothing more for men than they would do for other men.

12 And Jesus walked again within the temple courts.

13 The priests and scribes were much emboldened by the council of Caiaphas and the other men in power, and so they came to Jesus and they said,

14 Who gave you the authority to do as you have done? Why did you drive the merchants from the temple yesterday?

15 And Jesus answered them and said, If you will answer what I ask, then I will answer you; Was

John, the harbinger, a man of God, or was he a seditious man?

16 The scribes and Pharisees were loath to answer him; they reasoned thus among themselves:

17 If we shall say, John was a prophet sent from God, then he will say,

18 John testified for me, that I am son of God; why do you not believe his words?

19 If we should say, John was a bold, seditious man, the people will be angered, for they think he was a prophet of the living God.

20 And so they answered Jesus and they said, We do not know; we cannot tell.

21 Then Jesus said, If you will tell me not, then I will tell you not who gave me power to drive the robbers from the house of God.

22 And then he spoke a parable to them; he said, A man once made a feast inviting all the rich and honored people of the land.

23 But when they came, they found the door into the banquet hall was low, and they could enter not except they bowed their heads and fell down on their knees.

24 These people would not bow their heads and fall down on their knees, and so they went away; they went not to the feast.

25 And then the man sent forth his messengers to bid the common folks, and those of low estate, to come and feast with him.

26 These people gladly came; they bowed their heads and fell down on their knees, and came into the banquet hall and it was full, and every one rejoiced.

27 And then the master said, Behold, you priests and scribes, and Pharisees! the Lord of heaven and earth has spread a sumptuous feast, and you were bidden first of all;

28 But you have found the door into the banquet hall so low that you must bow your heads and fall down on your knees to enter in, and you have scorned the king who made the feast, refused to bow your heads and fall down on your knees, and you have gone your way;

29 But now God calls again; the common folks and those of low estate have come in multitudes, have entered in unto the feast and all rejoice.

30 I tell you, men, that publicans and courtesans go through the gates into the kingdom of the God of heaven, and you are left with-

31 John came to you in righteousness; he brought the truth, but you believed him not.

32 But publicans and courtesans believed, and were baptized and now have entered in unto the feast.

33 I tell you now, as I have told you many times, The many have been called, but chosen are the few.

CHAPTER 154.

Jesus teaches in the temple court. The parable of the householder and wicked husbandmen. Parable of the marriage feast and the guest without a wedding robe.

THE multitudes would hear what Jesus had to say, and so they built a platform in the temple court, and Jesus stood upon the place and taught. He spoke in parables; he said,

2 A man possessed a vast estate; he planted out a vineyard, placed a hedge about it, built a tower, installed the press for making wine.

3 He placed his vineyard in the hands of husbandmen and then he journeyed to a distant land. .

4 Now, in the vintage time the man sent forth a servant to receive and bring to him his portion of the fruitage of the vines.

5 The husbandmen came forth and beat the man; laid forty lashes on his back and cast him out beyond the vineyard gate.

6 And then the owner sent another man to bring to him his own. The husbandmen laid hold of him and sorely wounded him and cast him from the vineyard, leaving him half dead beside the way.

7 The owner sent another man to bring to him his own. The husbandmen seized hold of him and with a javelin they pierced his heart; then buried him beyond the hedge.

8 The owner was aggrieved. He thought within himself, What shall I do? and then he said, This will I do. My only son is here, and I will send him to the husbandmen,

9 They surely will respect my son and send me what is mine.

10 He sent his son; the husbandmen took counsel with themselves; they said, This is the only heir to all this wealth, and if we take his life the vast inheritance is ours.

11 They took his life and cast him out beyond the vineyard hedge.

12 The days will come; the owner will return to reckon with the husbandmen, and he will seize them every one, and cast them into scorching fires where they shall stay until they pay the debts they owe.

13 And he will place his vineyard in the care of honest men.

14 Then turning to the priests and scribes he said, Did not your prophets say,

15 The stone the builders cast away became the capstone of the arch?

16 You men who pose as men of God, as husbandmen, lo, you have

stoned and killed the messengers of God, his prophets and his seers, and now you seek to slay his son.

17　I tell you men, the kingdom shall be snatched away from you, and shall be given unto people who are not a people now, and to a nation that is not a nation now.

18　And men whose speech you cannot understand, will stand between the living and the dead, and show the way to life.

19　The chief priests and the Pharisees were deeply moved with anger when they heard this parable, and would have seized the Lord and done him harm, but they were sore afraid; they feared the multitude.

20　And Jesus spoke another parable; he said, The kingdom is a-like a certain king who made a feast in honor of the marriage of his son.

21　He sent his servants forth to call the people who had been invited to the feast.

22　The servants called; but then the people would not come.

23　And then the king sent other messengers abroad to say, Behold, my tables now are spread; my oxen and my fatlings are prepared.

24　The choicest viands and the richest wines are on my boards; come to the marriage feast.

25　The people laughed and treated with disdain his call, and went their way, one to his farm, another to his merchandise;

26　And others seized the servants of the king; abused them shamefully; and some of them they killed.

27　And then the king sent forth his soldiery who slew the murderers and burned their towns.

28　And then the king sent other servants forth; to them he said, Go to the corners of the streets, the partings of the ways, and to the marts of trade and say,

29　Whoever will may come up to the marriage feast.

30　The servants went their way and called; and lo, the banquet hall was filled with guests.

31　But when the king came in to see the guests, he saw a man who had not on a wedding robe; he called to him and said,

32　Friend, why are you here without a wedding robe? Would you dishonor thus my son?

33　The man was dumb; he answered not.

34　And then the king said to his guards, Take you this man and bind him hand and foot and cast him out into the darkness of the night.

35　The many have been called, but none are chosen to be guests who have not clad themselves in wedding robes.

CHAPTER 155.

Jesus recognizes the justice of paying secular taxes. He teaches a lesson on family relationships in the life beyond. The greatest of the commandments is comprised in love. He warns his disciples against the hypocrisy of scribes and Pharisees.

AS Jesus spoke, the Pharisees came up to question him; they thought to criminate him by what he said.

2　A strict Herodian spoke and said, My Lord, you are a man of truth; you show the way to God, and you do not regard the personality of men;

3　Tell us, what do you think; should we, who are the seed of Abraham, pay tribute unto Cæsar? or should we not?

4　And Jesus knew his wickedness of heart and said, Why do you come to tempt me thus? Show me the tribute money that you speak about.

5 The man brought forth a piece of coin on which an image was engraved.

6 And Jesus said, Whose image and whose name is on this coin?

7 The man replied, 'Tis Cæsar's image and his name.

8 And Jesus said, Give unto Cæsar that which is Cæsar's own; but give to God the things of God.

9 And they who heard him said, He answers well.

10 And then a Sadducee, who thinks there is no resurrection of the dead, came up and said, Rabboni, Moses wrote that if a married man shall die, and have no child, his widow shall become his brother's wife.

11 Now, there were seven brothers and the eldest had a wife; he died and had no child; a brother took his widow for his wife, and then he died;

12 And every brother had this woman for his wife; in course of time the woman died;

13 Now which will have this woman for a wife in the resurrection day?

14 And Jesus said, Here in this plane of life men marry just to gratify their selfish selfs, or to perpetuate the race; but in the world to come, and in the resurrection day, men do not take upon themselves the marriage vows,

15 But, like the angels and the other sons of God, they form not unions for the pleasure of the self, nor to perpetuate the race.

16 Death does not mean the end of life. The grave is not the goal of men, no more than is the earth the goal of seeds.

17 Life is the consequence of death. The seed may seem to die, but from its grave the tree arises into life.

18 So man may seem to die, but he lives on, and from the grave he springs up into life.

19 If you could comprehend the word that Moses spoke about the burning bush that burned and still was not consumed, then you would know that death cannot destroy the life.

20 And Moses said that God is God of Abraham, of Isaac, and of Israel.

21 God is not God of dead men's bones, but of the living man.

22 I tell you, men, man goes down to the grave, but he will rise again and manifest the life;

23 For every life is hid with Christ in God, and man shall live while God shall live.

24 The Pharisees and scribes who heard the Lord, exclaimed, He speaks the truth; and they were glad to have the Sadducees discomfited.

25 And then an honest scribe came forth and said to Jesus, Lord, you speak as one whom God has sent, and may I ask,

26 Which is the greatest and the first of the Commandments of the Law?

27 And Jesus said, The first is: Hear O Israel, the Lord our God is one; and you shall love the Lord your God with all your heart, with all your mind, with all your soul, with all your strength;

28 And you shall love your neighbor as yourself.

29 These are the greatest of the ten, and on them hang the Law, the Prophets and the Psalms.

30 The scribe replied, My soul gives witness that you speak the truth, for love fulfills the law, and

far transcends burnt offerings and sacrifice.

31 And Jesus said to him, Lo, you have solved a mystery; you are within the kingdom and the kingdom is in you.

32 To his disciples Jesus spoke, and all the people heard; he said, Beware you of the scribes and Pharisees who pride themselves in wearing long and richly decorated robes,

33 And love to be saluted in the market place, and seek the highest seats at feasts, and take the hard-earned wages of the poor to satisfy their carnal selves, and pray in public, long and loud.

34 These are the wolves who clothe themselves to look like sheep.

35 And then he said to all, The scribes and Pharisees are placed by law in Moses' seat, and by the law they may interpret law;

36 So what they bid you do, that do; but do not imitate their deeds.

37 They say the things that Moses taught; they do the things of ~~~~~~~~~~~.

38 They talk of mercy, yet they bind on human shoulders burdens grievous to bear.

39 They talk of helpfulness, and yet they put not forth the slightest helpful efforts for their brother man.

40 They make a show of doing things, and yet they do not anything but show their gaudy robes, and broad phylacteries, and smile when people call them honored masters of the law.

41 They strut about and show their pride when people call them father, so and so.

42 Hear, now, you men, Call no man father here. The God of heaven and earth, and he alone, is Father of the race of men.

43 Christ is the hierarch, the high, exalted master of the sons of men.

44 If you would be exalted, sit down at the master's feet and serve. He is the greatest man who serves the best.

CHAPTER 156.

The scribes and Pharisees are angered. Jesus rebukes them for their hypocrisy. He laments over Jerusalem. The widow's mite. Jesus delivers his farewell address to the people in the temple.

THE scribes and Pharisees were wild with rage; and Jesus said,

2 Woe unto you, you scribes and Pharisees, you hypocrites! you stand within the way; you block the door; you will not go into the kingdom and you turn aside the pure in heart who are about to enter in.

3 Woe unto you, you scribes and Pharisees, you hypocrites! you compass sea and land to make one proselyte, and when he has been made he is a son of hell, just like yourselves.

4 Woe unto you who call yourselves the guides of men! and you are guides, blind guides;

5 For you pay tithes of cummin, mint and dill, and leave undone the weightier matters of the law; of judgment, justice, faith.

6 You filter out the gnats before you drink; but then you swallow camels and the like.

7 Woe unto you, you scribes and Pharisees, you hypocrites! you clean and scour the outside of the cup, while it is full of filth, extortion and excess.

8 Go to and clean the inside of the cup, and then the poisonous

fumes will not defile the outside of the cup.

9 Woe unto you, you scribes and Pharisees, you hypocrites! you are yourselves like whitewashed sepulchres; your outer garbs are beautiful, but you are full of dead men's bones.

10 You seem to men to be divine; but in your hearts you nourish lust, hypocrisies and vile iniquities.

11 Woe unto you, you scribes and Pharisees, you hypocrites! you build and then adorn the tombs of holy men of old and say,

12 If we had lived when these men lived, we would have guarded them, would not have acted as our fathers did, when they maltreated them and put them to the sword.

13 But you are sons of them who slew the holy men, and you are not a whit more just than they.

14 Go forth and fill the measure of your fathers who were steeped in crime.

15 You are the offsprings of the vipers, and how can you be but serpents of the dust?

16 God now has sent again to you his prophets and his seers, his wise men and his holy men, and you will scourge them in your synagogues, and stone them in the streets, and nail them to the cross.

17 Woe unto you! for on your heads will come the blood of all the holy men who have been slain upon the earth,

18 From righteous Abel down to Zacharias, son of Barachias, who was slain within the Holy Place before the altar of the Lord.

19 Behold, I say that these things all shall come upon this nation and the people of Jerusalem.

20 And Jesus looked about and said, Jerusalem, Jerusalem, thou cruel city of Jerusalem, that slays the prophets in the streets and kills the holy men whom God has sent to you!

21 Lo, I would oft have gathered you as children to the fold of God; but you would not.

22 You have rejected God, and now your house is desolate, and you shall see me not again till you can say,

23 Thrice blessed is the son of man who comes as son of God.

24 Then Jesus went and sat beside the treasury and watched the people as they paid their tithes.

25 The rich men came and gave of their abundance; and then he saw a poor but loyal widow come and put a farthing in the treasure box.

26 And then he said to his disciples who were standing by, Behold, for this poor widow who has put a farthing in the treasury has done more than they all;

27 For she has given all she had; the rich have given just a little share of what they have.

28 A company of Grecian Jews were at the feast, and they met Philip, who could talk with them, and said, Sir, we would see the Lord, this Jesus, who is called the Christ.

29 And Philip led the way, and brought them to the Christ.

30 And Jesus said, The hour has come; the son of man is ready to be glorified, and it cannot be otherwise.

31 Except a grain of wheat fall into earth and die it can be nothing but a grain of wheat; but if it die it lives again, and from its grave a hundred grains of wheat arise.

32 My soul is troubled now; What shall I say? And then he cast his eyes to heaven and said,

33 My Father-God, I would not ask to be relieved of all the burdens

I must bear; I only ask for grace and strength to bear the burdens whatso'er they be,

34   This is the hour for which I came to earth. O Father, glorify thy name!

35   And then the place was lighted with a light more brilliant than the noonday sun; the people stood a-back; they were afraid.

36   And then a voice that seemed to come from heaven said,

37   I have both glorified my name and yours, and I will honor them again.

38   The people heard the voice, and some exclaimed, Behold, a distant thunder! Others said, An angel spoke to him.

39   But Jesus said, This voice was not for me; it was for you, that you might know that I am come from God.

40   Now is the judgment of the world at hand; the prince of darkness shall be manifest and go unto his own.

41   The son of man will now be lifted up from earth, and he will draw all men unto himself.

42   The people said, The law declares that Christ abides forever more. How can you say, The son of man will now be lifted up? Who is the son of man?

43   And Jesus said to them, The light is shining now; walk in the light while you still have the light.

44   The darkness comes; but he who walks in darkness cannot find the way.

45   Again I say, Walk in the light while you still have the light, that men may know that you are sons of light.

46   And Jesus stood out in the temple porch, and made his last appeal unto the multitudes; he said,

47   He who believes in me, be-lieves in God who sent me forth to do his will, and he who sees me now beholds my Father-God.

48   Behold, I came a light unto the world; he who believes in me shall walk in light, the light of life.

49   You men who hear me now, If you believe me not, I judge you not.

50   I am not come to judge the world, but I am come to save the world.

51   God is the only judge of men; but what I speak will stand against you in the day when God will judge the world;

52   For from myself I do not speak; I speak the words that God has given me to speak.

53   And then he said, Jerusalem, with all your glory and your crimes, Farewell.

CHAPTER 157.

The Christines upon Mount Olives. Jesus prophecies the destruction of Jerusalem, and of terrible disasters that will mark the conclusion of the age. He exhorts his disciples to faithfulness.

THEN Jesus with the twelve went forth and sat upon Mount Olives, just beyond the city's gate.

2   And his disciples said, Behold the wondrous city of Jerusalem! its homes are all so beautiful! its temples and its shrines are clothed in such magnificence!

3   And Jesus said, The city is the glory of my people, Israel, but, lo, the time will come when every stone will be cast down, and it will be a hiss and byword for the nations of the earth.

4   And the disciples asked, When will this desolation come?

5   And Jesus said, This round of human life will not be full until the

armies of the conqueror will thunder at her gates, and they will enter in, and blood will flow like water through the streets.

6 And all the precious furnishings of temple, court and palaces will be destroyed, or carried off to deck the palaces and courts of kings.

7 Behold, these days are not at hand. Before they come, lo, you shall be maltreated by the scribes and Pharisees, the high priests and the doctors of the law.

8 Without a cause you will be haled into the courts; you will be stoned; you will be beaten in the synagogues; will stand condemned before the rulers of this world, and governors and kings will sentence you to death.

9 But you will falter not, and you will testify for truth and righteousness.

10 And in these hours be anxious not about your speech; you need not think of what to say;

11 For, lo, the Holy Breath will overshadow you and give you words to say.

12 But then the carnage will go on, and men will think that they are pleasing God by killing you, and nations far and near will hate you for the sake of Christ.

13 And men will stir up evil thoughts among your kin, and they will hate you and will give you up to die.

14 And brothers will be false to brothers; fathers will stand forth and testify against their own, and children will drive parents to the funeral pile.

15 When you shall hear the Roman eagle screaming in the air, and see his legions streaming o'er the plain, then know the desolation of Jerusalem is near.

16 Then let the wise wait not, but flee. Let him who is upon his house wait not to enter in the house to gather up his wealth, but let him flee.

17 And he who labors in the field must not return, but leave his all to save his life.

18 And woe to mothers with their little children in that day; none shall escape the sword.

19 The tribulation of these days cannot be told in words, for such has never been since God created man upon the earth.

20 The conqueror will carry many of the sons of Abraham away as captives into foreign lands, and they who know not Israel's God will tread the highways of Jerusalem until the anti-Jewish times have been fulfilled.

21 But when the people have been punished for their crimes, the tribulation days will end; but lo, the time will come when all the world will rise, like gladiators in a ring, and fight just for the sake of shedding blood.

22 And men will reason not; they will not see, nor care to see a cause for carnage, desolation, thefts; for they will war with friend or foe.

23 The very air will seem surcharged with smoke of death; and pestilence will follow close upon the sword.

24 And signs that men have never seen will then appear in heaven and earth; in sun, and moon, and stars.

25 The seas will roar, and sounds will come from heaven that men can never comprehend, and these will bring distress of nations with perplexity.

26 Hearts of the strongest men will faint in fear, in expectation of

the coming of more frightful things upon the earth.

27 But while the conflicts rage on land and sea, the Prince of Peace will stand above the clouds of heaven and say again:

28 Peace, peace on earth; good will to men; and every man will throw away his sword, and nations will learn war no more.

29 And then the man who bears the pitcher will walk forth across an arc of heaven; the sign and signet of the son of man will stand forth in the eastern sky.

30 The wise will then lift up their heads and know that the redemption of the earth is near.

31 Before these days shall come, behold, false Christs and poor deluded prophets will arise in many lands.

32 And they will show forth signs, and do a multitude of mighty works; and they will lead astray the many who are not wise; and many of the wise will be deceived.

33 And now I tell you once again, When men shall say, The Christ is in the wilderness, go you not forth.

34 And if they say, The Christ is in the secret place, believe it not; for when he comes the world will know that he has come.

35 For as the morning light comes from the east and shines unto the west; so shall be the coming of the age and son of man.

36 The wicked of the earth will weep when they shall see the son of man come down upon the clouds of heaven, in power.

37 Take heed you, O take heed, for you know not the hour nor the day when comes the son of man.

38 Let not your hearts be overcharged with sensuous things, nor with the cares of life, lest that day come and find you unprepared.

39 Keep watch at every season of the year; and pray that you may meet the Lord with joy and not with grief.

40 Before these days shall come our Father-God will send his messengers abroad, yea, to the corners of the earth, and they will say,

41 Prepare you, O prepare; the Prince of Peace shall come, and now is coming on the clouds of heaven.

42 When Jesus had thus said, he went with his disciples back to Bethany.

CHAPTER 158.

Jesus and the twelve at prayer in Olivet. Jesus reveals to his disciples the deeper meanings of secret doctrines. He tells them what to teach the people. Relates a number of parables. They return to Bethany.

THE morning of the Wednesday of the week was come, and Jesus with the twelve went out to Olivet to pray; and they were lost in prayer for seven hours.

2 Then Jesus called the twelve close to his side and said, This day the curtain parts and we will step beyond the veil into the secret courts of God.

3 And Jesus opened up to them the meaning of the hidden way, and of the Holy Breath, and of the light that cannot fail.

4 He told them all about the Book of Life, the Rolls of Graphael, the Book of God's Remembrance where all the thoughts and words of men are written down.

5 He did not speak aloud to them; he told the secrets of the masters in an undertone, and when he spoke the name of God there was a silence in the courts of heaven for

half an hour, for angels spoke with
bated breath.

6 And Jesus said, These things
may not be spoken out aloud; they
never may be written down; they
are the messages of Silenceland;
they are the Breathings of the inner
heart of God.

7 And then the master taught
the twelve the lessons they should
teach to other men. He sometimes
taught in parables; he said,

8 You call to mind the words of
yesterday about the coming of the
son of man. Now, you shall teach
to other men what I have spoken
and am speaking unto you;

9 Teach them to pray and not
to faint; to be prepared at every
moment of the day, for when they
least expect him, then the Lord will
come.

10 A man went to a distant land
and left his house and all his wealth
in care of servants; five to guard his
house and five to guard his barns
and herds.

11 The servants waited long for
his return, but he came not, and
they grew careless in their work;
some spent their time in revelings
and drunkenness, and some slept
at their posts.

12 And night by night the robbers came and carried off the wealth
from house and barn, and drove
away the choicest of the herds.

13 And when they knew that
much of all the wealth that they
were left to guard had been pur-
loined, they said,

14 We cannot be to blame; if
we had known the day and hour
when our lord would come again
we would have guarded well his
wealth, and suffered not the thieves
to carry it away; he surely is at
fault because he told us not.

15 But after many days the

lord returned, and when he knew
that thieves had robbed him of his
wealth, he called his servants and
he said to them,

16 Because you have neglected
what was given you to do, have
spent your time in revelings and
sleep, behold you all are debtors
unto me.

17 What I have lost by your
neglect, you owe to me. And then
he gave them heavy tasks to do,
and bound them to their posts with
chains, where they remained till
they had paid for all the goods
their lord had lost through their
neglect.

18 Another man locked up his
wealth and went to sleep, and in the
night time robbers came, unlocked
his doors, and when they saw no
guard, they entered in and carried
off his wealth.

19 And when the man awoke
and found his doors ajar and all his
treasures gone, he said, If I had
known the hour when the thieves
would come I would have been on
guard.

20 Beware, my friends, beware!
and be prepared at every hour, and
if your Lord shall come at midnight
or at dawn, it matters not, for he
will find you ready to receive.

21 And then, behold, a marriage
was announced, and virgins, ten of
them, were set apart to meet the
bridegroom when he came.

22 The virgins clothed themselves in proper garbs, and took
their lamps and sat in waiting for
the watch to say, Behold, the bridegroom comes!

23 Now, five were wise; they
filled their lamps with oil; and five
were foolish, for they carried empty
lamps.

24 The groom came not at the

expected time; the virgins were a-weary with their watch and slept.

25 At midnight came the cry, Behold, the bridegroom comes!

26 The virgins rose; the wise ones quickly trimmed their lamps and went forth ready to receive the groom.

27 The foolish virgins said, We have no oil, our lamps burn not.

28 They sought to borrow from the wise, who said, We have no oil to spare; Go to the merchantmen and buy and fill your lamps and then come forth to meet the groom.

29 But while they went to purchase oil, the bridegroom came; the virgins who were ready with their lamps all trimmed went with him to the marriage feast.

30 And when the foolish virgins came the door was shut, and though they knocked and called aloud, the door was opened not.

31 The master of the feast exclaimed, I know you not! and in disgrace the virgins went their way.

32 Again I say to you, and you shall say to them who follow you,

33 Be ready every moment of the day and night, because when you expect him not, the Lord will come.

34 Behold, when he will come with all his messengers of light, the Book of Life, and that of Records, shall be opened up—the books in which the thoughts and words and deeds are written down.

35 And every one can read the records he has written for himself, and he will know his doom before the judge shall speak, and this will be the sifting time.

36 According to their records men will find their own.

37 The judge is Righteousness, the king of all the earth, and he will separate the multitudes as shepherds separate the sheep and goats.

38 The sheep will find their places on the right, the goats upon the left, and every man will know his place.

39 And then the judge will say, to those upon the right, You blessed of the Father-God, come unto your inheritance, which was prepared for you from times of old.

40 You have been servants of the race; and I was hungry and you gave me bread; was thirsty and you gave me drink; was naked and you gave me clothes;

41 Was sick, you ministered to me; and was in prison and you came to me with words of cheer; I was a stranger and in your homes I found a home.

42 Then will the righteous say, When did we see you hungry, thirsty, sick, imprisoned or a stranger at our gates and ministered to you?

43 And then the judge will say, You served the sons of men, and whatsoever you have done for these, that you have done for me.

44 The judge will say to those upon the left, Depart from me; you have not served the sons of men.

45 I was hungry and you gave me naught to eat; was thirsty and you gave me naught to drink; I was a stranger and you drove me from your door; I was imprisoned and was sick, you did not minister to me.

46 Then these will say, When did we thus neglect to care for you? When did we see you hungry, thirsty, sick, a stranger or in prison and did not minister to you?

47 And then the judge will say, Your life was full of self; you served the self and not your fellow man,

and when you slighted one of these, you slighted and neglected me.

48 Then will the righteous have the kingdom and the power, and they who are unrighteous shall go forth to pay their debts, to suffer all that men have suffered at their hands.

49 They who have ears to hear and hearts to understand will comprehend these parables.

50 When he had finished all these parables he said, You know that in two days the great passover feast will come, and lo, the son of man will be betrayed into the hands of wicked men.

51 And he will give his life upon the cross, and men will know that he, the son of man, is son of God.

52 Then Jesus and the twelve returned to Bethany.

SECTION XVIII.

TZADDI.

The Arrest and Betrayal of Jesus.

CHAPTER 159.

The Christines attend a feast in Simon's house. Mary anoints the master with a costly balm, and Judas and others rebuked her for profligacy. Jesus defends her. The rulers of the Jews employ Ananias to arrest Jesus. Ananias bribes Judas to aid him.

BAR-SIMON, who was once a leper and was cleansed by Jesus by the sacred Word, abode in Bethany.

2 In honor of the Christine Lord he gave a feast, and Lazarus was among the guests, and Ruth and Martha served.

3 And as the guests reclined about the table, Mary took a cruse of rich perfume and poured it out on Jesus' head and feet.

4 And then she knelt and with her hair she wiped his feet; the odor of the rich perfume filled all the room.

5 Now, Judas, always looking at the selfish side of life, exclaimed, For shame! why did you waste that costly perfume thus?

6 We might have sold it for three hundred pence, and had the money to supply our wants and feed the poor.

7 (Now, Judas was the treasurer, and carried all the money of the Christine band.)

8 And others said, Why, Mary, what a profligate you are! you should not throw such wealth away.

9 But Jesus said, You men, be still; let her alone; you know not what you say.

10 The poor are with you constantly; at any time you can administer to them; but I will not be with you long.

11 And Mary knows the sadness of the coming days; she has anointed me beforehand for my burial.

12 The gospel of the Christ will everywhere be preached, and he who tells the story of the Christ will tell about this day; and what was done by Mary at this hour will be a sweet memorial to her wherever men abide.

13 And when the feast was over Jesus went with Lazarus to his home.

14 Now, in Jerusalem the priests and Pharisees were busy with their plans to seize the Lord and take his life.

15 The high priest called in counsel all the wisest men and said, This deed must be accomplished in a secret way.

16 He must be taken when the multitudes are not a-near, else we may cause a war; the common people may stand forth in his defense and thus pollute this sacred place with human blood.

17 And what we do, that we must do before the great day of the feast.

18 And Ananias said, I have a plan that will succeed. The twelve with Jesus every day go forth alone to pray;

19 And we will find their trysting place; then we can seize the man and bring him here without the knowledge of the multitudes.

20 I know one of the twelve, a man who worships wealth, and for a sum I think that he will lead the way to where the man is wont to pray.

21 And then Caiaphas said, If you will lead the way and bribe the man of whom you speak, to aid in seizing Jesus in a secret place, then we will give to you a hundred silver pieces for your hire.

22 And Ananias said, 'Tis well.

23 And then he went to Bethany and found the twelve at Simon's house, and calling Judas to the side he said,

24 If you would care to make a sum of money for yourself hear me:

25 The high priest and the other rulers in Jerusalem would like to talk with Jesus when alone, that they may know about his claims;

26 And if he proves himself to be the Christ, lo, they will stand in his defense.

27 Now, if you will but lead the way to where your master is to-morrow night that they may send

a priest to talk with him alone, there is a sum of silver, thirty pieces, that the priests will give to you.

28 And Judas reasoned with himself; he said, It surely may be well to give the Lord a chance to tell the priests about his claims when he is all alone.

29 And if the priests would do him harm he has the power to disappear and go his way as he has done before; and thirty pieces is a goodly sum.

30 And so he said to Ananias, I will lead the way, and by a kiss make known which person is the Lord.

CHAPTER 160.

Jesus and the twelve eat the passover alone in Nicodemus' house. Jesus washes the disciples' feet. Judas leaves the table and goes forth to betray the Lord. Jesus teaches the eleven. He institutes the Lord's supper.

ON Thursday morning Jesus called to him the twelve disciples, and he said to them, This is God's remembrance day, and we will eat the pascal supper all alone.

2 And then he said to Peter, James and John, Go now into Jerusalem and there prepare the pasch.

3 And the disciples said, Where would you have us go to find the place where we may have the feast prepared?

4 And Jesus said, Go by the fountain gate and you will see a man who has a pitcher in his hand. Speak unto him and say: This is the first day of unleavened bread;

5 The Lord would have you set apart your banquet hall where he may eat his last passover with the twelve.

6 Fear not to speak; the man

whom you will see is Nicodemus, a ruler of the Jews, and yet a man of God.

7 And the disciples went and found the man as Jesus said, and Nicodemus hastened to his home; the banquet hall, an upper room, was set apart, the supper was prepared.

8 Now, in the afternoon the Lord and his disciples went up to Jerusalem and found the feast in readiness.

9 And when the hour had come to eat the feast, the twelve began to strive among themselves, each anxious to secure the honored seats.

10 And Jesus said, My friends, would you contend for self just as the shadows of this night of gloom comes on?

11 There is no honored seat at heaven's feast except for him who humbly takes the lowest seat.

12 And then the Lord arose and took a basin full of water and a towel, and bowing down, he washed the feet of all the twelve and dried them with the towel.

13 He breathed upon them and he said, And may these feet walk in the ways of righteousness forevermore.

14 He came to Peter and was about to wash his feet, and Peter said, Lord, would you wash my feet?

15 And Jesus said, You do not comprehend the meaning of the thing I do, but you will comprehend.

16 And Peter said, My master, no, you shall not stoop to wash my feet.

17 And Jesus said, My friend, if I wash not your feet you have no part with me.

18 And Peter said, Then, O my Lord, wash both my feet, my hands, my head.

19 And Jesus said to him, He who has taken first his bath is clean, and has no need to wash, except his feet.

20 The feet are truly symbols of the understanding of the man, and he who would be clean must, in the living stream of life, wash well his understanding every day.

21 Then Jesus sat with his disciples at the table of the feast and said, Behold the lesson of the hour:

22 You call me master; such I am. If, then, your Lord and master kneel and wash your feet, should you not wash each other's feet and thus show forth your willingness to serve?

23 You know these things, and if you do them, blessed thrice are you.

24 And then he said, This is an hour when I can truly praise the name of God, for I have greatly wished to eat with you this feast before I pass the veil;

25 For I will eat it not again until anew I eat it with you in the kingdom of our Father-God.

26 And then they sung the Hebrew song of praise that Jews were wont to sing before the feast.

27 And then they ate the pasch and as they ate, the master said, Behold, for one of you will turn away this night and will betray me into wicked hands.

28 And the disciples were amazed at what he said; they looked into each other's face in wonderment; they all exclaimed, Lord, is it I?

29 And Peter said to John, who sat beside the Lord, To whom does he refer?

30 And John put forth his hand and touched the master's hand and said, Which one of us is so depraved as to betray his Lord?

31 And Judas said, Lord, is it I?

32 And Jesus said, He is the one who now has put his hand with mine into the dish. They looked, and Judas' hand was with the hand of Jesus in the dish.

33 And Jesus said, The prophets cannot fail; the son of man must be betrayed, but woe to him who shall betray his Lord.

34 And from the table Judas rose at once; his hour had come.

35 And Jesus said to him, Do quickly what you are to do. And Judas went his way.

36 And when the pasch was done the Lord with the eleven sat a while in silent thought.

37 Then Jesus took a loaf of bread that had been broken not and said, This loaf is symbol of my body, and the bread is symbol of the bread of life;

38 And as I break this loaf, so shall my flesh be broken as a pattern for the sons of men; for men must freely give their bodies up in willing sacrifice for other men.

39 And as you eat this bread, so shall you eat the bread of life, and never die. And then he gave to each a piece of bread to eat.

40 And then he took a cup of wine and said, Blood is the life; this is the life-blood of the grape; it is the symbol of the life of him who gives his life for men.

41 And as you drink this wine, if you shall drink in faith, you drink the life of Christ.

42 And then he supped and passed the cup, and the disciples supped; and Jesus said, This is the feast of life, the great passover of the son of man, the Supper of the Lord, and you shall often eat the bread and drink the wine.

43 From henceforth shall this bread be called Remembrance bread; this wine shall be Remembrance wine; and when you eat this bread and drink this wine remember me.

CHAPTER 161.

Jesus teaches the eleven. Tells them that they will all be estranged from him, and that Peter will deny him thrice before the morning. He speaks final words of encouragement. Promises the Comforter.

NOW, after Judas had gone forth to meet the emissaries of the priests and to betray his Lord,

2 The master said, The hour has come, the son of man will now be glorified.

3 My little children, I am with you yet a little while; soon you will seek me and will find me not, for where I go you cannot come.

4 I give to you a new command: As I love you and give my life for you, so shall you love the world, and give your life to save the world.

5 Love one another as you love yourselves, and then the world will know that you are sons of God, disciples of the son of man whom God has glorified.

6 And Peter said, Lord, where you go there I will go, for I would lay my life down for my Lord.

7 And Jesus said, Boast not of bravery, my friend; you are not strong enough tonight to follow me.

8 Now, Peter, hear! you will deny me thrice before the cock shall crow tomorrow morn.

9 And then he looked upon the eleven and said, You all will be estranged from me this night.

10 The prophet said, Lo, he will smite the shepherd of the sheep; the sheep will flee and hide away.

11 But after I am risen from the

dead, lo, you will come again, and I will go before you into Galilee.

12 And Peter said, My Lord, though every other man forsake you I will not.

13 And Jesus said, O Simon Peter, lo, your zeal is greater than your fortitude! Behold, for Satan cometh up to sift you as a pan of wheat, but I have prayed that in your faith you shall not fail; that after trial you may stand a tower of strength.

14 And the disciples all exclaimed, There is no power on earth that can estrange,, or cause us to deny our Lord.

15 And Jesus said, Let not your hearts be sad; you all believe in God; believe in me.

16 Behold, for there are many mansions in my Fatherland. If there were not I would have told you so.

17 I go unto my Fatherland, and will prepare a place for you that where I am there you may be. But now you do not know the way unto my Fatherland.

18 And Thomas said, We do not know where you intend to go; how could we know the way?

19 And Jesus said, I am the way, the truth, the life; I manifest the Christ of God. No man can reach my Fatherland except he comes with me through Christ.

20 If you had known and comprehended me, then you would know my Father-God.

21 And Philip said, Show us the Father and we will be satisfied.

22 And Jesus said, Have I been with you all these years and still you know me not?

23 He who has seen the son has seen the Father, for in the son the Father has revealed himself.

24 Lo, I have told you many times that what I speak and what I do are not the words and works of man;

25 They are the words and works of God, who lives in me and I in him.

26 Hear me, you faithful men: He who believes in me and in my Father-God shall say and do what I have said and done.

27 Yea, more, he shall do greater works than I have ever done, because I go to him whose works we do, and then I can reach forth my hand in helpfulness.

28 And in my name, through Christ, you may petition God and he will grant you your request.

29 Do you believe what I have said? Yes, you believe, and if you love the Christ and follow me then you will keep my words.

30 I am the vine; you are the branches of the vine; my Father is the husbandman,

31 The branches that are worthless, bearing naught but leaves, the husbandman will cut away and cast into the fire to be burned.

32 And he will prune the branches that bear fruit that they may yield abundantly.

33 The branch cannot bear fruit if separated from the vine; and you cannot bear fruit when separate from me.

34 Abide in me, and do the works that God, through me, has taught you how to do, and you will bear much fruit, and God will honor you as he has honored me.

35 And now I go my way, but I will pray my Father-God and he will send another Comforter to you, who will abide with you.

36 Behold, this Comforter of God, the Holy Breath, is one with God, but she is one the world cannot

receive because it sees her not; it knows her not.

37 But you know her, and will know her, because she will abide within your soul.

38 I will not leave you desolate, but in the Christ, which is the love of God made manifest to men, I will be with you all the way.

CHAPTER 162.

Jesus reveals more fully the mission of the Holy Breath. Tells his disciples plainly that he is about to die, and they are sad. He prays for them and all the world of believers. They leave the banquet hall.

NOW, John was deeply grieved because the master said, I go away, and where I go you cannot come.

2 He wept and said, Lord, I would go with you through every trial and to death.

3 And Jesus said, And you shall follow me through trials and through death; but now you cannot go where I will go; but you shall come.

4 And Jesus spoke again unto the eleven and said, Grieve not because I go away, for it is best that I should go away. If I go not the Comforter will not come to you.

5 These things I speak while with you in the flesh, but when the Holy Breath shall come in power, lo, she will teach you more and more, and bring to your remembrance all the words that I have said to you.

6 There are a multitude of things yet to be said; things that this age cannot receive, because it cannot comprehend.

7 But, lo, I say, Before the great day of the Lord shall come,

the Holy Breath will make all mysteries known—

8 The mysteries of the soul, of life, of death, of immortality; the oneness of a man with every other man and with his God.

9 Then will the world be led to truth, and man will be the truth.

10 When she has come, the Comforter, she will convince the world of sin, and of the truth of what I speak, and of the rightness of the judgment of the just; and then the prince of carnal life will be cast out.

11 And when the Comforter shall come I need not intercede for you; for you will stand approved, and God will know you then as he knows me.

12 The hour has come when you will weep; the wicked will rejoice, because I go away; but I will come again, and all your sorrows shall be turned to joy;

13 Yea, verily, you will rejoice as one who welcomes back a brother from the dead.

14 And the disciples said, Our Lord, speak not in proverbs any more; speak plainly unto us; we know that you are wise and know all things.

15 What is the meaning of your words, I go away, but I will come again?

16 And Jesus said, The hour is come when you will all be scattered forth, and every man will be afraid;

17 Will flee to save his life and leave me all alone; yet I will not be all alone; my Father-God is with me all the way.

18 And wicked men will take me to the judgment seat of wicked men, and in the presence of the multitudes I will give up my life, a pattern for the sons of men.

19 But I will rise again and come to you.

20 These things I speak that you may be established in the faith when they shall come to pass.

21 And you shall bear the buffetings of men, and follow in the thorny path I tread.

22 Be not dismayed; be of good cheer. Lo, I have overcome the world, and you shall overcome the world.

23 Then Jesus lifted up his eyes to heaven and said, My Father-God, the hour has come;

24 The son of man must now be lifted from the earth, and may he falter not, that all the world may know the power of sacrifice;

25 For as I give my life for men, lo, men must give their lives for other men.

26 I came to do thy will, O God, and in the sacred name, the Christ is glorified, that men may see the Christ as life, as light, as love, as truth,

27 And through the Christ become themselves the life, the light, the love, the truth.

28 I praise thy name because of these whom thou hast given me, for they have honored thee and they will honor thee;

29 And none of them are lost, and none are gone away, except the blinded son of carnal life, who hath gone forth to sell his Lord.

30 O God, forgive this man, because he knows not what he does.

31 And now, O God, I come to thee, and am no more in mortal life; keep thou these men to whom I have made known thy wisdom and thy love.

32 As they believe in me, and in the words I speak, may all the world believe in them and in the words they speak.

33 As thou hast sent me forth into the world, so I have sent them

forth. I pray that thou wouldst honor them as thou hast honored me.

34 I do not pray that thou wouldst take them from the world, but that they may be guarded from the evil of the world, and not be subject to temptations that are too great for them to bear.

35 They once were of the world, but now are of the world no more, as I am of the world no more.

36 Thy word is truth, O God, and by thy word let them be sanctified.

37 I do not pray for these alone, O God; I also pray for all who will believe on me, and will accept the Christ because of what they do and say, that they may all be one.

38 As I am one with thee, and thou art one with me, may they be one with us,

39 That all the world may know that thou hast sent me forth to do thy will, and that thou lovest them as thou hast ever loved me.

40 When Jesus had thus said, they sung the Jewish song of praise, and then arose and went their way.

CHAPTER 163.

Jesus visits Pilate, who urges him to flee from the country to save his life. Jesus refuses to do so. He meets his disciples in Massalian's orchard. The scene in Gethsemane. The Jewish mob led by Judas appears.

AS Jesus and the eleven went out, a Roman guard approached and said, All hail! Is one of you the man from Galilee?

2 And Peter said, We all are men from Galilee; whom do you seek?

3 The guard replied, I seek for Jesus, who is called the Christ.

4 And Jesus answered, Here am I.

5 The guard spoke out and said, I do not come in an official way; I bear to you a message from the governor.

6 Jerusalem is all alive with vengeful Jews who swear that they will take your life, and Pilate would confer with you, and he would have you come to him without delay.

7 And Jesus said to Peter and the rest, Go to the vale, and by the Kidron wait for me, and I will go alone and see the governor.

8 And Jesus went up with the guard, and when he reached the palace, Pilate met him at the gate and said,

9 Young man, I have a word to say that may be well for you. I have observed your works and words three years and more;

10 And I have often stood in your defense when your own countrymen would fain have stoned you as a criminal.

11 But now the priests, the scribes and Pharisees have stirred the common people to a stage of frenzied wantonness and cruelty, and they intend to take your life,

12 Because, they say, that you have sworn to tear their temple down; to change the laws that Moses gave; to exile Pharisee and priest and seat yourself upon a throne.

13 And they aver that you are full in league with Rome.

14 The streets of all Jerusalem are filled this moment with a horde of madmen all intent to shed your blood.

15 There is no safety for you but in flight; wait not until the morning sun. You know the way to reach the border of this cursed land.

16 I have a little band of guards, well horsed and armed, and they will take you out beyond the reach of harm.

17 You must not tarry here, young man, you must arise and go.

18 And Jesus said, A noble prince has Cæsar in his Pilate Pontius, and from the point of carnal man your words are seasoned with the wise man's salt; but from the point of Christ your words are foolishness.

19 The coward flees when danger comes; but he who comes to seek and save the lost must give his life in willing sacrifice for those he comes to seek and save.

20 Before the pasch has been consumed, lo, all this nation will be cursed by shedding blood of innocence; and even now the murderers are at the door.

21 And Pilate said, It shall not be; the sword of Rome will be unsheathed to save your life.

22 And Jesus said, Nay, Pilate, nay; there are no armies large enough in all the world to save my life.

23 And Jesus bade the governor farewell, and went his way; but Pilate sent a double guard with him lest he should fall into the hands of those who were alert to take his life.

24 But in a moment Jesus disappeared; the guards saw him no more, and in a little while he reached the brook of Kidron where the eleven were.

25 Now, just beyond the brook there was an orchard and a home where one, Massalian, lived, where Jesus oft had been.

26 Massalian was his friend, and he believed that Jesus was the Christ that Jewish prophets long ago had said would come.

27 Now, in the orchard was a

sacred knoll; Massalian called the place Gethsemane.

28 The night was dark, but in the orchard it was doubly dark and Jesus bade the eight disciples tarry by the brook,

29 While he, with Peter, James and John went to Gethsemane to pray.

30 They sat beneath an olive tree, and Jesus opened up the mysteries of life to Peter, James and John. He said,

31 The Spirit of eternity is One unmanifest; and this is God the Father, God the Mother, God the Son in One.

32 In life of manifests the One became the Three, and God the Father is the God of might; and God the Mother is omniscient God, and God the Son is love.

33 And God the Father is the power of heaven and earth; and God the Mother is the Holy Breath, the thought of heaven and earth; and God the Son, the only son, is Christ, and Christ is love.

34 I came as man to manifest this love to men,

35 As man I have been subject unto all the trials and temptations of the human race; but I have overcome the flesh, with all its passions and its appetites.

36 What I have done all men can do.

37 And I am now about to demonstrate the power of man to conquer death; for every man is God made flesh.

38 I will lay down my life, and I will take it up again, that you may know the mysteries of life, of death, and of the resurrection of the dead.

39 I lay me down in flesh, but I will rise in spirit form with power to manifest myself so mortal eyes can see.

40 So in a trinity of days I will show forth the all of life, the all of death, the meaning of the resurrection of the dead.

41 And what I do all men can do.

42 And you, my three, who constitute the inner circle of the Church of Christ, will show to men the attributes of all the Gods.

43 And Peter shall make known the Power of God; and James shall show the Thought of God; and John shall demonstrate the Love of God.

44 Be not afraid of men, for you have been sent forth to do the mighty works of God the Father, God the Mother, God the Son.

45 And all the powers of carnal life cannot destroy your life until your work is done.

46 I leave you now, and I will go out in the darkness all alone and talk with God.

47 By sorrow I am overwhelmed. I leave you here to watch with me.

48 Then Jesus went three hundred cubits toward the east, and fell upon his face and prayed; he said,

49 My God! my God! is there a way by which I may escape the horrors of the coming hours? My human flesh shrinks back; my soul is firm; so not my will, but thine, O God, be done.

50 In agony he prayed; the strain upon the human form was great; his veins were burst asunder, and his brow was bathed in blood.

51 And then he went back to the three, and found them all asleep; he said,

52 O Simon, Simon, do you sleep! Could you not watch with me a single hour? Be vigilant, and watch and pray that your temptations be not too great for you to bear.

53 I know the spirit is alert and willing; but the flesh is weak.

54 And then he went again and prayed, O Father, God! if I must drink this bitter cup, give me the strength of body, as I have the strength of soul; for not my will, but thine be done.

55 And when he went again to his disciples; lo, he found them still asleep. He wakened them and said to James,

56 Have you been sleeping while your master has been wrestling with the greatest foe of men? Could you not watch with me a single hour?

57 And then he went again and prayed. O God, I yield to thee; thy will be done.

58 And then again he went back to the three, and still they slept. He said to John,

59 With all the love you have for me, could you not watch with me a single hour?

60 And then he said, It is enough; the hour has come, and my betrayer is at hand; arise and let us go.

61 And when they came again to Kidron, lo, the eight disciples were asleep, and Jesus said, You men, awake; behold, for the betrayer of the son of man is come.

CHAPTER 164.

Judas betrays his Lord with a kiss. Jesus is seized by the mob and the disciples flee to save their lives. Jesus is taken unto Jerusalem. Peter and John follow the mob.

THE Lord with the eleven were in the orchard of Massalian, and as they talked they saw a band of men with lanterns and with swords and clubs approaching them.

2 And Jesus said, Behold the emissaries of the evil one! and Judas leads the way.

3 And the disciples said, Lord, let us flee to save our lives.

4 But Jesus said, Why should we flee to save our lives when this is the fulfillment of the words of prophets and of seers?

5 And Jesus went alone to meet the men; and as they came he said, Why are you here, you men? whom do you seek?

6 And they replied, We seek the man from Galilee. We seek for Jesus, one who calls himself the Christ.

7 And Jesus answered, Here am I.

8 And then he raised his hands and with a mighty thought he brought the ethers to the state of light; and all the orchard was aglow with light.

9 The frenzied men were driven back and many fled and tarried not until they reached Jerusalem; and others fell upon their faces on the ground.

10 The bravest men, and they with hardest hearts, remained, and when the light had paled, the Lord again inquired, Whom do you seek?

11 And Ananias said, We seek the man from Galilee; we seek for Jesus, he who calls himself the Christ.

12 And Jesus answered him and said, I told you once before; but now I tell you once again that I am he.

13 By Ananias, Judas stood; but in a moment he had gone and coming up behind the Lord he said, My Lord; and then he kissed him as a sign that he was Jesus whom they sought.

14 And Jesus said, Do you, Iscariot, come and thus betray your master with a kiss?

15 This thing must need be done; but woe to him who does betray his Lord.

16 Your carnal greed has seared your conscience and you know not what you do; but in a little time your conscience will assert itself, and in remorse, lo, you will close your span and take your life.

17 Then the eleven came, laid hold of Judas and would have done him harm; but Jesus said,

18 You must not harm this man; you have no right to judge this man; his conscience is his judge, will sentence him and he will execute himself.

19 And then the mob led on by Malchus, servant of Caiaphas, laid hold of Jesus, and was binding him with chains.

20 And Jesus said, Why do you come in dead of night with swords and clubs to take me in this sacred place?

21 Have I not spoken in the public places of Jerusalem? Have I not healed your sick, and opened up your blinded eyes, and made your lame to walk, your deaf to hear? You could have found me any day.

22 And now you try to bind me down with chains; what are these chains but links of reeds? And then he raised his hands; the chains were broken and they fell to earth.

23 And Malchus thought the Lord would flee to save his life, and with a club he fain would smite him in the face.

24 But Peter had a sword, and rushing up he smote the man and wounded him.

25 But Jesus said, Stay, Peter, stay; put up your sword; you are not called to fight with swords and clubs. Whoever wields the sword shall perish by the sword.

26 I do not need protection by the sons of men, for I could call this moment and a legion, yea, twelve legions of the messengers of God, would come and stand in my defense; but then it is not well.

27 And then he said to Malchus, Man, I would not have you harmed. And then he laid his hand upon the wound that Peter made, and it was healed.

28 Then Jesus said, Be not concerned lest I should tear myself away from you and flee to save my life. I have no wish to save my life; do with me as you wish.

29 And then the mob rushed up to seize the eleven to take them back to stand for trial as the aids of Jesus in his crimes.

30 But the disciples, every one of them, deserted Jesus, and they fled to save their lives.

31 Now, John was last to flee; the mob laid hold of him and tore his garments all to shreds; but he escaped in nakedness.

32 Massalian saw the man, and took him to his home and gave him other clothes; and then he followed after them who led the Lord away.

33 And Peter was ashamed because of his weak cowardice, and when he was himself again he joined with John and followed close behind the mob, and came into Jerusalem.

SECTION XIX.

KOPH.

The Trial and Execution of Jesus.

CHAPTER 165.

Jesus before Caiaphas. Peter denies his Lord thrice. The indictment, signed by seven ruling Jews. A hundred perjured witnesses testify to the truth of the charges.

CAIAPHAS was the high priest of the Jews; the mob led Jesus to his palace hall.

2 The court had been convened, and all the galleries were packed with scribes and Pharisees already sworn as witnesses against the Lord.

3 The maid who kept the palace door knew John, and this disciple asked that he and Peter be admitted to the hall.

4 The maid permitted them to enter in, and John went in; but Peter was afraid and tarried in the outer court.

5 The woman said to Peter, as he stood beside the door, Are you a follower of this man from Galilee?

6 And Peter said, No, I am not.

7 The men who had brought Jesus to the hall sat by a fire in the outer court, because the night was cool, and Peter sat with them.

8 Another maid who waited in the place saw Peter and she said to him, You surely are from Galilee; your speech is that of Galilee; you are a follower of this man.

9 And Peter said, I know not what you mean; I do not even know this man.

10 And then a servant of Caiaphas, one of those who seized the Lord and brought him to the court, saw Peter and he said to him,

11 Did I not see you in the orchard of Massalian with this seditious Nazarene? I'm sure I did, and you are one of those who followed him.

12 Then Peter rose and stamped upon the floor, and swore by every sacred thing, that he knew not the criminal.

13 Now, John was standing near and when he heard the words and knew that Peter had denied his Lord, he looked at him in sheer astonishment.

14 Just then a cock crew loud beneath the court, and Peter called to mind the words the Lord had said,

15 Before the cock shall crow tomorrow morn you will deny me thrice.

16 And Peter's conscience smote him heavily, and he went out into the night and wept.

17 Caiaphas sat in state; before him stood the man from Galilee.

18 Caiaphas said, You people of Jerusalem, who is the man that you accuse?

19 They answered: In the name of every loyal Jew we do accuse this man from Galilee, this Jesus, who assumes to be our king, as enemy of God and man.

20 Caiaphas said to Jesus, Man, you are permitted now to speak and tell about your doctrines and your claims.

21 And Jesus said, You priest of carnal man, why do you ask about my words and works?

22 Lo, I have taught the multitudes in every public place; I have restored your sick to health: have

opened up your blinded eyes; have
caused your deaf to hear, your lame
to walk, and I have brought your
dead to life again.

23 My works have not been
done in secret place but in your
public halls and thoroughfares.

24 Go ask the people, who have
not been bought with gold or glit-
tering promises, to tell about my
words and works.

25 When Jesus had thus said
a Jewish guard came up and smote
him in the face and said, How dare
you speak thus unto him, the high
priest of the Jews?

26 And Jesus said, If I have
spoken falsely bear witness unto
what I say; if I have told the truth
why did you smite me thus?

27 And then Caiaphas said,
What'er you do, do in a legal way,
for we must answer to a higher
court for everything we do or say.

28 Let the accusers of this man
present their charges in a legal
form.

29 And then Caiaphas' scribe
stood forth and said, I have the accusations here in legal form; the
charges made and signed by scribes
and priests and Pharisees.

30 Caiaphas said, Be still, you
men, and hear the charges read.
The scribe took up a roll and read:

31 To the Sanhedrim of the Jews
and to Caiaphas the high priest,
most honored men:

32 The highest duty man can
render to his nation and his own is
to protect them from their foes.

33 The people of Jerusalem are
conscious that a mighty foe is in
their very midst.

34 A man named Jesus has
come forth and claims to be the heir
to David's throne.

35 As an impostor he is foe, and

in the name of every loyal Jew we
here submit these charges, which
we are competent to prove:

36 And first, he blasphemes
God; he says he is the son of God;
that he and God are one;

37 And he profanes our holy
days by healing, and by doing other
work upon the Sabbath days;

38 And he proclaims himself the
king, successor of our David and
our Solomon;

39 And he declares that he will
tear our temple down and build it
up again in form more glorious in
three days;

40 And he declares that he will
drive the people from Jerusalem,
as he drove out the merchants from
the temple court; and bring to occupy our sacred hills a tribe of men
that know not God;

41 And he avers that every doctor, scribe and Pharisee and Sadducee, shall go in exile, and shall
nevermore return;

42 And to these charges we do
set our hands and seals.

Annas.	Simon.
Abinadab.	Annanias.
Joash.	Azaniah.
	Hezekiah.

43 Now, when the scribe had
read the charges, all the people
called for blood; they said, Let such
a wretch be stoned; let him be crucified.

44 Caiaphas said, You men of
Israel, do you sustain the charges of
these men?

45 A hundred men who had
been bribed, stood forth to testify;
they swore that every charge was
true.

46 Caiaphas said to Jesus, Man,
have you a word to say? are you
the son of God?

47 And Jesus said, So you have
said; and then he said no more.

CHAPTER 166.

Jesus before the Sanhedrim. Nicodemus pleads for justice; he shows the incompetency of the witnesses. The council fail to declare Jesus guilty, but Caiaphas, the presiding judge, declares him guilty. The mob maltreat Jesus. He is taken to Pilate's court.

WHEN Jesus would not speak, Caiaphas stood before the Jewish mob and said,

2 Bind fast the prisoner, for he must go before the great Sanhedrim of the Jews to answer for his life.

3 We cannot execute a criminal until our findings have been verified by this, the highest council of the Jews.

4 As soon as it was day the highest council of the people met; the Lord and his accusers stood before the bar.

5 Caiaphas was the chief; he rose and said, Let the accusers of this man from Galilee bring forth their charges and their evidence.

6 Caiaphas' scribe stood forth and read the charges and the names of those who had accused the man from Galilee.

7 And all the witnesses were made to stand and testify before the council of the Jews.

8 And then the lawyers weighed the evidence, and Nicodemus stood among the men who plead.

9 He raised his hands and said, Let justice now be done, though every scribe and Pharisee and priest and Sadducee, as well as Jesus, the accused, be judged a liar.

10 If we can prove this Jesus to be foe and traitor to our laws and land, let him be judged a criminal and suffer for his crimes.

11 If it be proved that these who testify are perjurers in the sight of God and man, then let them be adjudged as criminals, and let the man from Galilee go free.

12 And then he brought the testimonies of the witnesses before the judges of the law; no two of them agreed. In heat of passion, or for gain, the men had testified.

13 The council would have gladly judged that Jesus was a criminal and sentence him to death; but in the face of all the evidence they were afraid.

14 And then Caiaphas said, You man from Galilee, Before the living God, I now command that you shall answer me, Are you the Christ, the son of God?

15 And Jesus said, If I would answer, Yes, you would not hear, nor yet believe,

16 If I would answer, No, I would be like your witnesses, and stand a liar in the sight of man and God. But this I say,

17 The time will come when you will see the son of man upon the throne of power and coming in the clouds of heaven.

18 And then Caiaphas rent his clothes and said, Have you not heard enough? Did you not hear his vile blasphemous words? What further need have we of witnesses? What shall we do with him?

19 The people said, Put him to death. And then the mob rushed up and spit into his face, and struck him with their hands.

20 And then they bound a cloth about his eyes and smote him in the face and said, You are a prophet; tell us who it was who smote you in the face.

21 And Jesus answered not and like a lamb before his shearer he, the man from Galilee, resisted not.

22 Caiaphas said, We cannot

put a man to death until the Roman ruler shall confirm the sentence of this court;

23 So take this criminal away and Pilate will endorse what we have done.

24 And then was Jesus dragged along the way up to the palace of the Roman governor.

CHAPTER 167.

Jesus before Pilate. Is pronounced not guilty. Jesus before Herod and is tortured and returned to Pilate, who again declares him innocent. The Jews demand his death. Pilate's wife urges her husband to have nothing to do with the punishment of Jesus. Pilate weeps.

INTO the palace of the Roman governor the Jews would enter not lest they become defiled and be unworthy to attend the feast; but they led Jesus to the palace court, and Pilate met them there.

2 And Pilate said, Why this commotion in the early day? What is your prayer?

3 The Jews replied, We bring before you one, an evil and seditious man.

4 He has been tried before the highest council of the Jews and has been proven traitor to our laws, our state and to the government of Rome.

5 We pray that you will sentence him to death upon the cross.

6 And Pilate said, Why do you bring him unto me? Go to, and judge him for yourselves.

7 You have a law, and by the sanction of the Roman law, you have a right to judge and right to execute.

8 The Jews replied, We have no right to execute a man upon the cross, and since this man is traitor

to Tiberius, our counsellors believe that he should meet the most humiliating death—the death upon the cross.

9 But Pilate said, No man can be found guilty of a crime by Roman law until the testimony all is in, and the accused has been permitted to defend himself;

10 So I will take your bill of charges, with the evidence you have, and judge by Roman law.

11 The Jews had made a copy of the accusations in the language of the Roman court, and they had added to the bill:

12 We charge that Jesus is an enemy of Rome; that he demands that men shall pay no tribute to Tiberius.

13 And Pilate took the bill; his guards led Jesus up the steps into the palace hall.

14 And Jesus stood before the Roman governor, and Pilate read to him the charges of the Jews, and said,

15 What is your answer to this bill? These charges, are they true or false?

16 And Jesus said, Why should I plead before an earthly court? The charges have been verified by perjured men; what need I say?

17 Yes, I am king; but carnal men cannot behold the king, nor see the kingdom of the God; it is within.

18 If I had been a king as carnal man is king, my servants would have stood in my defense, and I would not have willingly surrendered to the minions of the Jewish law.

19 I have no testimony from the sons of men. God is my witness, and my words and deeds bear witness to the truth;

20 And every man who comprehends the truth will hearken to my

words, and in his soul give witness unto me.

21 And Pilate said, What is the truth?

22 And Jesus said, Truth is the God who knows. It is the changeless one. The Holy Breath is truth; she changes not and cannot pass away.

23 And Pilate went again unto the Jews and said, This man is guilty of no crime; I cannot sentence him to death.

24 And then the Jews grew boisterous; they cried aloud and said, Our council surely knows. The wisest men of all the land have found him guilty of a score of crimes.

25 He would pervert the nation of the Jews; would overthrow the Roman rule and make himself the king. He is a culprit come from Galilee; he must be crucified.

26 And Pilate said, If Jesus is from Galilee he is a subject of the governor of Galilee, who should be judge.

27 Now, Herod had come down from Galilee and with his suite was in Jerusalem.

28 And Pilate sent to him the Lord in chains; he also sent a copy of the charges, and of the testimonies of the Jews, and asked that he would pass in judgment on the case.

29 And Herod said, I have heard much about this man and I am pleased to see him in my court.

30 And then he asked the Lord about his claims, about his doctrines and his aims.

31 And Jesus answered not a word; and Herod was enraged; he said, Do you insult the ruler of the land by answering not?

32 And then he called his guards and said, Take you this man and torture him until he answers me.

33 The guards took Jesus and they smote him; mocked him; wrapped him in a royal robe; they made a crown of thorns and put it on his head; they put a broken reed into his hands;

34 And then they said deridingly, All hail, thou royal king! Where are your armies and your guards? Where are your subjects and your friends?

35 But Jesus answered not a word. Then Herod sent him back to Pilate with this note of courtesy:

36 Most worthy counsellor of Rome, I have examined all the charges and the testimonies that you sent to me regarding this seditious man from Galilee, and while I might adjudge him guilty of the crimes as charged,

37 I yield to you my rights as judge, because you are superior to me in power. I will approve of any judgment you may render in this case.

38 Now, Pilate and the tetrarch had been foes, but the experience of this hour destroyed their enmity and they were friends in after days.

39 When Jesus had been brought again to Pilate's court, the Roman governor stood forth before the accusers of the Lord and said,

40 I cannot find this Nazarene to be a criminal as charged; there is no evidence that he should suffer death; so I will scourge him well and let him go.

41 The Jews cried angrily, It is not mete that such a dangerous man should live; he must be crucified.

42 Then Pilate said, I bid you wait a little time. And then he

went into an inner room and sat in silent thought.

43 And as he mused his wife, a godly woman, chosen from among the Gauls, came in and said,

44 I pray you, Pilate, hearken unto me: Beware of what you do this hour. Touch not this man from Galilee; he is a holy man.

45 If you should scourge this man you scourge the son of God. Last night I saw it all in vision far too vivid to be set aside as idle dream.

46 I saw this man walk on the waters of the sea; I heard him speak and calm an angry storm; I saw him flying with the wings of light;

47 I saw Jerusalem in blood; I saw the statues of the Cæsars fall; I saw a veil before the sun, and day was dark as night.

48 The earth on which I stood was shaken like a reed before the wind. I tell you, Pilate, if you bathe your hands in this man's blood then you may dread the frowns of great Tiberius, and the curses of the senators of Rome.

49 And then she left, and Pilate wept.

CHAPTER 168.

Pilate's final effort to release Jesus fails. He washes his hands in feigned innocence. Delivers Jesus to the Jews for execution. The Jewish soldiers drive him to Calvary.

A SUPERSTITIOUS people are the Jews. They have a faith that they have borrowed from the idol worshippers of other lands, that at the end of every year,

2 They may heap all their sins upon the head of some man set apart to bear their sins.

3 The man becomes a scapegoat for the multitudes; and they believe that when they drive him forth into the wilds, or into foreign lands, they are released from sin.

4 So every spring before the feast they chose a prisoner from the prisons of the land, and by a form their own, they fain would make him bear their sins away.

5 Among the Jewish prisoners in Jerusalem were three who were the leaders of a vile, seditious band, who had engaged in thefts and murders and rapine, and had been sentenced to be crucified.

6 Barabbas bar Jezia was among the men who were to die; but he was rich and he had bought of priests the boon to be the scapegoat for the people at the coming feast, and he was anxiously in waiting for his hour to come.

7 Now, Pilate thought to turn this superstition to account to save the Lord, and so he went again before the Jews and said,

8 You men of Israel, according to my custom I will release to you today a prisoner who shall bear your sins away.

9 This man you drive into the wilds or into foreign lands, and you have asked me to release Barabbas, who has been proven guilty of the murder of a score of men.

10 Now, hear me men, Let Jesus be released and let Barabbas pay his debt upon the cross; then you can send this Jesus to the wilds and hear no more of him.

11 At what the ruler said the people were enraged, and they began to plot to tear the Roman palace down and drive in exile Pilate, and his household and his guards.

12 When Pilate was assured that civil war would follow if he heeded not the wishes of the mob, he took a bowl of water and in the

presence of the multitude he washed his hands and said,

13 This man whom you accuse, is son of the most holy Gods, and I proclaim my innocence.

14 If you would shed his blood, his blood is on your hands and not on mine.

15 And then the Jews exclaimed, And let his blood be on our hands and on our children's hands.

16 And Pilate trembled like a leaf, in fear. Barabbas he released and as the Lord stood forth before the mob the ruler said, Behold your king! And would you put to death your king?

17 The Jews replied, He is no king; we have no king but great Tiberius.

18 Now, Pilate would not give consent that Roman soldiers should imbue their hands in blood of innocence, and so the chief priests and the Pharisees took counsel what to do with Jesus, who was called the Christ.

19 Caiaphas said, We cannot crucify this man; he must be stoned to death and nothing more.

20 And then the rabble said, Make haste! let him be stoned. And then they led him forth toward the hill beyond the city's gates, where criminals were put to death.

21 The rabble could not wait until they reached the place of skulls. As soon as they had passed the city's gate, they rushed upon him, smote him with their hands, they spit upon him, stoned him and he fell upon the ground.

22 And one, a man of God, stood forth and said, Isaiah said, He shall be bruised for our transgressions and by his stripes we shall be healed.

23 As Jesus lay all bruised and mangled on the ground a Pharisee

called out, Stay, stay you men! behold, the guards of Herod come and they will crucify this man.

24 And there beside the city's gate they found Barabbas' cross; and then the frenzied mob cried out, Let him be crucified.

25 Caiaphas and the other ruling Jews came forth and gave consent.

26 And then they lifted Jesus from the ground, and at the point of swords they drove him on.

27 A man named Simon, from Cyrene, a friend of Jesus, was a-near the scene and since the bruised and wounded Jesus could not bear his cross, they laid it on the shoulders of this man and made him bear it on to Calvary.

CHAPTER 169.

Judas is filled with remorse. Hurries to the temple and throws the thirty pieces of silver at the feet of the priests who take it and buy a potter's field. Judas hangs himself. His body is buried in the potter's field.

NOW, Judas who betrayed his Lord, was with the mob; but all the time he thought that Jesus would assert his power and demonstrate the strength of God that he possessed, and strike to earth the fiendish multitudes and free himself;

2 But when he saw his master on the ground and bleeding from a score of wounds, he said,

3 O God, what have I done? I have betrayed the son of God; the curse of God will rest upon my soul.

4 And then he turned and ran with haste until he reached the temple door; he found the priests, who gave to him the thirty silver pieces to betray the Lord, and said,

5 Take back your bribe; it is the cost price of my soul; I have betrayed the son of God.

6 The priests replied, That matters not to us.

7 Then Judas threw the silver on the floor, and, bowed with grief, he went away, and on a ledge beyond the city's walls he hanged himself and died.

8 In time the fastenings gave way, his body fell into the Hinnon vale and after many days they found it there a shapeless mass.

9 The rulers could not put the price of blood into the treasury, and so they took the thirty silver pieces with which they bought a potter's field,

10 Where they might bury those who had no rights to lie within their sacred burial grounds.

11 And there they put the body of the man who sold his Lord.

CHAPTER 170.

The crucifixion. Jesus prays for his murderers. Pilate puts an inscription above the cross. Jesus speaks words of encouragement to the penitent thief. Commits to John the care of his mother and Miriam. The soldiers divide his garments among themselves.

THE Jewish mob pushed on toward Calvary and as they went the Marys, Miriam, and other women not a few, were close beside the Lord.

2 They wept aloud. When Jesus saw them weeping and lamenting thus he said,

3 Weep not for me, for though I go away, go through the gateway of the cross, yet on the next day of the sun, lift up your hearts, for I will meet you at the sepulchre.

4 The great procession came to Calvary. The Roman soldiers had already bound the two state prisoners to the cross.

5 (They were not nailed, but simply bound.)

6 Four soldiers of the Roman guard that Herod brought from Galilee were called to execute the orders of the court.

7 These were the men who had been set apart to torture Jesus and secure from him confession of his guilt.

8 These were the men who scourged him, put a crown of thorns upon his head, a broken reed into his hands, and wrapped him in a royal robe, and bowed in mockery, before him as a king.

9 These soldiers took the Lord and stripped him, laid him on the cross and would have bound him there with cords; but this would not suffice.

10 The cruel Jews were near with hammer and with nails; they cried, not cords, but nails; drive fast the nails and hold him to the cross.

11 And then the soldiers took the nails and drove them through his feet and hands.

12 They offered him a sedative to drink, a draught of vinegar and myrrh; but he refused to drink the draught.

13 The soldiers had prepared a place in which to plant Barabbas' cross between the other criminals; and here they raised the cross of Jesus, who was called the Christ;

14 And then the soldiers and the mob sat down to watch him die.

15 And Jesus said, My Father-God, forgive these men; they know not what they do.

16 Now, Pilate had prepared a

tablet to be placed upon the cross on which was written in the tongues of Hebrew, Latin and the Greek these words of truth: JESUS THE CHRIST, KING OF THE JEWS.

17 And this was placed upon the cross. The priests were angered when they read these words upon the tablet of the cross.

18 And then they prayed that Pilate would not say, He is the Christ, king of the Jews; but say, He claims to be the Christ, king of the Jews.

19 But Pilate said, What I have written, I have written; let it stand.

20 The Jewish multitudes who saw the Lord upon the cross were wild with joy; they said, All hail, fake king!

21 You who would tear the temple down and in three days would build it up again, why don't you save yourself?

22 If you are Christ, the son of God, come from the cross; then all men will believe.

23 The priests and scribes and Pharisees looked on the scene and scoffed; they said, He rescued others from the grave; why don't he save himself?

24 The Jewish soldiers and the Roman guards who came from Galilee were loud in mocking and deriding him.

25 One of the other men upon the cross joined in the mockery; he said, If you are Christ, you have the power; just speak the Word, and save yourself and me.

26 The other man upon the cross rebuked the man; he said, You wretch! have you no fear of God?

27 This man is innocent of any crime while you and I are guilty and are paying up the debts we owe.

28 And then he said to Jesus,

Lord, I know thy kingdom comes, the kingdom that the world can never comprehend;

29 And when thou comest on the clouds of heaven, remember me.

30 And Jesus said, Behold, for I will meet you in the realm of souls this day.

31 Now, standing near unto the cross were many women from Judea and from Galilee. Among them were the mother of the Lord and Miriam,

32 And Mary, mother of the two apostles, James and John, and Mary Magdalene, and Martha, Ruth and Mary, and Salome.

33 When Jesus saw his mother and the singer Miriam standing close beside the cross and John anear, he said to John,

34 In your most tender care I leave my mother and my sister Miriam.

35 And John replied, While they shall live my home shall be the home of your thrice blessed mother and your sister Miriam.

36 According to a custom of the Jews, to those who were the executioners of law and took the lives of criminals, belonged the garments of the criminals.

37 So when the Lord was crucified, the Roman guards divided up among themselves the garments of the Lord.

38 But when they found his coat it was a seamless coat and highly prized.

39 For it the guards cast lots, and thus determined who should have the prize.

40 And thus the scripture was fulfilled, which said, And they divided all my robes among themselves, and for my vesture they cast lots.

CHAPTER 171.

Concluding scenes of the crucifixion. Joseph and Nicodemus, by consent of Pilate, take the body of Jesus from the cross and lay it in Joseph's tomb. A guard of one hundred Jewish soldiers are placed about the sepulcher.

NOW, at the sixth hour of the day, although the sun was at its height, the day became as dark as night;

2 And men sought lanterns and they builded fires upon the hills that they might see.

3 And when the sun refused to shine and darkness came, the Lord exclaimed, *Heloi! Heloi! lama sabachthani?* (Thou sun! thou sun! why hast thou forsaken me?)

4 The people did not understand the words he spoke; they thought he spoke the name Elijah and they said,

5 He calls upon Elijah in his hour of need; now we will see if he will come.

6 And Jesus said, I thirst. A Roman soldier dipped a sponge in vinegar and myrrh, and placed it to his lips.

7 Now, at the ninth hour of the day the earth began to quake, and in the darkness of that sunless day, a flood of golden light appeared above the cross;

8 And from the light a voice was heard which said, Lo, it is done.

9 And Jesus said, My Father-God, into thy hands I give my soul.

10 A Roman soldier in compassion said, This agony is all too great; relief shall come. And with a spear he pierced his heart and it was done; the son of man was dead.

11 And then the earth was shocked again; the city of Jerusalem rocked to and fro; the hills were rent and tombs were opened up;

12 And people thought they saw the dead arise and walk the streets.

13 The temple quivered and the veil between the sanctuary and the Holy Place was rent in twain, and consternation reigned through all the place.

14 The Roman guard who watched the body on the cross exclaimed, This surely was the son of God who died.

15 And then the people hurried down from Calvary. The priests, the Pharisees and scribes were filled with fear.

16 They sought the cover of their synagogues and homes and said, Behold, the wrath of God!

17 The great day of the Jewish pasch was near, and Jews could not by law permit a criminal to hang upon the cross upon the Sabbath day.

18 And so they prayed that Pilate would remove the bodies of the men that had been crucified.

19 And Pilate sent his guards to Calvary to note if all the men were dead.

20 And when the guards were gone, two aged Jews came to the palace door to see the governor, and they were members of the highest council of the Jews;

21 Yet they believed that Jesus was a prophet sent from God.

22 The one was Rabbi Joseph, the Arimathean counsellor, and he was just and loved the law of God.

23 And Nicodemus was the other one who came.

24 These men fell down at Pilate's feet and prayed that they might take the body of the Nazarene and lay it in a tomb.

25 And Pilate gave consent.

26 Now, Joseph had prepared a

costly mixture to embalm the body of the Lord, about a hundred pounds of aloes and of myrrh, and this they took and hastened out to Calvary.

27 And when the guards returned they said, The Nazarene is dead; the malefactors are alive.

28 And Pilate told the guards to go and smite the living men so they would die, and then to give their bodies to the flames; but give the body of the Nazarene to rabbis who would call for it.

29 The soldiers did as Pilate said.

30 The rabbis came and took away the body of the Lord and when they had prepared it with the spices they had bought,

31 They laid it in the new-made tomb that had been made for Joseph in a solid rock.

32 And then they rolled a stone up to the sepulcher.

33 The priests were fearful lest the friends of Jesus would go forth at night and take away the body of the Nazarene, and then report that he had risen from the dead, as he had said;

34 And they requested that the governor would send his soldiers to the tomb to guard the body of the dead.

35 But Pilate said, I will not send a Roman guard; but you have Jewish soldiers and may send a hundred men with a centurion to guard the tomb.

36 And then they sent a hundred soldiers out to guard the tomb.

SECTION XX.

RESH.

The Resurrection of Jesus.

CHAPTER 172.

Pilate places the Roman seal upon the stone door of the tomb. At midnight a company of the silent brothers march about the tomb. The soldiers are alarmed. Jesus preaches to the spirits in prison. Early Sunday morning he rises from the tomb. The soldiers are bribed by the priests to say that the disciples had stolen the body.

THE tomb in which they laid the body of the Lord was in a garden, rich with flowers, the garden of Siloam, and Joseph's home was near.

2 Before the watch began Caiaphas sent a company of priests out to the garden of Siloam that they might be assured that Jesus' body was within the tomb.

3 They rolled away the stone; they saw the body there, and then they placed the stone again before the door.

4 And Pilate sent his scribe who placed upon the stone the seal of Rome, in such a way that he who moved the stone would break the seal.

5 To break this Roman seal meant death to him who broke the seal.

6 The Jewish soldiers all were sworn to faithfulness; and then the watch began.

7 At midnight all was well, but suddenly the tomb became a blaze of light, and down the garden walk a troupe of white clad soldiers marched in single file.

8 They came up to the tomb

and marched and countermarched before the door.

9   The Jewish soldiers were alert; they thought the friends had come to steal the body of the Nazarene. The captain of the guard cried out to charge.

10   They charged; but not a white clad soldier fell. They did not even stop; they marched and countermarched among the frightened men.

11   They stood upon the Roman seal; they did not speak; they unsheathed not their swords; it was the Silent Brotherhood.

12   The Jewish soldiers fled in fear; they fell upon the ground.

13   They stood apart until the white clad soldiers marched away, and then the light about the tomb grew dim.

14   Then they returned; the stone was in its place; the seal was not disturbed, and they resumed their watch.

15   Now, Jesus did not sleep within the tomb. The body is the manifest of soul; but soul is soul without its manifest.

16   And in the realm of souls, unmanifest, the Lord went forth and taught.

17   He opened up the prison doors and set the prisoners free;

18   He broke the chains of captive souls, and led the captives to the light;

19   He sat in council with the patriarchs and prophets of the olden times;

20   The masters of all times and climes he met, and in the great assemblies he stood forth and told the story of his life on earth, and of his death in sacrifice for man,

21   And of his promises to clothe himself again in garb of flesh and

walk with his disciples, just to prove the possibilities of man;

22   To give to them the key of life, of death, and of the resurrection of the dead.

23   In council all the masters sat and talked about the revelations of the coming age,

24   When she, the Holy Breath, shall fill the earth and air with holy breath, and open up the way of man to perfectness and endless life.

25   The garden of Siloam was silent on the Sabbath day; the Jewish soldiers watched and no one else approached the tomb; but on the following night the scene was changed.

26   At midnight every Jewish soldier heard a voice which said, *Adon Mashich Cumi,* which meant, Lord Christ arise.

27   And they supposed again that friends of Jesus were alert, were coming up to take the body of their Lord away.

28   The soldiers were alert with swords unsheathed and drawn, and then they heard the words again.

29   It seemed as though the voice was everywhere, and yet they saw no man.

30   The soldiers blanched with fear, and still to flee meant death for cowardice, and so they stood and watched.

31   Again, and this was just before the sun arose, the heavens blazed with light, a distant thunder seemed to herald forth a coming storm;

32   And then the earth began to quake and in the rays of light they saw a form descend from heaven, They said, Behold an angel comes.

33   And then they heard again, *Adon Mashich Cumi.*

34   And then the white-robed form tramped on the Roman seal,

and then he tore it into shreds; he took the mighty stone in hand as though it were a pebble from the brook, and cast it to the side.

35 And Jesus opened up his eyes and said, All hail the rising sun! the coming of the day of right-

36 And then he folded up his burial gown, his head bands and his coverings and laid them all aside.

37 He rose, and for a moment stood beside the white-robed form.

38 The weaker soldiers fell upon the ground, and hid their faces in their hands; the stronger stood and watched.

39 They saw the body of the Nazarene transmute; they saw it change from mortal to immortal form, and then it disappeared.

40 The soldiers heard a voice from somewhere; yea, from everywhere, it said,

41 Peace, peace on earth; good will to men.

42 They looked, the tomb was empty and the Lord had risen as he said.

43 The soldiers hastened to Jerusalem, and to the priests, and said,

44 Behold, the Nazarene has risen as he said; the tomb is empty and the body of the man is gone; we know not where it is. And then they told about the wonders of the night.

45 Caiaphas called a council of the Jews; he said, the news must not go forth that Jesus has arisen from the dead;

46 For if it does all men will say, He is the son of God, and all our testimonies will be proven false.

47 And then they called the hundred soldiers in and said to them,

48 You know not where the body of the Nazarene is resting now, so if you will go forth and say that his disciples came and stole the body while you slept,

49 Each one of you shall have a silver piece, and we will make it right with Pilate for the breaking of the Roman seal.

50 The soldiers did as they were paid to do.

SECTION XXI.

SCHIN.

Materialization of the Spiritual Body of Jesus.

CHAPTER 173.

Jesus appears, fully materialized, to his mother, Miriam, Mary of Magdala and to Peter, James and John.

NOW, when the rabbis took the body of the Lord and laid it in the tomb the mother of the Lord, and Mary Magdalene, and Miriam were there.

2 And when the body was entombed they went to Joseph's home and there abode.

3 They did not know that Jewish soldiers had been sent to guard the tomb, nor that the Roman seal was placed upon the stone;

4 So in the morning of the first day of the week they hastened to the tomb with spices to embalm the Lord.

5 But when they reached the tomb they found the terror-stricken soldiers running frantically about.

6 The women did not know the cause; but when they found an

empty tomb they were excited and aggrieved.

7 The soldiers did not know what had transpired; they could not tell who took the body of the Lord away.

8 And Mary Magdalene ran with haste toward Jerusalem to tell the news to Peter and the rest.

9 She met, just by the gateway, Peter, James and John; she said, Some one has rolled away the stone and carried off the body of the Lord.

10 And then the three disciples ran toward the tomb; but John was fleet of foot and was the first to reach the tomb; he found it empty; the body of his Lord was gone.

11 When Peter came he went into the tomb, and found the grave clothes neatly folded up and laid aside.

12 Now, the disciples did not comprehend the scene. They did not know the meaning of their Lord when he informed them just before his death that he would rise from death upon the first day of the week.

13 The three disciples went back to Jerusalem; the mother of the Lord and Miriam went not away.

14 And Mary looked within the tomb, and saw two masters sitting there; they said, Why do you weep?

15 And Mary said, Because my Lord is gone; some one has carried off the body of my Lord; I know not where it is.

16 Then she arose and looked around; a man stood near and said, Why do you weep? whom do you seek?

17 And Mary thought it was the gardener and said, If you have borne away the body of my Lord, O tell me where it is that I may lay it in a sacred tomb.

18 And then the man came near and said, My mother! and Mary said, My Lord!

19 The eyes of Miriam were opened up and she beheld the Lord.

20 And Jesus said, Behold, I told you as we walked along the way up to the cross that I would meet you at the sepulcher upon the first day of the week.

21 Now, Mary Magdalene was sitting not a great way off, and Jesus went to her and said,

22 Why seek the living 'mong the dead? Your Lord has risen as he said. Now, Mary, look! behold my face!

23 Then Mary knew it was the Lord; that he had risen from the dead.

24 And then Salome, and Mary, mother of the two disciples, James and John, Joanna, and the other women who had come out to the tomb, saw Jesus, and they talked with him.

25 And Mary Magdalene was filled with joy. She sought again for Peter, James and John; she found them and she said,

26 Lo, I have seen the Lord; and Miriam has seen the Lord; the mother of the Lord has seen the Lord; and many more have seen his face; for he has risen from the dead.

27 But the disciples thought that she had simply seen a vision of the Lord. They did not think that he had risen from the dead.

28 Then Mary found the other members of the company and told them all about the risen Lord; but none of them believed.

29 Now, Peter, James and John were in the garden of Siloam; were talking with the gardener about the happenings of the day when John beheld a stranger coming up the walk.

30 The stranger lifted up his

hands and said, I am. Then the disciples knew it was the Lord.

31 And Jesus said, Behold, for human flesh can be transmuted into higher form, and then that higher form is master of things manifest, and can, at will, take any form.

32 And so I come to you in form familiar unto you.

33 Go speak to Thomas, and the other men whom I have called to be apostles unto men, and say to them,

34 That he whom Jews and Romans thought was dead is walking in the garden of Siloam;

35 Will stand again before the priests and Pharisees within the temple in Jerusalem;

36 And will appear unto the sages of the world.

37 Tell them that I will go before them into Galilee.

38 Then Peter, James and John went forth and found their brethren, and said, Behold, the Lord is risen from the dead, and we have seen him face to face.

39 The brethren were amazed at what the three disciples said; but still they looked upon their words as idle talk and they believed them not.

CHAPTER 174.

Jesus appears, fully materialized, to Zachus and Cleophas as they journey to Emmaus, but they know him not. He tells them many things about Christ. He eats the evening meal with them, and reveals himself to them. They go to Jerusalem and tell the news.

TOWARDS the evening of the resurrection day, two friends of Jesus, Zachus and Cleophas of Emmaus, seven miles away, were going to their home.

2 And as they walked and talked about the things that had occurred a stranger joined their company.

3 He said, My friends, you seem discouraged and are sad. Has some great grief upon you come?

4 Cleophas said, Are you a stranger in Judea, and know not of the thrilling things that have transpired here?

5 The stranger said, What things? To what do you refer?

6 Cleophas said, Have you not heard about the man from Galilee who was a prophet mighty in both word and deed?

7 A man whom many thought had come to found again the kingdom of the Jews, and drive the Romans from the city of Jerusalem and be himself the king?

8 The stranger said, Tell me about this man.

9 Cleophas said, His name was Jesus; he was born in Bethlehem; his home was up in Galilee. He loved the people as he loved himself.

10 He was, in truth, a master sent from God, for he had matchless power. He healed the sick and made the deaf to hear, the blind to see, the lame to walk, and even raised the dead.

11 The Jewish scribes and Pharisees were jealous of his fame and power, and they arrested him; by perjured witnesses they proved him guilty of a score of crimes,

12 And on last Friday he was taken to the place of skulls and crucified.

13 He died and he was buried in a rich man's tomb, out in the garden of Siloam.

14 This very morning when his friends went to the tomb they found

it empty; the body of the Lord was gone.

15 And now the news has spread abroad that he has risen from the dead.

16 The stranger said, Yes, I have heard about this man; but it seems strange that after all the things that Jewish prophets long ago foretold concerning him that when he came men knew him not.

17 This man was born to demonstrate the Christ to men, and it is just to say that Jesus is the Christ.

18 According to the Word, this Jesus came to suffer at the hands of men, to give his life as pattern for the sons of men;

19 To rise from death that men might know the way to rise from death.

20 And then the stranger told the two disciples all about the Law, the Prophets and the Psalms, and read to them a multitude of things that had been written of this man from Galilee.

21 And now the men had reached their home and as the night was near they importuned the stranger to abide with them.

22 And he went in with them and as they sat about the table at the evening meal, he took a piece of bread, and blessed it in the name of Christ.

23 And instantly their eyes were opened up, and they perceived that he, the stranger, was the Lord, the man from Galilee; that he had risen from the dead; and then the form of Jesus disappeared.

24 When he had gone, the two disciples were amazed. They said, Did not our hearts burn with delight while he was talking to us by the way and opening up the testimonies of the Law, the Prophets and the Psalms?

25 Then Zachus and Cleopas went back to Jerusalem, and everywhere they went they said, Lo, we have seen the Lord;

26 He walked with us to Emmaus; he ate with us the evening meal, and broke for us the bread of life.

CHAPTER 175.

Jesus appears, fully materialized, to the ten apostles in Simon's house, and to Lazarus and his sisters.

THE evening of the resurrection day had come; the ten apostles were in Simon's house in Bethany. The lawyer, Thomas, was not there.

2 The doors were closed and barred, because the Jews had said that they would drive the Galileans from the land.

3 And as they talked, lo, Jesus came and stood forth in their midst, and said, Peace! peace!

4 And the disciples shrank in fear; they thought it was a phantom that they saw.

5 And Jesus said, Why are you troubled thus? why do you fear? I am no phantom form. I am your Lord, and I have risen from the dead.

6 I often said, I will arise; but you believed me not; and now come here and see. A phantom has not flesh and bones and brawn, like I possess.

7 Come now, and clasp my hands, and touch my feet, and lay your hands upon my head.

8 And every one came up and clasped his hands, and touched his feet, and laid his hands upon his head.

9 And Jesus said, Have you here anything to eat?

10 And they brought out a fragment of a fish; he ate it in the pres-

ence of them all, and then the ten believed.

11 Nathaniel said, And now we know that he has risen from the dead; he stands a surety of the resurrection of the dead. And Jesus disappeared.

12 Now, Mary, Martha, Ruth and Lazarus were in their home, and they had heard the rumor that their Lord had risen from the dead, and Martha said,

13 It cannot be, for such a thing has never happened since the world began.

14 But Mary said, Did not the Lord bring back our brother from the dead? and he could surely bring himself to life again.

15 And as they talked, the Lord stood in their midst and said,

16 All hail! for I am risen from the dead, first fruitage of the grave!

17 And Martha ran and brought the chair in which the Lord had ever loved to sit, and Jesus sat down on the chair.

18 And for a long, long time they talked about the trial, and the scenes of Calvary and of the garden of Siloam.

19 Then Jesus said, Fear not, for I will be your boon companion all the way; and then he disappeared.

CHAPTER 176.

Jesus appears, fully materialized, to the eastern sages in the palace of Prince Ravanna in India. To the magian priests in Persia. The three wise men speak in praise of the personality of the Nazarene.

RAVANNA, prince of India, gave a feast. His palace in Orissa was the place where men of thought from all the farther East were wont to meet.

2 Ravanna was the prince with whom child Jesus went to India many years ago.

3 The feast was made in honor of the wise men of the East.

4 Among the guests were Mengste, Vidyapati and Lamaas.

5 The wise men sat about the table talking of the needs of India and the world.

6 The door unto the banquet hall was in the east; a vacant chair was at the table to the east.

7 And as the wise men talked a stranger entered, unannounced, and raising up his hands in benediction said, All hail!

8 A halo rested on his head, and light, unlike the light of sun, filled all the room.

9 The wise men rose and bowed their heads and said, All hail!

10 And Jesus sat down in the vacant chair; and then the wise men knew it was the Hebrew prophet who had come.

11 And Jesus said, Behold, for I am risen from the dead. Look at my hands, my feet, my side.

12 The Roman soldiers pierced my hands and feet with nails; and then one pierced my heart.

13 They put me in a tomb, and then I wrestled with the conqueror of men. I conquered death, I stamped upon him and arose;

14 Brought immortality to light and painted on the walls of time a rainbow for the sons of men; and what I did all men shall do.

15 This gospel of the resurrection of the dead is not confined to Jew and Greek; it is the heritage of every man of every time and clime; and I am here a demonstration of the power of man.

16 Then he arose and pressed the hand of every man and of the royal host, and said,

17 Behold, I am not myth made of the fleeting winds, for I am flesh and bone and brawn; but I can cross the borderland at will.

18 And then they talked together there a long, long time. Then Jesus said,

19 I go my way, but you shall go to all the world and preach the gospel of the omnipotence of man, the power of truth, the resurrection of the dead;

20 He who believes this gospel of the son of man shall never die; the dead shall live again.

21 Then Jesus disappeared, but he had sown the seed. The words of life were spoken in Orissa, and all of India heard.

22 The magian priests were in the silence in Persepolis, and Kaspar, and the magian masters who were first to greet the child of promise in the shepherd's home in Bethlehem, were with the priests.

23 And Jesus came and sat with them; a crown of light was on his head.

24 And when the silence ended Kaspar said, A master from the royal council of the Silent Brotherhood is here; let us give praise.

25 And all the priests and masters stood and said, All hail! What message from the royal council do you bring?

26 And Jesus said, My brothers of the Silent Brotherhood, peace, peace on earth; good will to men!

27 The problem of the ages has been solved; a son of man has risen from the dead; has shown that human flesh can be transmuted into flesh divine.

28 Before the eyes of men this flesh in which I come to you was changed with speed of light from human flesh. And so I am the message that I bring to you.

29 To you I come, the first of all the race to be transmuted to the image of the AM.

30 What I have done, all men will do; and what I am, all men will be.

31 But Jesus said no more. In one short breath he told the story of his mission to the sons of men, and then he disappeared.

32 The magi said, Some time ago we read this promise, now fulfilled, upon the dial plate of heaven.

33 And then we saw this man who has just demonstrated unto us the power of man to rise from carnal flesh and blood to flesh of God, a babe in Bethlehem.

34 And after many years he came and sat with us in these same groves;

35 He told the story of his human life, of trials, sore temptations, buffetings and woes.

36 He pressed along the thorny way of life till he had risen and o'erthrown the strongest foes of God and man; and he is now the only master of the human race whose flesh has been transmuted into flesh divine.

37 He is the God-man of today; but every one of earth shall overcome and be like him, a son of God.

CHAPTER 177.

Jesus appears, fully materialized, in the temple in Jerusalem. Rebukes the rulers of the Jews for their hypocrisy. Reveals himself to them and they fall back in fear. He appears to the apostles in Simon's house. Thomas is convinced.

IT was the Sabbath day and many priests and scribes and Pharisees were in the temple in Jerusalem. Caiaphas, Annas and some other ruling Jews were there.

2 A stranger came in garb of fisherman and asked, What has become of Jesus who is called the Christ? Is he not teaching in the temple now?

3 The Jews replied, That man from Galilee was crucified a week ago, because he was a dangerous man, a vile, seditious man.

4 The stranger asked, Where did you put the body of this man from Galilee? where is his tomb?

5 The Jews replied, We do not know. His followers came at night and stole the body from the tomb in which it lay and carried it away, and then declared that he had risen from the dead.

6 The stranger asked, How do you know that his disciples stole the body from the tomb? was any one a witness of the theft?

7 The Jews replied, We had a hundred soldiers at the place, and every one of them declares that his disciples stole the body from the tomb.

8 The stranger asked, Will any one of all your hundred men stand forth and say, I saw the body stolen from the tomb?

9 The Jews replied, We do not know; these men are men of truth; we cannot doubt their word.

10 The stranger said, You priests and scribes and Pharisees hear me: I was a witness of the facts, was in the garden of Siloam, and stood among your hundred men.

11 And this I know that not a man among your hundred men, will say, I saw the body stolen from the tomb.

12 And I will testify before the God of heaven and earth, The body was not stolen from the tomb; the

man from Galilee is risen from the dead.

13 And then the priests and scribes and Pharisees rushed up to seize the man and cast him out.

14 But instantly the fisherman became a radiant form of light, and priests and scribes and Pharisees fell back in deadly fear; they saw the man from Galilee.

15 And Jesus looked upon the frightened men and said, This is the body that you stoned beyond the city's gates and crucified on Calvary.

16 Behold my hands, my feet, my side and see the wounds the soldiers made.

17 If you believe that I am phantom made of air, come forth and handle me; ghosts do not carry flesh and bones.

18 I came to earth to demonstrate the resurrection of the dead, the transmutation of the flesh of carnal man to flesh of man divine.

19 Then Jesus raised his hands and said, Peace be to every one of you; good will to all mankind. And then he disappeared.

20 Now, Thomas had not seen the Lord since he had risen from the dead, and when the ten averred that they had seen and talked with him he said,

21 Until I see the nail prints in his hands and feet, the spear wound in his side, and talked with him as I have talked with him before, I cannot have a reason to believe that he is risen from the dead.

22 At Simon's house in Bethany the men from Galilee had met. It was the evening of the first day of the week, and on the morrow all would turn their faces toward their homes.

23 The eleven apostles all were there; the doors were closed and

.rred, and Jesus came and said,
:ace be to all!

24 And then he said to Thomas,
·iend, you do not know that I
ιve risen from the dead; the time
ιs come for you to know.

25 Come here and see the nail
ints in my hands, the spear
ound in my side, and talk with
ιe as you have often talked with
me.

26 And Thomas came and saw,
ιnd then exclaimed, My master,
ɾɪ̣d my Lord! I do not now be-
l eve, I know that you are risen
from the dead.

27 And Jesus said, Because you
see me you believe, and blessed are
your eyes;

28 But blessed thrice are they
who see me not and yet believe.

29 Then Jesus vanished from
their sight, but the disciples were
established in their faith.

CHAPTER 178.

*Jesus appears, fully materialized,
before Apollo and the Silent Brotherhood in Greece. Appears to
Claudas and Juliet on the Tiber
near Rome. Appears to the priests
in the Egyptian temple at Heliopolis.*

APOLLO, with the Silent Brotherhood of Greece, was sitting
in a Delphian grove. The Oracle
had spoken loud and long.

2 The priests were in the sanctuary and as they looked the Oracle became a blaze of light; it seemed
to be on fire, and all consumed.

3 The priests were filled with
fear. They said, A great disaster
is to come; our gods are mad; they
have destroyed our Oracle.

4 But when the flames had spent
themselves, a man stood on the
orac pedestal and said,

5 God speaks to man, not by an
oracle of wood and gold, but by the
voice of man.

6 The gods have spoken to the
Greeks, and kindred tongues,
through images made by man; but
God, the One, now speaks to man
through Christ the only son, who
was, and is and evermore will be.

7 This Oracle shall fail; the Living Oracle of God, the One, will
never fail.

8 Apollo knew the man who
spoke; he knew it was the Nazarene
who once had taught the wise men
in the Acropolis and had rebuked
the idol worshippers upon the
Athen's beach;

9 And in a moment Jesus stood
before Apollo and the Silent Brotherhood, and said,

10 Behold, for I have risen from
the dead with gifts for men. I
bring to you the title of your vast
estate.

11 All power in heaven and
earth is mine; to you I give all
power in heaven and earth.

12 Go forth and teach the nations of the earth the gospel of the
resurrection of the dead and of
eternal life through Christ, the love
of God made manifest to men.

13 And then he clasped Apollo's
hand and said, My human flesh was
changed to higher form by love divine and I can manifest in flesh, or
in the higher planes of life, at will.

14 What I can do all men can
do. Go preach the gospel of the
omnipotence of man.

15 Then Jesus disappeared; but
Greece and Crete and all the nations
heard.

16 Claudas and Juliet, his wife,
lived on the Palatine in Rome and
they were servants of Tiberius; but
they had been in Galilee;

17 Had walked with Jesus by

the sea, had heard his words and seen his power; and they believed that he was Christ made manifest.

18 Now Claudas and his wife were on the Tiber in a little boat; a storm swept from the sea, the boat was wrecked and Claudas and his wife were sinking down to death.

19 And Jesus came and took them by the hands and said, Claudas and Juliet, arise and walk with me upon the waves.

20 And they arose and walked with him upon the waves.

21 A thousand people saw the three walk on the waves, and saw them reach the land, and they were all amazed.

22 And Jesus said, You men of Rome, I am the resurrection and the life. They that are dead shall live, and many that shall live will never die.

23 By mouth of gods and demigods God spoke unto your fathers long ago; but now he speaks to you through perfect man.

24 He sent his son, the Christ, in human flesh, to save the world, and as I lifted from the watery grave and saved these servants of Tiberius,

25 So Christ will lift the sons and daughters of the human race, yea, every one of them, from darkness and from graves of carnal things, to light and everlasting life.

26 I am the manifest of love raised from the dead; Behold my hands, my feet, my side which carnal men have pierced.

27 Claudas and Juliet, whom I have saved from death, are my ambassadors to Rome.

28 And they will point the way and preach the gospel of the Holy Breath and of the resurrection of the dead,

29 And that was all he said, but Rome and all of Italy heard.

30 The priests of Heliopolis were in their temple met to celebrate the resurrection of their brother Nazarite; they knew that he had risen from the dead.

31 The Nazarite appeared and stood upon a sacred pedestal on which no man had ever stood.

32 This was an honor that had been reserved for him who first would demonstrate the resurrection of the dead.

33 And Jesus was the first of all the human race to demonstrate the resurrection of the dead.

34 When Jesus stood upon the sacred pedestal the masters stood and said, All hail! The great bells of the temple rang and all the temple was ablaze with light.

35 And Jesus said, All honor to the masters of this Temple of the Sun.

36 In flesh of man there is the essence of the resurrection of the dead. This essence, quickened by the Holy Breath, will raise the substance of the body to a higher tone,

37 And make it like the substance of the bodies of the planes above, which human eyes cannot behold.

38 There is a holy ministry in death. The essence of the body cannot be quickened by the Holy Breath until the fixed is solved; the body must disintegrate, and this is death.

39 And then upon these pliant substances God breathes, just as he breathed upon the chaos of the deep when worlds were formed,

40 And life springs forth from death; the carnal form is changed to form divine.

41 The will of man makes possible the action of the Holy Breath.

When will of man and will of God are one, the resurrection is a fact.

42　In this we have the chemistry of mortal life, the ministry of death, the mystery of deific life.

43　My human life was wholly given to bring my will to tune with the deific will; when this was done my earth-tasks all were done.

44　And you, my brothers, know full well the foes I had to meet; you know about my victories in Gethsemane; my trials in the courts of men; my death upon the cross.

45　You know that all my life was one great drama for the sons of men; a pattern for the sons of men. I lived to show the possibilities of man.

46　What I have done all men can do, and what I am all men shall be.

47　The masters looked; the form upon the sacred pedestal had gone, but every temple priest, and every living creature said, Praise God.

CHAPTER 179.

Jesus appears, fully materialized, to the apostles at the sea of Galilee. Appears to a multitude of people. Tells his apostles to go again to Jerusalem and he would meet them there.

NOW, the apostles were at home in Galilee; the women tarried in Judea until the Pentecost,

2　And Peter, James and John, and Andrew, Philip and Nathaniel were in Capernaum. They joined with Jonah and with Zebedee, and in their boats went out to fish,

3　They toiled all night and when the morning came they had no fish.

4　And as they neared the shore a man stood on the shore and said, How many fish have you?

5　And Peter answered, None.

6　Again the man called out and said, A school of fish is passing now upon the right side of your boat; cast out your net.

7　They cast their net, and it was filled; and John exclaimed, It is the Lord who stands upon the shore.

8　And Peter plunged into the sea and swam to shore. The other men brought in the net, and it contained a hundred fifty and three fish and yet it did not break.

9　And Jesus said, My children, let us break our fast together here.

10　They found some living coals upon the beach and Peter brought and dressed the fish; they had some bread.

11　And when the meal had been prepared they broke their fast, and Jesus ate of both the fish and bread.

12　Now, after breakfast all the men were sitting on the beach, and Jesus said to Peter, Do you love the Lord your God with all your heart, and do you love your neighbor as you love yourself?

13　And Peter said, Yea, Lord, I love the Lord my God with all my heart; I love my neighbor as I love myself.

14　And Jesus said, Then feed my sheep.

15　And then he said to James, Do you love her, the Holy Breath, with all your heart, and do you love your neighbor as you love yourself?

16　And James replied, Yea, Lord, I love the Holy Breath with all my heart; I love my neighbor as I love myself.

17　Then Jesus said, Protect my sheep.

18　And then he said to John, Do you love Christ, the love divine made manifest, with all your heart, and do you love your neighbor as you love yourself?

19   And John replied, Yea, Lord, I love the Christ with all my heart; I love my neighbor as I love myself.

20   And Jesus said, Then feed my lambs.

21   Then Jesus rose and said to Peter, Follow me. And Peter followed him.

22   When Peter saw that John was following him he said to Jesus, Lord, behold, John follows you! What shall he do?

23   Now Peter did not hear the master when he said to John, Then feed my lambs.

24   And Jesus spoke to Peter and he said, It matters not to you what John shall do; not even though I will that he remain until I come again.

25   Just do your duty; follow me.

26   And Jesus passed, they knew not where he went.

27   The news soon spread through all Capernaum that Jesus had arisen from the dead, that he had walked with his disciples by the sea, and ate with them the morning meal. The multitudes came forth to see.

28   Now Peter, James and John, together with the other men who had been called to be apostles of the Lord, went to the mountains near Capernaum to pray,

29   And as they prayed the master came; they saw him and they talked with him.

30   He said to them, The Pentecost is near at hand; go to Jerusalem and I will meet you there.

31   And as he talked, a multitude of people came; they saw the Lord; they said,

32   Behold, for now we know that he, the Nazarene, has risen from the dead for we have seen him face to face.

CHAPTER 180.

Jesus appears, fully materialized, to the apostles in Jerusalem. Gives them his instructions. Promises them a special endowment for their work on Pentecost. Goes to Mount Olives and in full view of many disciples ascends to heaven. The disciples return to Jerusalem.

THE eleven apostles of the Lord were in Jerusalem and in a spacious room that they had chosen by the Lord's command.

2   And as they prayed the Lord appeared to them and said,

3   Peace be to all; good will to every living thing. And then he talked with them a long, long time.

4   And the disciples asked, Will you restore the kingdom unto Israel now?

5   And Jesus said, Be not concerned about the governments of men; the masters will direct.

6   Do that which has been given you to do, and wait and murmur not.

7   All power in heaven and earth is given unto me, and now I bid you go to all the world and preach the gospel of the Christ, the unity of God and man, the resurrection of the dead, and of eternal life.

8   And as you go and preach, baptize the people in the name of Christ.

9   They who believe and are baptized shall rise up in the newness of the life of Christ, and they who disbelieve shall rise not in the newness of the life of Christ.

10   And you shall give to men the power I give to you.

11   They who believe and are baptized shall heal the sick; shall cause the blind to see, the deaf to hear, the lame to walk;

12   Shall cast the unclean spirits

out of those obsessed; shall tread on deadly serpents and be not harmed; shall pass through flames and not be burned; and if they drink a poisonous draught it shall not kill.

13 You know the sacred Word, which is the word of power.

14 The secret things that I have told to you that may not now be told to all the world, you shall make known to faithful men who shall in turn reveal them unto other faithful men,

15 Until the time shall come when all the world may hear and comprehend the words of truth and power.

16 And now I will ascend to God, as you and all the world will rise to God.

17 Behold, upon the day of Pentecost you all shall be endowed with power from on high.

18 But here you shall remain till then in holy thought and prayer.

19 Then Jesus went to Olivet, and his disciples followed him, and in a place not far removed from Bethany, he met the Marys and Salome;

20 Met Martha, Ruth and Miriam; met Lazarus and a host of others who had come from Galilee.

21 And Jesus stood apart and raised his hands and said,

22 The benedictions of the Holy Ones, of the Almighty God, and of the Holy Breath, of Christ the love of God made manifest,

23 Will rest upon you all the way till you shall rise and sit with me upon the throne of power.

24 And then they saw him rise upon the wings of light; a wreath encircled him about; and then they saw his form no more.

25 But as they gazed up into heaven two men, in robes of white, appeared and said,

26 You men of Galilee, why gaze you thus so anxiously upon the ascending Lord? Lo, he will come again from heaven as you have seen him go to heaven.

27 Then the eleven and Lazarus, and the other men from Galilee, together with the faithful women, not a few, returned unto Jerusalem and there abode.

28 And they were constantly in prayer and holy thought. They waited for the Holy Breath, and for the coming of the promised power from on high.

SECTION XXII.

TAU.

Establishment of the Christine Church.

CHAPTER 181.

The eleven apostles make choice of Matthias to fill the place made vacant by the deflection of Judas. The Christines are glad. Miriam sings a song of praise. Apostolic roster.

THE fact that Jesus had arisen from the dead was not denied by many of the rulers of the Jews.

2 And Pilate gave an order that the followers of the Nazarene be not molested in their worship any place in his domain.

3 The day of Pentecost was near at hand and every one was looking for a manifest of Spirit power.

4 Now, in Jerusalem the eleven had met to choose a man to fill the place of Judas who betrayed his Lord.

5 And Peter said, The Lord called to this ministry twelve men as twelve foundation stones on which the Christine temple should be built.

6 This Judas, who betrayed his Lord, has gone to his own place beyond the veil.

7 Of him the prophet wrote: His habitation shall be desolate; no man shall dwell therein; his office let another take.

8 From those who have accompanied us from Gilgal, where the harbinger baptized, until this day, shall one be chosen to complete the number twelve, to fill the place from which our brother by transgression fell.

9 And then the eleven spent a long, long time in prayer, and when they cast their lots, Matthias, from the valley of the Nile, was chosen for the place.

10 Matthias was an Israelite indeed; but he was learned in all the wisdom of Egyptian schools, and he had taught the mysteries of Mizraim in Jericho.

11 He was among the first to greet the harbinger; among the first to recognize the Nazarene as Christ, the son of God;

12 He had been with the Christine band in all their journeys in the land of Galilee, Judea and Samaria.

13 A messenger was sent who found Matthias, and he came and joined the eleven, and for a time the twelve were lost in silent prayer.

14 The Christines who had come from Galilee and places in Judea, about six score, were there, and Peter told them of Matthias, and how, by lot, he had been chosen an apostle of the Lord.

15 The Christines all were glad and praised the name of God; and Miriam sung a song of praise.

16 These are the names of the apostles of the Lord: Peter, John and James; Philip, Andrew and Nathaniel;

17 Thomas, James the son of Alpheus and Simon Zelotes; Matthew, Jude, the son of Alpheus and Matthias.

CHAPTER 182.

Events of the day of Pentecost. Endowment of the apostles. The Christine Church is established. Peter preaches the introductory sermon. The sermon. Three thousand people are baptized and become members of the church.

NOW, when the day of Pentecost had come Jerusalem was filled with pious Jews and proselytes from many lands.

2 The Christines all were met and were in perfect harmony.

3 And as they sat in silent prayer they heard a sound a-like the distant murmur of a coming storm.

4 The sound grew loud, and louder still, until, like thunder peals, it filled the room where the apostles sat.

5 A brilliant light appeared, and many thought, The building is afire.

6 Twelve balls, that seemed like balls of fire, fell from heaven—a ball from every sign of all the circle of the heavens, and on the head of each apostle there appeared a flaming ball of fire.

7 And every ball sent seven tongues of fire toward heaven, and each apostle spoke in seven dialects of earth.

8 The ignorant rabble treated lightly what they heard and saw; they said, These men are drunk, and know not what they say.

9 But men of learning were

amazed; they said, Are not these men who speak all Jews? how is it that they speak in all the languages of earth?

10 And Peter said, You people of Jerusalem, and you who live beyond the city's gates; Peace be to you, and all mankind.

11 This is the time that holy men of old desired to see; by faith they saw this hour, and now they stand with us in ecstasy.

12 The prophet Joel in the olden times told of the things you see and hear. The Holy Breath spoke with his tongue and said,

13 And it shall come to pass in latter days, that I will breathe upon the sons of men, and fill them with the blessedness of holiness.

14 Your sons and daughters will stand forth and prophesy; your young men will be seers; your old men will dream dreams.

15 And I will show forth wonders in the heavens above, and marvelous signs in earth.

16 Sounds will proceed from heaven and voices will be heard that men will fail to comprehend.

17 The sun will fail to shine, the moon will wade in blood before the coming of the great day of the Lord.

18 And it will come to pass that they who call upon the name of God in faith shall be redeemed.

19 This is the day of Christine power; the day that he, the man from Galilee, is glorified.

20 He came as babe in Bethlehem and from his day of birth the kings of earth went forth intent to take his life.

21 God held him in the hollow of his hand.

22 Men called him Jesus, and they called him well, for he was sent to seek and save the lost.

23 And Jesus grew to manhood and was subject unto all the trials and temptations of the sons of men, that he might know the loads that men must bear, and know the way to succor them.

24 In distant lands he lived and by the sacred Word he healed the sick, threw prison doors ajar, and set the prisoners free, and everywhere he was proclaimed, Immanuel.

25 But wicked men despised him and rejected him, and by bribed men they proved him guilty of a score of crimes;

26 And in the presence of a multitude of men who hear me now, they nailed him to a cross;

27 They sealed him with the seal of death; but death was all too weak to hold him in the tomb and when immortal masters said, Adon mashich cumi, he burst the bands of death, and rose again to life.

28 He showed himself alive, not only to the rulers in Jerusalem, but to the many in the distant parts of earth;

29 And then, before the wondering eyes of many who now hear me speak, attended by a retinue of courtiers of the angel world, he ascended to the throne of God.

30 And being now exalted high, and having breathed to full the Holy Breath, he breathes again on us, and thus sheds forth what you now see and hear.

31 You men of Israel, know that God has made this man from Galilee whom you abused and crucified, both Lord and Christ.

32 And then the people said, What shall we do?

33 And Peter said, This Christine Lord has sent us forth to open up the gates of dawn. Through Christ all men may enter into light and life.

34 The Christine Church stands

on the postulates that Jesus is the love of God made manifest; that love is savior of the sons of men.

35   This Christine Church is but the kingdom of the Holy One within the soul, made manifest.

36   This day the Christine Church is opened up, and whosoever will may enter in, and, by the boundless grace of Christ, be saved.

37   Again the people said, How may we enter in that we may share the boundless grace of Christ?

38   And Peter said, Reform and be baptized, and turn away from sin and lead the life deep hid with Christ in God, and you shall enter in and be redeemed.

39   Three thousand people turned away from sin and were baptized and sought to lead the life deep hid with Christ in God.

40   And in one day the Christine Church became a mighty power; and Christ became a mighty word that thrilled the multitudes in many lands.

RETURN TO the circulation desk of any
University of California Library

or to the

NORTHERN REGIONAL LIBRARY FACILITY
Bldg. 400, Richmond Field Station
University of California
Richmond, CA 94804-4698

ALL BOOKS MAY BE RECALLED AFTER 7 DAYS

- 2-month loans may be renewed by calling
  (510) 642-6753
- 1-year loans may be recharged by bringing
  books to NRLF
- Renewals and recharges may be made
  4 days prior to due date

DUE AS STAMPED BELOW

MAY 1 2 2004

DD20 15M 4-02

UNIVERSITY OF CALIFORNIA, BERKELEY
FORM NO. DD6, 60m, 3/80   BERKELEY, CA 94720

74029551R00148

Made in the USA
San Bernardino, CA
12 April 2018